CW01079860

Dr Klaus Schmidt

The Quest for Identity

*CORPORATE IDENTITY
STRATEGIES, METHODS AND EXAMPLES*

CASSELL

Cassell

Wellington House   215 Park Avenue South
125 Strand   New York
London WC2R 0BB   NY 10003

© Dr Klaus Schmidt 1995
First published 1995

British Library Cataloguing-in-Publication Data
A catalogue record for this book is available from
the British Library.

ISBN 0-304-33411-1

Printed and bound in Great Britain by Cambridge University Press

Contents

Corporate identity is due for a redefinition and a renaissance. From a company's understanding of its own purpose and values, through its culture and behaviour, to its outward expression, corporate identity deals with matters of core strategic concern. These matters affect everyone inside a company and everyone in its range of external contacts. Special management skills must be adopted, and these are revealed in the unique case studies contained in this book.

For many years, corporate identity has been associated with visual presentation, with logotypes, with new colours and with vast implementation costs. Now culture is beginning to be mentioned in the context of identity and is, in some minds, the new holy grail.

But these one-dimensional views of identity are simply not relevant any more in the rapidly changing, shifting world in which all organisations must now operate. Economic and social developments on a global scale are placing severe new demands on companies and the international competitiveness of European companies, in particular, is suffering. European unification itself and globalisation of markets has increased competition and forced far-reaching changes. Structural problems are evident: costs are too high, flexibility is lacking and innovation lags behind. At the same time, companies must reorient themselves, away from products and towards customers, who themselves are more and more demanding and who increasingly adopt values which make them aware and critical of corporate ecological behaviour and social awareness.

Of course, productivity needs to be significantly improved, innovation stepped up, foreign markets penetrated and flexibility enhanced. The prerequisite, though, for success through all these changes is the formulation, expression and application of corporate aims and values both inside and outside an organisation. The internal effect is a flexible, motivated workforce with a readiness to accept change as the critical factor for success. The external effect is to appeal to all target audiences, building a loyal customer base and attracting new customers, as well as influencing wider opinions.

It is exactly in the formulation, expression and application of corporate aims and values that holistic corporate identity is proving to be a vital success factor in achieving competitive advantage. If companies are to benefit fully from this, we need to take stock of our ideas and expectations of corporate identity, and produce a definition which reflects the real needs of companies and which takes into account all relevant dimensions, not just those of practitioners who have historically thrived on peddling narrowly specialised offers, for example those based only on design or marketing. To understand those needs better, and to gain insights on companies' perceptions of corporate identity, its nature and benefits, Henrion, Ludlow & Schmidt have, since 1989, carried out a series of pan-European studies. The aim has been to determine the knowledge and attitudes of managers responsible for corporate identity, including their various understandings of the subject and their evaluation of its importance and benefits. We wanted to know what they considered was its practical relevance, what experience they had gained of it and what they expected from it.

Through presenting a picture of the results of these studies, and real-life examples, this book gives a view of the level of development and state of knowledge of corporate identity in Europe, and describes attitudes, circumstances and critical success factors relevant to the state of international corporate identity.

The first part of the book, under the heading 'Strategies and methods', deals with the historical development of corporate identity, our understanding of it and its potential. The first chapter sets out the main driving forces in the development of corporate identity, from coats of arms, through early industrial applications in Europe to its rôle in the internationalisation of companies and the globalisation of markets. It mentions companies such as AEG, IBM, Coca-Cola and KLM, which take their place as pioneers and classics of corporate identity. As examples of globalisation, the identity developments of Coopers & Lybrand and Mitsubishi Motors are featured. Another theme of the chapter is the basic differences in the expectations and demands of corporate identity, the different prerequisites and circumstances which result from the varied activities of different corporations, such as those in capital goods, raw materials or services. Relevant situations for consideration of corporate identity, which result from the development of an organisation and the economic and social framework common to all companies, are addressed. The potential of corporate identity is defined, including what can, and what cannot, realistically be expected of it.

The second chapter presents the rich and fascinating results of the three pan-European studies. The studies give keys to the factors for success in international corporate identity development. Definitions of corporate identity are given, along with perceived advantages or benefits, and relevant image and identity factors. Satisfaction with, as well as the importance and implementation of, the individual aspects of identity are described. Target groups are identified and prioritised. The relevance of corporate identity to internationalisation, and in a recession, is presented. And ratings of exemplary and successful international corporate identities are described and commented on, in both pan-European and national form.

The important insights which have been gained from these studies, combined with practical experience over many years of international consulting, have led us to a 'holistic' understanding of corporate identity, which is based on the real needs of companies. This understanding forms the basis for the structure and process models of holistic corporate identity development which are introduced in the third chapter. We show how, through a target positioning, the relevant identity elements of corporate culture, corporate behaviour, market conditions and strategies, products and services, and communications and design, can be planned and developed.

The phased process of structured analysis, concept and development for complex corporate identity tasks is described in detail, together with a range of helpful methods. With checklists and examples from corporate identity practice, guidance is given on desk research, survey methods in status quo and strengths-and-weaknesses analysis, management and target group investigations, positioning strategies and on measures for the development of corporate identity.

The second part of the book is a series of detailed, practical examples of successful corporate identities and their development, among them some of the 'Top Ten' identified in our survey, including ABB, Ford and Siemens. In addition, a number of medium and small companies' identities are presented, which contain points of particular interest. Experienced businessmen, entrepreneurs, top managers and others responsible for corporate identity from marketing, public relations, personnel, communications and design backgrounds give an inside view into the 'works' of corporate identity and explain how it comes into existence and how it is given form.

ABB's Vice President of Communications explains the reasons behind the 1988 merger between the Swedish ASEA and the Swiss Brown Boveri. The development of a global image was a top priority for the merged organisation, which is highly decentralised. The rôle of corporate identity in creating and communicating a mission and values is described, as well as the way in which it meets both global and local needs.

Ford of Europe's Director of Corporate Affairs and Internal Communications recounts the development of Ford's global identity, then goes on to explain the restructuring and cultural repositioning of the Company under increasing pressure of competition, and how Ford has developed internal pan-European communications through the medium of a pioneering internal television service.

The Governor of the **Henriettenstiftung**, a charitable institution in Hanover, Germany, describes their repositioning through identity and how they reconciled Christian founding principles with their present-day rôle as a service company in the business of caring for sick and elderly people.

IBM's identity story is historically described and then brought up to date, showing how, against a background of global upheaval in the computer industry, basic beliefs held good, and how core identity was still of value, but how responsiveness to competition and changing customer demands must be created and communicated.

The Dean of **INSEAD**, one of the best known and most respected of international business schools, tells of its success, but also of the individually-generated tensions within the organisation which made development of a unifying corporate identity a necessity.

The Staff Director of **Keller**, an international foundations engineering group, tells the identity story of a management buyout and subsequent flotation, which involved the creation of a credible presence and perceived shareholder value for a new and complex international organisation.

KLM's Corporate Identity Director traces the development of the airline's classic visual identity, then goes on to describe the interdependence of aspects such as behaviour and quality in forming a basis for customer differentiation and choice in an ultra-competitive global market.

The Brand Director of **Krups**, the German household appliance company, describes the difficult market situation in which the Company found itself at the beginning of the 90s, and how the 'corporate identity of a brand' was developed, based on a positioning which centred on the customer as its focal point.

London Underground's Design and Advertising and Publicity Managers give their account of the struggle to achieve a culture of customer service within the organisation and explain how identity helps to motivate and inform in the face of an ageing infrastructure and the difficulties of day-to-day operations.

Migros' Director of Public Relations and Information, together with a company spokesperson, jointly describe the unconventional principles of Switzerland's largest cooperative supermarket chain, whose founders laid down a social, cultural, business and political mission which still governs and expresses its corporate identity.

The former Group Marketing Manager of **RTZ Pillar** explains the identity problem of Pillar Electrical, a group of electrical companies in which one predominated to the detriment of the whole, how the development of an identity structure expressed the Group and supported its brands, and how 'Black Monday' affected the choice of a new name.

The development of **Siemens**' identity, one of the pioneering classics mentioned in Chapter 1, is described, with its principles of internationality and cultural openness, and its focus on a design 'credo' which expresses corporate values, attitudes and continuity in areas as diverse as products and buildings.

The Chairman of the Board of **Veitsch-Radex**, an international market leader in refractory products, points to the value of holistic corporate identity as an instrument of crisis management in a merger situation, when the pressing need was to promote integration and cooperation between former cut-throat competitors.

Vitra's Managing Director writes about his company's ideals and about the creative personalities of the individuals who contribute to the identity of Vitra through supplying the stimulus and innovation which makes the principle of creative variety into a feature of identity.

Fascinating parallels and certain contradictions exist in this series of case histories, but all have in common the comprehensiveness of a holistic approach or the inter-dependence of relevant aspects and dimensions. Individually and in total, they prove the necessity for a holistic corporate identity strategy.

I would like to thank all of the authors of the case histories who, through their collaboration, have made this book possible. I would also like especially to thank all those at Henrion, Ludlow & Schmidt who have participated in the creation of the book. In addition, I thank Gerd Günter Lange who, through his stimulating ideas, has contributed to the 'identity' of the book, and I thank our publishers Cassell, who have patiently watched over the birth of this complex volume.

Dr Klaus Schmidt
London, November 1995

Corporate identity: development, understanding and potential

DR KLAUS SCHMIDT

Corporate identity is a relatively recent arrival on the strategic management scene, which its state of development betrays. For some, it is at the heart of successful management; others perceive it as merely one of any number of modern management ideas. What is certain is that awareness of corporate identity among top managers has increased tremendously in recent years.

The growing discussion about matters related to the identities of corporations is founded on global changes: internationalisation of markets and production, plus the rush of developing technologies. On the one hand, the number of products and services is increasing all the time and corporations are getting bigger and more complex. On the other hand, products and prices, target groups and distribution systems – and with that, corporations them-selves – are relentlessly converging, some already seeming virtually interchangeable.

Added to this, changing values and greater environmental awareness are leading to target groups becoming more and more critical and seeking subjective values and points of identification. This is also true for employees, whose own identification with the company increasingly depends on subjective aspects alongside financial and career expectations.

It is axiomatic that customers don't just see a product or service in isolation; they see the company as a whole, including all aspects and dimensions of its identity, from its products and services, through its cultural, social, environmental and market behaviour, to its communications and design. Identity in this comprehensive sense is an absolute prerequisite for acceptance and success in the market.

Corporate identity, used as a strategic planning and management tool, is an expression of developed economic and corporate culture. Understanding of corporate identity depends on the state of economic development and, along with that, the range of a country's marketing methods.

The origins

Royal and civic coats of arms, army uniforms and the 'ex libris' of book printers were, and are, marks of identity. With these marks, there were often actual or implied statements. Mottoes and watchwords in coats of arms, transmitted a shared spirit and a common cause. Flag and uniform signalled affiliation, to be identified by, even if it was not always possible to identify with them. And printers' marks spoke of origin and quality, like the signs and symbols of today's companies.

It was always about identity and identifi-cation, about symbolising ideas and claims, about marking territories or communicating aims, about differentiation and presence, recognition and profile. In the beginning, it was about identities for ideologies or claims to power. Then, with the growth of trade, manufacturing and, finally, industrialisation, the need for identity and identification increased greatly.

It was with industrialisation that the necessity for corporate identity really developed. The first activities stemmed from design and marketing, and were directed towards creating a particular image in the market, as well as in the minds of staff and customers. By present understanding, this represents only corporate design coordination and development of the visual image.

Antecedents

There are antecedents to the modern concept of corporate identity, and many of them demonstrate strong development of various aspects and dimensions. In Britain in the nineteenth century, railway companies were fiercely independent and competitive. To express their power, and also to develop a strong esprit de corps – perhaps as an encouragement to the acceptance of draconian employment terms – they developed identities which encompassed visual aspects, from the hardware used to the colours, and behavioural aspects.

Differentiation was achieved through product appearance (each company designed and manufactured most of its own locomotives and rolling stock), operating policies related to frequency and speed, architectural style, graphic design of colours and markings, uniform styles, information policies and so on. The North Eastern Railway Company even produced a visual identity manual well before the First World War.

Meanwhile in Germany, at the beginning of the century, one of the first industrial coordinated design 'programmes' was being developed by AEG, the Allgemeine Elektrizitätsgesellschaft, literally 'General Electricity Company'.

The first impetus for this came in 1907 through the appointment of architect and designer Peter Behrens as 'artistic consultant'. Behrens formed a team including, among others, the young Walter Gropius and Mies van der Rohe. Encouraged and supported by AEG's chief, Rathenau, this team designed the whole visual appearance of what was, in those days, Europe's largest energy and electrical engineering company. This involved everything from the business card and letterhead, through light-bulbs and turbines to workshops and office buildings. All of this was planned in a standardised style, which could be seen as the forerunner of Bauhaus thinking. Even then, the efforts made towards consistent, appealing design were not the whim of an art-loving company boss, but

were the means to an end: an expression of quality and self-esteem.

This 'corporate identity era' at AEG came to an end at the outbreak of the First World War. However, the idea of corporate design lived on: the total appearance of a company in all its detail following a coordinated style and thus giving the company a unique, characteristic profile.

International developments

After the Second World War, it was principally Anglo-American companies and consultants who spread and practised corporate identity worldwide.

One of the first classic developments of corporate identity was surely IBM: proceeding from a vision of corporate philosophy, the identity was developed, spanning corporate culture, design and communications. If you were to describe IBM's identity in two words, they would be 'quality' and 'professionalism'. IBM's success lies in consistent implementation of these prerequisites in all areas and aspects of the company. Thus, quality awareness extends not only to products, services and clients, but also to the company's own people and to society in general. For the 'father' of the IBM identity, Thomas Watson Senior, the key to success was the enshrinement of quality thinking in staff: 'You don't succeed with any company if you're not convinced it's the best in the world. You have to put your soul into the business and the business into your soul.'

IBM's consistent corporate identity-oriented policy has helped it to gain a remarkable market position in information technology, and to use its goodwill potential in difficult times and crises. IBM's corporate identity programme serves as a model for companies of this size and is just as valid today as it was decades ago. Coca-Cola, too, is an example of classic international corporate identity development. The emphasis is on product and packaging as well as promotion. 'Coca-Cola is a religion.' Although this quote from former Coca-Cola president Robert Woodruff might sound a little exaggerated, it comes close to the truth about what is probably the world's most famous brand. If you buy a 'Coke', you don't get any old caffeinated soft drink. You get lifestyle: enjoyment , fun, energy, verve and freedom.

By combining unique flavour (Pepsi does taste different), the bottle (one of the few packs which is sexy and recognisable in the dark), unmistakable corporate design, a widespread and cleverly-devised distribution system and one of the world's largest advertising budgets, Coca-Cola has created a symbol of western post-war culture. 'You can drink their identity', said one of the respondents in our last pan-European corporate identity study.

Of course, American companies coming to Europe were facing a special situation. Because of the different cultures and the varying states of economic development, the preconditions were diverse and complex. If one doesn't regard corporate identity as a matter for national navel-gazing, one must admit that the state of its development and knowledge of it is very different in different countries.

In the course of their internationalisation, American multinational companies were the ones who realised the significance of corporate identity activities most clearly. This was enhanced by fast growth and the importance of success and acceptance in international markets, which were marked by their varied requirements and conditions. In the USA, corporate identity was developed and nurtured by most multinational companies. IBM, already mentioned, was one of them, as

were corporations such as Westinghouse, General Motors, Ford and Xerox, as well as the big banks, insurance companies, oil companies and airlines.

In the aftermath of the Second World War, the internationalisation of German companies was delayed. This meant that the possibilities and significance of corporate identity activities as a management tool were recognised much later. An important influence on the development of identity had been the designer Otl Aicher, whose identity for the 1972 Olympic Games in Munich became an essential expression of the character of the games. Out of this came an epoch-making impetus for a 'German' corporate design style. There came to be model examples of corporate identity or corporate design development in Germany – often medium-sized companies which shaped and developed distinctive corporate identities on the basis of their products. They include Lamy, Erco, Bulthaup and Vitra. Product design constitutes the nucleus and foundation of these identities, and design dictates the visual style of the items of communication.

A classic of corporate identity history

One of the first critical appraisals of planned corporate identity work can be found in the FHK Henrion and Alan Parkin book *Design Coordination and Corporate Image* (1967), in which the potential synergetic effects of corporate identity are demonstrated. In the book, the identity concept for KLM Royal Dutch Airlines is described, developed in 1959 by FHK Henrion, a definite pioneer in corporate identity.

Then as now, the market was characterised by increasing convergence of activities. Faced with this situation, KLM, the world's first commercial airline, was also one of the first to recognise the need for successful differentiation from other airlines through an actively service-oriented culture. This new awareness was spread by means of a comprehensive concept which went far beyond superficial measures, to embrace aspects from corporate culture to visual image. At first, the design concept did not pass without criticism. Feelings ran high about the radical reworking of the crown, symbol of the Dutch royal family, which was part of the airline's existing insignia. The crown had to retain its emotional appeal as a symbol; at the same time the impact and recognition value needed improvement. The new crown became a vital identification feature in the corporate design concept. Almost forty years later, the mark remains unchanged and vindicates the courageous decision made then.

Another reason for the enduring success of this particular corporate identity is surely its dynamism. Over the last thirty years, the visual image has been constantly monitored for its validity and modernity, then carefully developed. By aligning itself to individual market conditions, KLM has always managed to keep its corporate identity up-to-date, both visually and through its service culture. Long-lasting relevance is the proof of a good corporate identity – an essential criterion when one considers the investment necessary. Taking other airlines into account, for example British Airways, which changed its identity three times in the same period, KLM's approach seems not only more credible, but also more economical.

Global influence from London

In the 70s, FHK Henrion's practice in London, known then as HDA International, did mostly international corporate identity consultancy work. On the client list, KLM was still present along with companies such as Audi NSU, Volkswagen, InterRent, C&A, Philips, Olivetti

and Braun. For such clients, the company worked on global corporate identity projects or on individual tasks.

One of the most innovative projects of that time was the renewal of the worldwide identity of Beiersdorf AG, owners of Nivea and other well-known brands, a text-book case study. After the US management consultants Booz Allen & Hamilton had conceptualised new fields of business and corporate structures, the corporate identity work supported the implementation of these recommendations and the worldwide positioning and presentation of the company in relation to its brands. As an essential foundation and reference point for all corporate identity activities, we already at that time developed corporate guidelines. Through pragmatic interpretation, these guidelines had immediate relevance to attitudes and day-to-day activities, as well as design and communications, at Beiersdorf.

For Henrion, Ludlow & Schmidt, as the company became known in 1981, Mitsubishi and Coopers & Lybrand followed as corporate identity tasks of global proportions, breaking new ground in cultural considerations, business areas and scope of implementation.

Searching for successful market penetration strategies, one soon discovers Japanese car manufacturers and their European 'campaign of conquest' which they have pursued since the late 70s. Typical of this phenomenon is Mitsubishi Motors Corporation. A major part of the company's success rests on its con-tracted dealers. They are what the customer is first aware of in the front line, next to the products, and they decisively influence the image of the company in the marketplace. Therefore the development of a corporate identity, which coordinated and integrated the different cultural backgrounds between the manufacturer and the dealers in Europe, was a critical success factor both there and worldwide. The corporate identity concept of Mitsubishi Motors exists to bridge Japanese and European values and perceptions and, by joining them, to create synergies. The concept, first implemented in Europe, was so successful that after a time it was adopted in other parts of the world, even Japan. The corporate identity established Mitsubishi Motors as global brand.

In the corporate identity for Coopers & Lybrand, one of the 'big six' globally-active accounting and management consulting firms, multicultural ethos and acceptance were also essential factors. How can one advertise without advertising? Coopers & Lybrand managed the squaring of this particular circle through corporate identity. As professional ethics and some national professional accountancy bodies forbade advertising activities or frowned on them, Coopers & Lybrand decided to support the Firm's worldwide presence in the market through the medium of corporate identity – in 1980 an absolute novelty in the area of professional services.

One of the most important elements of this corporate identity programme was its consistent implementation. By means of a carefully-considered worldwide logistics concept, internal acceptance was assured and by both global and local recognition in the market, 'goodwill' was increased. A flexible system of identity elements made it possible to cope with the particular and varied demands of more than 400 offices in over 100 countries around the world.

The worldwide, homogeneous appearance so created is an outstanding example of combining appropriate professional reserve with strong communicative effectiveness. It matches the market circumstances and supports the communication of international standards to which all member firms of Coopers & Lybrand around the world

subscribe. Corporate identity has given Coopers & Lybrand a globally-accepted profile and presence in the intensely competitive professional services sector.

Expectations of corporate identity

What is expected from corporate identity is heavily dependent on the specific corporate situation, which could be a merger or an acquisition, a management buyout, or a much-needed differentiation and profiling in the market. The situation could be related to the local, national acceptance of a multi-national computer company or the inter-nationalisation plans of a pharmaceuticals and chemicals corporation. The problem could be about survival in a recession or a structural change caused by increasing competition.

Companies which are able to develop their entire identities through product identity have already been mentioned. More complex and problematic is the development of identity for companies in capital goods markets and primary industry, as well as in the service sector, which have intangible or commodity products of inherently low interest. The products themselves offer little or nothing which could be given form by design to serve as a visual basis for the development of an identity. But it is particularly such companies – machine tool makers, construction companies, raw materials suppliers, airlines, insurance companies and brokers, banks, software and systems houses, local government administrations, public amenities, utilities – who need comprehensive, holistic identities to make their offer, their products and services, visible and tangible, from the design of product brochures to the behaviour of customer services departments. Offer and performance are becoming more and more similar and even interchangeable. What distinguishes one airline today from any other? All fly to the same destinations, with the same planes at the same prices. What differentiates this bank from that? They all deal in money matters, lend and claim interest on comparable terms.

It is corporate identity which can differentiate them: it is the fitting out of planes or retail branches, the visual presence, the service, the customer care, the product features and presentation as well as the marketing and corporate communications which create differentiation and profile. A comprehensive corporate identity strategy taking account of all aspects and dimensions is vital in achieving a desired positioning in the market and acceptance by target groups.

Corporate identity-oriented management

Corporate identity management is change management, especially in times of economic or cultural crisis. Those companies and employees who are most receptive to the change process which corporate identity can promote are those who are under pressure, for example in identity crises such as changes of management, loss of leadership vision, changes in market demand, financial losses, or extremes of fluctuation. Worry about employment and position can also make people open to change. But also, top management's conviction that corporate identity can develop potential and resources, and through this improve corporate performance, can act as the launch pad for corporate identity measures. The following points summarise some typical situations where consideration of corporate identity would be appropriate.

- A new company is founded.
- A merger, de-merger or management buyout takes place.

- An existing corporate identity no longer corresponds with the desired positioning, or the necessary differentiation from the competition.
- A company's brands are known and established in the market, but the company behind them is not.
- At the time of a flotation, a company needs to assure investors and others of its competence, capabilities and credibility.
- At the time of change of ownership, management or generation when, as a consequence, new visions and strategies must be communicated in a lasting way.
- Through growth, diversification or acquisitions, a company's identity is no longer appropriate, coherent, transparent or communicative.
- A new strategic direction must be communicated internally to staff and externally to the market.
- Operating companies are known to the relevant target groups, but the holding company is not.
- A company has a constricting identity, not giving single business units enough freedom to respond to market dynamics.

In addition to these occasions and circumstances, there is a whole gamut of social and economic developments which make corporate identity increasingly important. The following have been especially relevant in recent times:

- changes in values and the related increase in environmental awareness
- opportunities and challenges of the European market
- the opening up of Eastern Europe
- globalisation of markets and production
- increasing competition among the 'Triad'
- the structural crises in many areas of industry
- the challenges of the recent recession

There are also other considerations. Staff and clients are increasingly discriminating in identifying with employers or with product or service providers. Identity facilitates identification, of course, but acceptance is the prerequisite. For staff, this means acceptance of the goals, values and mission of the company for which they work. For customers, identification comes through long-term acceptance of the products or services which they buy or use. Identification requires substance, symbols and form – a meaningful, tangible and visible image.

The 'triggers' for initiating corporate identity activities may be diverse, but corporate identity should always have commercial or social relevance and real economic or conceptual benefits. For the corporate identity process to be successful, goals and strategies, strengths and weaknesses, commonalities and conflicts as well as potential and resources must be recognised, handled and developed within a framework of interdependence.

If corporate identity work is to be realistic instead of dwelling in an imaginary world of idealised harmony, we must distance ourselves from the conventionally-assumed differences between the interests of staff and those of the corporation. The primary interests of staff could be said to be:

• recognition
• material needs
• self-fulfilment
• communication
• security

Primary corporate interests could be said to be:

• profits
• growth
• security of the business
• professional recognition
• social recognition

These lists came from an actual corporate identity workshop session. The development of a comprehensive corporate identity strives to safeguard corporate goals and to balance the interests of both parties.

As social entities, companies have special, individual cultures which contribute to the identities which differentiate them from others. Soft factors, like culture, are nowadays accepted alongside hard business factors as critical to success. A culture of working together towards commonly-accepted corporate goals helps to minimise interface losses and promotes synergy, motivation and identification, leading to job satisfaction and greater efficiency. The influence of the identity on the company cannot, if it is to be successful, serve as a kind of collective discipline, but has to be done within an integrated and integrating process of activities.

Corporate identity management should therefore not be seen as an ethically questionable means of domination, but as an integrative, culturally-aware activity. The formulation and communication of corporate goals are not to be indulged in for their own sake. Only goals and perspectives which are seen as meaningful, and with which people can identify, encourage long-term involvement. A shared understanding of what is meaningful and what is not is decisive for the basic acceptance. Thus, the 'meaning' of a company is at its core.

Corporate identity development should not aim simply at instilling those patterns of action which seem to be simple steps to success, but should be a process of mutually searching for goals, activities and meaningful ways of working together. A management which is aware of the significance of corporate identity sees in identity the potential and aims for business success. Staff and management are empowered to achieve performance as a group with shared goals and values. The development of a company's identity should be seen as a dynamic process, supported and influenced by staff, and at the same time forming them. A company's identity finds its expression in behaviour and can, indeed, form a code of behaviour.

When corporate identity became popular and started to be talked about

According to the individual understanding of corporate identity, different things happened in different countries in the 80s, the decade of the identity bubble. In Britain, perceptions of corporate identity remained firmly linked to design and, as design activities grew exponentially, so did corporate identity. In this superficial decade, design became symbolic of change, but cynicism became widespread as it was realised that real change consisted of more than a new logotype or new colours. The idea that the application of design could change the culture of a company also gained adherents. This was closely connected with certain theories of 'design management', a term which has been particularly espoused by very large organisations such as BT, British Rail (now dispersed) and London Transport. The London Business School was a very strong formative influence on this situation. However, by the end of the 80s, 'design' was beginning to be identified as one of the less acceptable manifestations of the 'boom', and corporate identity, being essentially seen as a branch of design (if an esoteric one), suffered the same fate.

Unfortunately, client companies also suffered. Many 'identities' were produced which were merely fashionable graphics. They dated quickly, having been produced without attention to interdependent dimensions, thus lacking true strategic content, cultural relevance and long-term value. At the beginning of the 80s corporate identity

became popular in Germany also and, in 1985, at the BDW (German Communications Association) Congress 'The future through communications', discussion on 'the one true corporate identity strategy' reached a high spot. 'Corporate identity specialists' who had previously been advertising consultants, graphic designers, packaging designers, textile engineers, or postcard designers styled themselves as corporate identity Popes and gurus preaching various creeds. CI, CD (Corporate Design), CB (Corporate Behaviour) and CC (for either Corporate Communications or Corporate Culture) were presented as mystic formulae. English terms were used, but were given a distinctively German definition. However, these 'corporate identity specialists' actually only sold standard services within the fields of advertising, PR, design or consulting as corporate identity services.

As in the UK, some companies who bought a narrow approach and paraded a 'new corporate identity', thereby appearing trendy, were not totally displeased. They had done something superficial towards polishing their image in the market and had been spared profound corporate analysis, which might have revealed sclerotic structures in leadership style, in relationships to the socio-economic background, in behaviour or in basic competence. But such analyses are necessary in order to ascertain the actual company identity with all its weaknesses – but also with its true strengths and potential. Aesthetic exercise or superficial spectacle is not a substitute for holistic corporate identity. Many companies were damaged by such activities and corporate identity lost its credibility or even became taboo.

In recent years, discussion of corporate identity became more subdued. Within companies, an objective need for such measures still existed, and so work was done, but the words 'corporate identity' were often only mentioned in secret. A comeback for corporate identity is predicted, and it is true that in crisis it is especially valuable. However, the only approaches seem to be one-dimensional and deal solely with single, isolated disciplines and problems. The term and the range of instruments of corporate identity are variously used and interpreted. This is true not only between experts and between companies, but also increasingly, at an international level, between countries.

It is difficult to measure the success of corporate identity, in financial as well as subjective terms. Corporate identity is often devalued because the term has been worn out and misused through wrong practice. A valuation of the relevance of individual aspects can only be made in the context of a specific corporate situation.

Competence and relevance, measurable results, facts and examples are all needed to be able to evaluate the sense and purpose of corporate identity. How do companies understand corporate identity? How do they implement corporate identity? Only as a means of market and product presentation? Or also as an instrument of planning and direction for internal and external communi- cations? At which target groups are corporate identity concepts directed? Is corporate identity seen as corporate communications, marketing communications or in its total complexity as a strategic planning instrument for corporate leader- ship? For which aspects of corporate leadership can corporate identity be enlisted? Which demands are placed on corporate identity, and what advantages and benefits are expected?

DR KLAUS SCHMIDT

A series of studies on corporate identity in Europe

With international corporate identity projects, it is repeatedly noticeable that extremely different ideas on and definitions of corporate identity exist, not only from country to country, but also inside companies and between companies. To develop an internationally-relevant corporate identity, knowledge of these differing definitions, expectations and conditions is a prerequisite, in order to reach a common understanding and successful implementation.

Increasingly, companies must internationalise and thus develop and implement corporate identities under multicultural conditions. If corporate identity is to succeed as an instrument of strategic planning and leadership, then the state of current knowledge and development must be recognised along with the cultural peculiarities of target markets, so facilitating development and implementation of successful programmes. Since there was no relevant information nor investigation on these questions at an international or European level, it was clear that we at Henrion, Ludlow & Schmidt had to initiate research ourselves.

We were, above all, wanting objective information, obtained empirically from companies, applicable to real corporate identity work. We wanted to establish a factual, rational basis and thereby make a contribution to the development and credibility of corporate identity. Our aim with this investigation was to research those dimensions and parameters of action which are particularly relevant for international corporate identity activities.

On the basis of the results, methods and means for the development and implementation of corporate identity programmes would be developed.

The following questions were considered appropriate:

- How is corporate identity defined and how is it understood?
- What benefits are expected from corporate identity and what demands are made of it?
- How do companies see themselves with regard to their positioning in national and international contexts?
- To what depth of complexity is corporate identity understood, and how effectively are corporate identity measures carried out?
- What sort of target groups are seen as relevant for corporate identity measures?
- Do companies have any formal corporate principles, and, if so, how are they communicated?
- What rôle does corporate identity play in internationalisation?
- How can corporate identity take cultural differences into account?
- Are there any typical characteristics present in international identities?
- What are the best existing examples of successful international identities, and what specific features do these identities have?

Knowing that the level of corporate identity development is related to the status of development of marketing and communications within the individual countries, we could establish a sample of representative countries.

We chose Europe for our research, because it is an easily-grasped economic area containing differently-developed economies which, through their varied national and cultural conditions, simulate a global situation. Germany, France, Britain, Austria, Scandinavia (Denmark, Finland, Norway, Sweden considered as one country) and Spain were chosen as representative.

The first pan-European study 1989

To cast light on the issues raised, in 1989 we commissioned the distinguished British research company MORI (Market & Opinion Research International) to carry out a pan-European study under the title 'Corporate identity in a multicultural market'. At that time, the European single market was in the course of formation and internationalisation of companies was in full spate. Over 240 managing directors and chairmen of leading companies in the nine countries chosen were interviewed by MORI. The companies were taken at random from the top 100 to 500 in the individual countries, but aiming at a cross-section of types and business areas. The 1989 study made it very apparent that there was a very divergent development and level of knowledge about corporate identity in Europe; and it became clear what problems and expectations companies have in relation to the development of international identities. In this sense, the results of the study did not really surprise us, but did present the objective proof of our practical experience.

The results can be summarised thus: The opinions about what corporate identity is were strongly divided and could be best described as to do with image. The principal benefits expected and the greatest potential effects of corporate identity were seen as being in the area of staff motivation (32%). Building of client trust was the second mentioned benefit.

Quality and competence, both inherent in the performance and products as well as in the identity itself (19%), Europe-wide presence (13%), and the ability to adapt to different cultures (12%) were seen as the main features of an international (European) identity. There were high expectations of corporate identity as an aid to the internationalisation of companies but hardly any specific ideas which were compatible internationally. There was relatively uniform attribution of importance to those aspects which concerned human resources. Great emphasis was put on cultural differences, but only vague ideas existed on the possibilities of overcoming them. Cooperation and flexibility were mentioned, and tolerance and adaptability were expected from the other side!

The league table of successful international corporate identities was, in 1989, led by IBM (17%), a non-European company whose strength was seen in its ability to adapt to the multicultural variety and differing national characteristics of Europe. Quality, competence, presence, continuity and adaptability of corporate activities, and of the Company's identity, were the apparent criteria for rating of successful and exemplary international identities. The overwhelming image most of the surveyed companies had of themselves was that of a national company with global market demands (39%). Fewer companies felt themselves to be 'European'.

Their satisfaction with their own identities was only average, although different aspects were valued in different ways. The focus of corporate identity activity was seen as being in internal and external communications as well as in the establishment of regional and European acceptance. The companies wanted to be seen as good Europeans and involved corporate citizens. In nominating relevant target groups for corporate identity, two thirds of those interviewed mentioned customers. Perhaps surprisingly, the majority of companies (82%) said they had a formal corporate philosophy. A large proportion (29%) said that the philosophy was communicated 'through the way of thinking of senior management'.

What is to be gleaned from these results? What are the essential insights for further development of corporate identity? What does this mean in concrete terms for companies and for our work as consultants? It was the cultural aspects, especially in relation to international companies' identities, which gave a new dimension in requirements and demanded corresponding awareness and new methods of problem solving. Thus, corporate identity was seen as a potentially effective management tool for the development of international acceptance and corporate culture, but at the same time a certain helplessness prevailed on the subject of how to carry it through.

As mentioned above, the results and findings from the study proved many of our actual experiences in international corporate identity work. They also proved that it is not only specific aspects which should be taken into consideration, but that special methods and instruments are necessary to match the complexity of the demands. Against this background and on the basis of years of experience, we developed a structure model for corporate identity. The model is described in Chapter 3.

We also ascertained through the study that, for us as consultants, it is vital to know the expectations which companies have towards international corporate identity activities. On the one hand this serves to match instruments and consultancy products more realistically to the demands. On the other hand we develop know-how, which for the companies themselves is difficult or impossible to obtain.

The second pan-European study 1991

With the far-reaching social and economic changes since the first study in 1989, demands on companies changed as well. It was reasonable to expect that the demands of companies towards corporate identity would also have changed. To track these changes,

we carried out the study again in 1991, but defining the sample somewhat differently than in 1989. In addition, some questions were modified. The sample in the first study consisted mostly of chairmen and managing directors, who had some responsibility for corporate identity, but, in the second study, we decided to identify each time the person who had ultimate responsibility for corporate identity.

From each of Britain, France, Germany and Scandinavia, 40 leading managers were interviewed, with 20 each from Austria, Spain and the Benelux countries (Belgium, Netherlands). The companies were chosen again from the top 100, 300 or 500 in each country.

The sample consequently became composed as follows, which was actually a result in itself:

Chairman of the Board, Managing Director	5 %
Public relations	31 %
Corporate communications	28 %
Marketing	16 %
Personnel	4 %
Advertising	8 %
Other	8 %

We discovered that in 1991 those interviewed were generally better informed about corporate identity than in 1989. We presumed that this resulted from the 'operational proximity' of managers to corporate identity. The age of those questioned must also have played a rôle: corporate identity is more strongly established and accepted in the minds of young managers.

Because the sample was different from that in 1989, the two studies cannot be freely compared. Nevertheless, some interesting comparisons are possible.

The different results noticeable are clearly related to the fact that the majority of interviewees were in the area of public relations, corporate communications and marketing. The political situation, too, and the changed economic climate, had an influence. Since the first study a series of radical changes and developments had taken place, for example:

- the unification of Germany
- the further opening and dramatic changes in Eastern Europe and the Soviet Union
- the Gulf War
- the beginning of recession in most European countries except Germany
- the planned integration of the EFTA countries into the European Union
- the ever-increasing globalisation of production and markets
- the decreasing influence of the United States along with the increasing wealth, presence and influence of Far-Eastern countries
- the increasing importance of Europe as a unified economic area within the Triad
- the European market as the future largest, with its special characteristic of cultural and national differences

On top of these events, additional socio-economic developments took place which were relevant to corporate identity, especially constantly-increasing environmental aware-ness and a growing regional cultural aware-ness whose aim was differentiation rather than integration and assimilation.

The results of the second study

'External image, public profile and recognition' was the most spontaneously-mentioned definition of corporate identity (74%). A quarter of those asked defined corporate identity as graphic presentation and design (24%). However, 22% described corporate identity using the terms 'culture' and 'values' and 17% expected internally-

oriented effects. Image, public profile (51%) and the building of trust in the financial world (27%) were seen as the main benefits of a strong identity, followed by staff motivation (26%) and attraction of customers (25%). Nearly a quarter of those asked (23%) expected support for products and brands. In comparison with the first survey, the external target groups had become more important than the internal under the early effects of the approaching recession. The main target groups for corporate identity were seen as customers and the financial sector, employees and general public being ranked as secondary.

The motivation of staff as an aim of corporate identity measures dropped back in times of recession. In Germany (13%) and Austria (20%) pressure groups played an important rôle as targets. In Austria, for example, this group was more often mentioned than the financial world, staff or government institutions. This is surely to be taken as a sign of increasing ecological awareness, although only 2% in Britain mentioned this target audience.

A large majority thought that corporate identity could play an important rôle in the internationalisation of companies and markets, although this was in terms of external goals. The benefits of corporate identity were seen in 'the opening up of new foreign markets' (27%), in 'the securing of international recognition' (25%) and in 'the establishment of an internationally consistent image' (23%).

Cultural aspects were seen as essential in internationalisation, and cultural differences were identified as the main obstacle in the development of international corporate identities. Bearing this in mind, it is astonishing that the potential of corporate culture to act as an integrating factor was hardly mentioned. The question about satisfaction with the company's own identity brought the response that corporate culture was seen as the greatest problem. In Germany and Austria, where more emphasis was placed on staff motivation, only 8% and 5% respectively were satisfied with their own corporate culture and only 5% and 15% respectively were satisfied with their internal communications. In Britain, 18% were satisfied with their corporate culture, 36% with their internal communications. These professionals also criticised the lack of awareness of the significance of corporate identity in their own companies. In Germany and Austria, those responsible for corporate identity even rated this aspect as the main obstacle to the development of international corporate identity concepts.

Corporate culture was rated by one third (33%) of those interviewed to be by far the most important aspect of corporate identity, followed by internal communications at 20% and marketing communications at 19%. Thus, the interdependence of corporate culture and internal communications does not seem to have been recognised. Most interviewees were clueless as to how an integrative corporate culture could be formed. The possibilities of communication as a means of influencing culture were too little seen.

It was surprising that none of those responsible for personnel argued spontaneously that corporate identity would increase staff motivation, help with recruitment or express corporate culture and values. The need here for much persuasion on the possibilities and potential of corporate identity measures was clearly hinted at.

The building of trust within the financial world (40%) and with customers (31%) are at the peak of satisfaction with elements of corporate identity, falling under the heading of 'very satisfied'. Satisfaction with corporate culture and internal communications was

relatively low. Only 15% and 17% respectively were 'very satisfied', with 22% and 30% respectively 'not satisfied'. There was also a large number who professed themselves 'quite satisfied' (60% with corporate culture and 52% with internal communication), which can actually be rated as dissatisfaction. Corporate advertising as well as marketing communications were also relatively poorly rated. Again, as in 1989, the majority of companies asked said they had a formulated corporate philosophy (88%). However, communication of this through the different levels of a company could not be ascertained.

IBM (38%) and Coca-Cola (31%) were rated as the companies with the most exemplary corporate identities. American companies were even more prevalent in 1991 than in 1989. In the upper ranks there were fewer car manufacturers. They were simply forced out by fast-moving consumer brands such as Coca-Cola and McDonald's. All in all, one could say that the demands on corporate identity had become more differentiated and definite since 1989.

In our markets for corporate identity consultancy, we have also experienced this change. Corporate identity projects are less and less often approached through superficial visual motives. The starting points and triggers for corporate identity work are more serious. So the full benefits of corporate identity are increasingly sought in cases of, for example, mergers and acquisitions and in business areas affected by deregulation. Crises have created necessities for the measures, have intensified awareness of the results and have demanded real consequences from implementation.

The third pan-European study 1993

In 1993, the barriers between the twelve EU countries fell. Within this great economic power block, which produces one quarter of the world's economic output with 6% of the world's population, a huge unified market has developed – the Single Market. This means free flow of goods, services, capital and people. In general Europe was, and is, in the process of restructuring. Seldom before had such radical changes taken place in such a short period of time, and never before had the companies of Europe faced such great challenges as:

- the intensification of the worldwide recession
- the relentless globalisation of markets and production
- the increasing presence of Far-Eastern industrial companies
- the further opening and dramatic changes in Eastern Europe
- the creation of the European economic area
- the intensification of the war in the former Yugoslavia
- the rejection of the values of the 80s and the adoption of the new values of the 90s: modesty and ecology, cost and quality awareness.

As already noted, when demands on companies change, so, too, do demands on corporate identity. To record these further changes, Henrion, Ludlow & Schmidt – again in collaboration with MORI – carried out the third pan-European survey in 1993.

In total, 223 top managers responsible for corporate identity were interviewed. To guarantee comparable results, questions from the 1991 survey were repeated. Questions referring to the rôle and benefits to be expected from corporate identity in the recession were added.

The configuration of the representative sample of countries matched, to a large extent, that of the 1991 study, and the companies were again chosen from the 100, 300 or 500 leading companies from each country.

Countries		Number of interviewees	
		1993	1991
Germany	(G)	42	40
Great Britain	(GB)	41	40
France	(F)	40	40
Scandinavia	(Sc)	40	40
Austria	(A)	20	20
Spain	(Sp)	20	20
Benelux	(BL)	20	20

The status of corporate identity had changed in comparison to 1991: more chairmen were adopting responsibility for corporate identity and there was a stronger focus of corporate identity responsibility on the fields of public relations, corporate communications and marketing at the expense of personnel and advertising.

As the first indication of this, the composition of the sample, in terms of the functions represented, was now as follows:

	1993	1991
Chairman, Managing Director	8%	5%
Public relations	35%	31%
Corporate communications	31%	28%
Marketing	19%	16%
Personnel	3%	4%
Advertising	2%	8%
Other	2%	8%

Definition of corporate identity

Again, in 1993 'image', 'company profile' and 'public presentation' were the most commonly-quoted definitions of corporate identity.

In Britain, more people mentioned 'visual presentation' and 'logotype' than in any other country (44%). By contrast, fewer mentioned culture, values or philosophy than in any other country (4%). This represents the narrowest view of corporate identity in Europe.

In Germany, on the other hand, definitions encompassed all essential dimensions of corporate identity: from the corporate culture and staff behaviour to the visual appearance, the public profile and the image.

How, briefly, would you define corporate identity?

	Total % 1993	GB %	F %	G %	Sc %	A %	BL %	Sp %	Total % 1991	Change %
Public image/ external projection	**50**	51	50	38	53	50	60	55	74	-24
Visual presentation/logo	**27**	**44**	10	33	**40**	15	5	20	24	+3
Expression of culture/values/ philosophy	**20**	4	20	**40**	13	**35**	20	15	22	-2
Internal projection/behaviour of staff	**18**	7	13	**38**	10	**45**	15	5	17	+1
Product/brand support	**4**	5	8	5	8	0	0	0	8	-4
Advertising/communications support	**4**	2	5	5	5	0	0	5	10	-6

Source: MORI, © Copyright: Henrion, Ludlow & Schmidt, 1993

Benefits of a strong corporate identity

Unchanged as an essential perceived benefit of a strong corporate identity is a clear public profile (52%). This benefit is valued by all countries more strongly than in 1991, even more so in Britain (68%). By contrast, all other benefit aspects experienced something of a decline.

A high rating for staff motivation was still given in Germany (36%) and Austria (30%), the advantages perceived corresponded with the definition of corporate identity. The low score given to staff motivation benefits in Britain (7%) reflects the British definition of corporate identity.

What do you see as the benefits of a strong corporate identity?

	Total % 1993	GB %	F %	G %	Sc %	A %	BL %	Sp %	Total % 1991	Change %
Public profile/recognition	**52**	**68**	40	50	43	60	**70**	45	51	+1
Staff motivation	**16**	7	23	**36**	8	**30**	0	0	26	-10
Attracts customers/aids customer relations	**13**	10	8	12	**33**	5	5	10	25	-12
Financial advantages/confidence among financial community	**12**	10	**28**	0	18	0	10	15	27	-15
Visual presentation/unity	**11**	17	8	**17**	10	10	0	5	13	-2
Product/brand support	**9**	5	13	5	13	0	5	20	23	-14
Expresses culture/values	**4**	5	0	7	3	**15**	0	0	12	-8
Advertising/communications support	**4**	2	5	0	5	10	5	5	10	-6
Attracts staff	**4**	0	5	5	8	0	5	0	9	-5

Source: MORI, © Copyright: Henrion, Ludlow & Schmidt, 1993

Satisfaction with aspects of corporate identity

How satisfied are you with the current state of each of the following in your organisation?

Logotypes and symbols were the aspects of corporate identity with which top managers were most satisfied two years previously. This pattern continued in 1993 (49% 'very satisfied').

Nearly a third were 'very satisfied' with their corporate design, only 16% indicating 'not satisfied' with this aspect.

A further trend was apparent: more of those questioned were 'very satisfied' with the cultures of their companies (23%). On the other hand, almost as many top managers (24%) were 'not satisfied' with the cultures of their companies. Evaluation of corporate culture in Germany, the country with the most

qualified corporate identity awareness, was particularly critical. Here only 17% of those interviewed were 'very satisfied' with the corporate culture, as opposed to 33% who were 'not satisfied' with this aspect. Basically, those questioned in all countries professed themselves more satisfied with their corporate identities than they were two years previously.

Only in Britain were the performances of aspects of corporate identity rated worse than in 1991. Only 15% were 'very satisfied' with the corporate culture, and remarkably few (39%) were happy with their logotypes and symbols, a surprising result given the importance attached to these aspects.

All countries	Very satisfied %	Fairly satisfied %	Not very satisfied %	Not at all satisfied %	No opinion %	Average %
Logotypes and symbols	49	38	8	4	1	1.2
Corporate design	31	45	14	2	8	1.0
Corporate culture	23	51	21	3	2	0.7
Marketing communications	21	49	17	1	11	0.8
Corporate advertising	19	39	21	4	17	0.6
Corporate communications	19	56	21	3	2	0.7

Source: MORI, © Copyright: Henrion, Ludlow & Schmidt, 1993

Importance of aspects of corporate identity

As in 1991, corporate culture was rated clearly the most important corporate identity aspect (37%). This referred to the internal as well as to the external effect of the corporate culture.

Further important aspects were internal communications (23%) and marketing communications (16%). At the bottom of the importance rating of corporate identity aspects were corporate advertising (6%), corporate design (5%) and logotypes and symbols (4%).

Which single aspect of corporate identity is of greatest underlying importance to the company?

	Total % 1993	GB %	F %	G %	Sc %	A %	BL %	Sp %	Total % 1991	Change %
Corporate culture	**39**	**46**	40	31	38	**50**	35	40	33	+6
Corporate communications	**23**	22	15	19	**33**	20	**40**	15	20	+3
Marketing communications	**16**	17	18	**24**	5	20	10	20	19	-3
Corporate advertising	**6**	2	15	5	5	5	0	5	2	+4
Corporate design	**5**	2	3	**12**	3	5	5	10	9	-4
Logotypes and symbols	**4**	5	0	0	10	2	5	5	12	-8

Source: MORI, © Copyright: Henrion, Ludlow & Schmidt, 1993

Satisfaction with current performance

How satisfied are you with your company's current performance on each of the following?

The European 'corporate identity responsibles' were generally satisfied with the performances of their corporate identities: 70% to 80% valued the impact of corporate identity activities in their companies in the relevant areas with the terms 'very satisfied' or 'satisfied'.

Especially positively valued was performance in the areas of 'building trust with existing customers' (40% 'very satisfied', 48% 'quite satisfied') and 'building trust with financial partners' (41% 'very satisfied', 40% 'quite satisfied'). Those questioned obviously thought that they were addressing themselves successfully to these, their main target groups.

Only a third of all questioned chairmen (35%) were satisfied with the degree to which corporate identity supported 'the acquisition of new customers'. To be set against that, nearly all (94%) argued their company was good in recruiting staff, a point to which half of the personnel managers agreed. Thus, only 63% of the personnel managers stated that corporate identity was influential in staff motivation, compared to the overall figure of 75%.

All countries	Very satisfied %	Fairly satisfied %	Not very satisfied %	Not at all satisfied %	No opinion %	Average %
Confidence among the financial community	41	40	10	1	8	1.2
Confidence among existing customers	40	48	8	0	4	1.2
Attracting potential employees	25	49	17	1	8	0.9
General image to external audiences	20	55	18	3	4	0.7
Staff motivation	19	57	19	1	4	0.8
Attracting new customers	15	51	19	1	14	0.7

Source: MORI, © Copyright: Henrion, Ludlow & Schmidt, 1993

Target audiences

Customers, existing and potential, were seen as the target group in the forefront of corporate identity efforts. For those questioned, in times of recession the maintenance and care of existing customer potential was the prime goal.

Further important target groups were shareholders and financial institutions as well as staff and the general public.

Which target audience or audiences is your corporate identity primarily targeted at?

	Total % 1993	GB %	F %	G %	Sc %	A %	BL %	Sp %	Total % 1991	Change %
Existing customers	**67**	41	**88**	74	70	60	65	65	56	+11
Potential customers	**57**	29	**78**	**67**	**73**	50	**75**	15	58	-1
Financial institutions/ shareholders	**38**	**56**	**53**	19	38	10	50	25	42	-5
Existing employees	**36**	17	43	**48**	40	45	**50**	5	30	+6
Potential employees	**24**	2	**35**	**36**	35	25	20	5	20	+4
General public	**20**	7	23	19	20	**40**	30	10	27	-7
Media	**15**	10	**28**	7	15	15	**30**	0	14	+1
Government	**12**	12	15	12	10	0	**25**	10	14	-2
Opinion leaders	**11**	5	18	17	0	20	20	0	14	-3
Suppliers	**9**	7	**20**	12	0	5	15	0	7	+2
Professional bodies	**8**	5	13	7	8	10	10	5	14	-6
Pressure groups	**7**	2	10	5	3	15	**25**	0	7	0
Average number of audiences	**3.1**	2.2	4.3	3.3	3.2	3.0	4.2	1.5	3.1	0

Source: MORI, © Copyright: Henrion, Ludlow & Schmidt, 1993

Corporate mission

Do you have a formulated corporate mission? If so, where is it communicated?

77% of all companies stated that they had a formal corporate mission. Surprisingly, Germany seemed to be lacking in this 'culture'. Germany (64%) and Britain (63%) were among the countries where companies were least likely to have a formal corporate mission. And when a philosophy did exist, then its implementation was in a bad way. From the information received from those questioned in Britain, the mission was communicated 'in the annual report' (39%),

'in the way of thinking of the top management' (7%) or 'somewhere else' (2%). In Germany, these scores were 19%, 17% and 40% respectively.

One of those questioned expressed the necessity of a corporate mission as follows: 'Without a true message corporate identity is senseless. All employees must have an awareness of the message of their corporate identity.'

	Total % 1993	GB %	F %	G %	Sc %	A %	BL %	Sp %	Total % 1991	Change %
Yes, total	**77**	63	77	64	**95**	75	**95**	75	88	-11
In the annual report	**30**	39	**43**	19	28	10	**50**	15	24	+6
In the corporate plan	**28**	5	23	12	**55**	**60**	35	30	31	-3
In the human resources/ personnel programme	**20**	22	28	10	23	20	30	5	16	+4
In the corporate identity	**20**	7	**40**	12	13	10	**45**	20	10	+10
In the minds of senior managers	**19**	7	**35**	17	28	15	25	0	21	-2
In the corporate advertising	**19**	15	**40**	12	10	10	**35**	10	19	0
Elsewhere	**13**	2	15	**40**	3	5	5	5	11	+2
Average number of sources	**1.9**	1.5	2.9	1.9	1.7	1.7	2.4	1.1	1.7	+0.2

Source: MORI, © Copyright: Henrion, Ludlow & Schmidt, 1993

The rôle of corporate identity in internationalisation

The necessity of adjusting to the single market and the tendency of companies and markets to globalise led to increasing demands on corporate identity. 85% saw corporate identity as an important instrument in the internationalisation of their companies. This rating had not changed since 1991. On the rôle of corporate identity in internationalisation, those interviewed had a clear judgement: 'Corporate identity supports companies introducing new products or new services in different markets. It is easier to penetrate a new market if the company is internationally known.' 70% had experience with the corporate identities of their companies in the process of internationalisation. Their judgement was thus based on concrete experience. Over one quarter of those asked (26%) saw recognition value and clear identification of the company as the most important contributions of corporate identity to internationalisation. Further highly valued aspects were the promotion of market position and of turnover through a strong image (17%) as well as support in the development of markets (15%). Here, too, the opinion stated in the question about definition of corporate identity was repeated, in that corporate identity is especially seen as an instrument for establishing profile, creating market presence and developing a desired image, or, as one interviewee said: 'Corporate identity promotes a good market position in different countries and internationally-successful sales. It helps to build a business basis of trust.'

How important a rôle would you say corporate identity can play in preparing a company for the single market and internationalisation in general?

	Total % 1993	GB %	F %	G %	Sc %	A %	BL %	Sp %	Total % 1991	Change %
Very important	**59**	56	**70**	38	63	60	50	**85**	64	-5
Fairly important	**26**	22	18	40	25	25	45	10	26	0
Not very important	**5**	7	0	7	3	10	5	5	5	0
Not at all important	**5**	10	8	10	0	0	0	0	3	+2
No opinion	**5**	5	5	5	10	5	0	0	2	+3
Helpful	**85**	78	88	78	88	85	**95**	**95**	90	-5
Not helpful	**10**	17	8	17	3	10	5	5	8	+2

Source: MORI, © Copyright: Henrion, Ludlow & Schmidt, 1993

No opinion

Not at all important

Not very important

Very important

5%

5%

5%

59%

26%

Source: MORI,
© Copyright: Henrion,
Ludlow & Schmidt, 1993

Fairly important

In what ways can corporate identity be important in this context?

	Total % 1993	GB %	F %	G %	Sc %	A %	BL %	Sp %	Total % 1991	Change %
Recognition/identification	**26**	31	17	22	25	26	20	**50**	25	+1
Strengthens market position	**17**	20	17	19	25	5	25	0	23	-6
Targeting foreign markets/ relevant to international marketplace	**15**	20	23	8	14	21	5	15	27	-12
Gains customers/investors	**9**	6	14	11	8	11	10	5	15	-6
Motivates/unifies employees	**7**	11	17	3	3	0	5	5	4	+3

Source: MORI, © Copyright: Henrion, Ludlow & Schmidt, 1993

Problems in translating corporate identity internationally

What are the main problems in translating corporate identity internationally?

Cultural differences were seen by 30% of those questioned as the main obstacle to the establishment of a successful, international identity. After a clear gap, language barriers and untranslatable names (14%) and costs (12%) followed.

In 1991, lack of understanding of corporate identity within management was one of the most essential problems in the implementation of international corporate identity concepts. In 1993, this aspect played no rôle. Instead, cost considerations had increased in intensity, especially in Germany, Scandinavia and Spain. 'It is only a question of time and money', confirmed one interviewee.

	Total %	GB %	F %	G %	Sc %	A %	BL %	Sp %	Total %	Change %
	1993								1991	
Cultural differences/barriers	**30**	34	**45**	24	33	30	30	5	49	-19
Language barriers/ translatable name	**14**	**27**	20	10	10	10	15	0	19	-5
Money/expense	**12**	10	8	14	18	5	0	**25**	9	+3
Research into different cultures/symbols/ standardisation of symbols	**10**	10	13	10	5	0	10	**25**	10	0
Symbol/logo must be identifiable	**6**	2	3	7	5	5	15	10	4	+2
Lack of understanding amongst internal management of the importance of corporate identity	**4**	2	0	10	5	5	0	0	11	-7
Adaptation of logo/products	**3**	2	3	5	5	0	0	0	16	-13

Source: MORI, © Copyright: Henrion, Ludlow & Schmidt, 1993

Characteristics of an international corporate identity

'An international corporate identity is successful when it represents and relates the interests of different cultures'. The main features of internationally-successful corporate identities were named as universality and global relevance (10%), followed by recognisable design and clear visual identity (13%) as well as aspects of recognition and identification of the company (13%). Besides these, the reliability of products and services was named by 11%. Features such as simplicity (9%), unification, integration and consistency (9%) were then mentioned, these being related to internal as well as external aspects.

What in your opinion are the most important characteristics for an international corporate identity to have?

	Total % 1993	GB %	F %	G %	Sc %	A %	BL %	Sp %	Total % 1991	Change %
Universality/ relevance to all nations	**16**	**27**	15	14	10	20	5	15	35	-19
Striking design/logo/ clear visual identity	**13**	**22**	5	12	13	10	5	20	19	-6
Instant recognition/ identification	**13**	**27**	10	17	5	5	20	0	17	-4
Reliability of products/services	11	0	**25**	5	15	10	20	5	16	-5
Strength/strong image	**9**	2	8	12	15	5	10	10	12	-3
Simplicity	**9**	20	3	2	10	0	10	15	5	+4
Uniformity/consistency	**9**	10	3	17	5	**20**	10	0	3	+6
Clear message	**8**	2	3	5	10	0	10	**35**	7	+1

Source: MORI, © Copyright: Henrion, Ludlow & Schmidt, 1993

Corporate identity and recession

How helpful do you think a strong corporate identity can be in protecting a company from the effects of economic slowdown and recession?

Similar high expectations were met with here as with the question on the rôle of corporate identity in internationalisation. An overwhelming majority of those interviewed (74%) stated that corporate identity could be of help in a recession ('very helpful': 41%, 'quite helpful': 33%). 'Companies with a strong corporate identity are less endangered or affected by temporary market shifts', was one conclusive statement. Looking internally, one respondent said, 'Staff are still motivated when times are bad: then they are better able to cope with difficulties'.

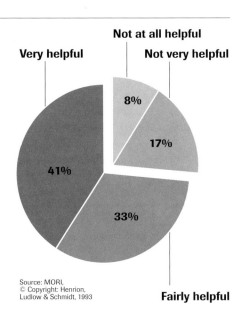

Source: MORI,
© Copyright: Henrion,
Ludlow & Schmidt, 1993

Benefits of corporate identity in a recession

In evaluating how corporate identity can be of help in the fight against the effects of recession, the aspect 'strong image' stood out in front with 34%. Here also the benefit was related externally to market profile and internally to staff.

Besides strong image, other aspects of long-term benefit were mentioned, such as customer and staff loyalty (26%), and the building of trust among customers, staff and shareholders (21%). 'In the case of market shrinkage, as happens for example in a recession, it is of great help to have loyal customers, which a company with a strong corporate identity usually has.'

In this question, it was confirmed that expectations and evaluations depend on the understanding of corporate identity in the individual countries. The British and Scandinavians, who defined corporate identity principally as logotypes and design, rated the rôle of corporate identity in the recession lower than the Austrians and French, who defined corporate identity through cultural and internal aspects; 80% and 90% respectively of those questioned saw corporate identity as helpful for motivation and customer loyalty.

So corporate identity was seen, when understood as a complex multi-dimensional phenomenon which takes into consideration various internal and external aspects, as a helpful instrument in the fight against the consequences of recession.

How helpful do you think a strong corporate identity can be in protecting a company from the effects of economic slowdown and recession?

	Total % 1993	GB %	F %	G %	Sc %	A %	BL %	Sp %
Very helpful	**41**	34	55	38	40	40	40	35
Fairly helpful	**33**	29	35	33	35	40	25	30
Not very helpful	17	24	3	12	18	15	35	25
Not at all helpful	8	12	8	14	3	5	0	10
Helpful	**74**	**63**	**90**	71	75	**80**	65	65
Not helpful	25	36	11	26	21	20	35	35

Source: MORI, © Copyright: Henrion, Ludlow & Schmidt, 1993

In what ways do you think a strong corporate identity can help in times of recession?

	Total %	GB %	F %	G %	Sc %	A %	BL %	Sp %
Reputation/strength of company	**34**	27	28	30	27	25	**62**	77
Trust/loyalty among customers/staff	**26**	**38**	22	**30**	23	31	15	15
Confidence among customers/staff/shareholders	21	19	**36**	13	**30**	6	15	0
Product/brand familiarity	**9**	**19**	8	10	13	0	0	0
Staff motivation	**9**	0	6	**17**	7	**31**	0	0

Source: MORI, © Copyright: Henrion, Ludlow & Schmidt, 1993

Successful international identities

Which companies come to mind when you think of an exemplary and successful international corporate identity?

Which companies were those whose identities were seen as exemplary? The Top Ten of the international corporate identities rated as successful and exemplary was again led by American companies. By a clear distance Coca-Cola was seen as the company with the best international corporate identity. 'You can drink their corporate identity' as one of those questioned put it. IBM exchanged its first place of 1991 for second. The Company fell back by ten percentage points to 28% in comparison to 1991 when it registered 38% of the nominations.

Well behind the two front runners there followed a whole clutch of companies: Daimler Benz/Mercedes-Benz (12%), Shell (11%), BP (10%), McDonald's (10%), Sony (9%), Ford (7%), ICI (6%) and British Airways (6%). Very different business areas were represented – from car manufacturing to fast-moving consumer goods, petrol, computers and chemicals. No single area predominated. In comparison to the 1991 survey, there were changes also outside the leading group. One of the biggest climbers was McDonald's with

an increase of 6 percentage points. Ford managed an increase of 5 percentage points.

The field of losers was led by IBM which lost 10 percentage points, with Daimler Benz/Mercedes-Benz, ICI and BMW each losing 4 percentage points. In comparison to 1991, car manufacturers in general had obviously lost reputation and popularity, which can be perhaps explained by the critical situation of the European motor industry. It is obvious that decreases in personnel numbers, worsened relationships with suppliers or weakened market position have a negative impact on the evaluation of an identity.

At first sight, IBM seemed to be the big loser. Looking at the results more closely, we recognised that IBM possessed considerable goodwill potential among those interviewed. Those who saw corporate identity particularly as an expression of culture and values had a significantly high regard for IBM. Some quotations on this: 'IBM has implemented all the factors that are related to a strong corporate philosophy'. 'A strong image transcends the problems of recent times.

Company		Total % 1993	GB %	F %	G %	Sc %	A %	BL %	Sp %	Total % 1991	Change %
1	**Coca-Cola**	**36**	32	23	29	**50**	30	40	**65**	31	+5
2	**IBM**	**28**	24	23	19	33	**45**	**35**	30	**38**	-10
3	**Daimler Benz/ Mercedes-Benz**	**12**	2	5	**33**	3	10	10	**25**	16	-4
4	**Shell**	**11**	24	3	0	8	15	**35**	5	8	+3
5	**BP**	**10**	**22**	0	2	8	15	**20**	10	7	+3
5	**McDonald's**	**10**	**22**	3	7	8	**25**	5	5	**4**	+6
7	**Sony**	**9**	5	15	12	8	10	5	0	8	+1
8	**Ford**	**7**	**22**	0	0	5	5	0	**15**	**2**	+5
9	**ICI**	**6**	**32**	0	0	0	0	0	0	10	-4
9	**British Airways**	**6**	**17**	0	2	3	5	0	**15**	2	+4
11	**Apple**	**4**	0	5	2	**13**	0	0	0	2	+2
11	**BMW**	**4**	5	3	**12**	3	0	0	0	8	-4
11	**Nestlé**	**4**	0	5	2	3	**15**	5	5	3	+1
11	**Siemens**	**4**	2	3	**10**	5	0	0	0	3	+1

Source: MORI, © Copyright: Henrion, Ludlow & Schmidt, 1993

They have grown out of their problems'. 'They seem to build a global unit and to have a strong esprit-de-corps.'

Striking among nominations for Coca-Cola was the fact that the valuations related to nearly all dimensions of identity, starting with the visual appearance and including the building of trust in the financial world. Product support and customer loyalty were put forward as positive features, but corporate identity aspects of internal relevance were hardly mentioned.

'Coca-Cola implements its corporate principles and guidelines globally. Its appearance is homogeneous in all countries.' 'A classical company with an evolved

corporate strategy instead of radical change.' 'A comprehensive concept for the whole world.'

At Daimler Benz/Mercedes-Benz the products were seen as a supporting factor of corporate identity. 'Solidity and quality', lasting, high-quality product lines. They have the reputation of selling more than just cars.

Regarding McDonald's, with an increase of 6 percentage points in comparison to 1991, the remarks referred to international, even global consistency, and acceptance of the concept and unity of brand and company. 'Their corporate identity transcends all cultural frontiers.' 'Their concept is accepted by different cultures.' 'The Company is the brand.'

Ford also belonged to the winners. With an increase of 5 percentage points the Company secured seventh place.

With Shell, uniform appearance was especially appreciated, the ratings coming from those interviewed for whom visual aspects were in the forefront of their corporate identity understanding.

In all countries, ICI's identity was rated lower than in the study of 1991. Its place in the Top Ten is only due to its ranking in Britain.

A third of British managers gave the opinion

that ICI has a successful international corporate identity. Internationally, this was not confirmed.

At this point, it is interesting to ask the question as to which companies were not represented. Where was, for example, Volkswagen, the biggest car manufacturer in Europe? Where was Rover? Where was Adidas, one of the big global brands? Where was BASF? Where were Audi, Fiat, Glaxo, or Hoechst? Or the big Japanese companies? All are international players, but their identities did not position them as such.

Top Ten by country

Which companies come to mind when you think of an exemplary and successful international corporate identity?

From a country-specific view of the results one can see that the ratings have become more international over the years. In 1991, a still very strongly-biased national selection could be seen. In 1993, Coca-Cola won in all countries with the exception of Germany and Austria. In France, the front runner was devalued by 7 percentage points and in Austria by 20 percentage points in

comparison to 1991 (1993: 50%, 1991: 30%). IBM managed to hold on to first position in Austria. In nearly all other countries IBM scored number two. The exceptions were Germany and Britain, where the Company slipped down to third place.

Shell's overall result was little different, but its score in the different countries changed

Britain	1993 %	1991 %
1 Coca-Cola	32	20
1 ICI	32	39
3 IBM	24	25
3 Shell	24	11
5 BP	22	18
5 Ford	22	7
5 McDonald's	22	2
8 British Airways	17	5
9 Pepsi	7	-
10 Sony	5	-

France	1993 %	1991 %
1 Coca-Cola	23	30
1 IBM	23	38
3 Sony	15	20
4 American Express	5	-
4 Apple	5	3
4 Daimler Benz	5	5
4 Michelin	5	-
4 Nestlé	5	-
4 Rhone-Poulenc	5	-
4 St. Gobain	5	-

Germany	1993 %	1991 %
1 Daimler Benz	33	43
2 Coca-Cola	29	13
3 IBM	19	35
4 BMW	12	20
4 Sony	12	5
6 Siemens	10	13
7 McDonald's	7	-
8 Benetton	5	-
8 Deutsche Bank	5	13
8 Volvo	5	-

quite significantly. In Germany and Spain Shell was devalued. In Britain, the Benelux countries, Austria and Scandinavia it gained points.

McDonald's improved generally in all countries. The development in Britain was remarkable. Whereas in 1991 only 2% of the British questioned mentioned the Company, in 1993 nearly a quarter (22%) thought McDonald's corporate identity was exemplary.

The slight overall decrease of Daimler Benz/ Mercedes-Benz was caused by strongly differing ratings in the individual countries: In Germany (1993: 33%, 1991: 43%) and in Austria (1993: 10%, 1991: 35%) Mercedes was severely devalued. In Spain, more of those questioned named the Company than two years previously. Here, there was an increase of 10 percentage points (1993: 25%, 1991: 15%).

For Ford and British Airways, too, a positive trend was recorded, which was essentially due to the extraordinarily good ratings of these two companies in Britain and Spain. The poor position of BMW is influenced by its score in specific countries. The most extreme devaluation took place in Austria, where in 1991 a fifth rated the corporate identity as exemplary. In 1993, no nominations were made for BMW.

Apple, Nestlé and Siemens were relatively consistent, but slightly negative. In Britain, the 1993 climbers were McDonald's (plus 20 percentage points), Ford (plus 15), Shell (plus 13), Coca-Cola (plus 12) and British Airways (plus 13).

In France, from fourth place downwards, all were newcomers. Most remarkable was that none of the big French car manufacturers ranked in the listing.

In Scandinavia, Coca-Cola increased strongly with 50% of the votes and pushed itself past

IBM (33%) to first place. In places four to seven, newcomers entered the lists: Apple (13%), Volvo (10%), BP (8%), Carlsberg (8%). With three Scandinavian companies in the Top Ten, once again a national influence could be detected. ABB lost two percentage points, but still remained at third place together with Apple.

Austrian managers, however, were totally internationally-oriented in their opinions. Not a single Austrian company reached the Top Ten. At the top stayed IBM with 45% of the votes. This position was supported by the slipping of Coca-Cola by 20 percentage points. McDonald's, BP and Nestlé increased in comparison to 1991, each by 10 percentage

Scandinavia		1993 %	1991 %
1	Coca-Cola	50	39
2	IBM	33	41
3	ABB	13	15
3	Apple	13	-
5	Volvo	10	-
6	BP	8	2
6	Carlsberg	8	-
6	McDonald's	8	5
6	Shell	8	7
6	Sony	8	5

Benelux		1993 %	1991 %
1	Coca-Cola	40	30
2	IBM	35	60
2	Shell	35	25
4	BP	20	-
5	Daimler Benz	10	5
5	Philips	10	5
5	Unilever	10	10
8	McDonald's	5	5
8	Nestlé	5	-
8	Sony	5	5

Austria		1993 %	1991 %
1	IBM	45	45
2	Coca-Cola	30	50
3	McDonald's	25	15
4	BP	15	5
4	Nestlé	15	5
4	Shell	15	-
7	Esso	10	-
7	Daimler Benz	10	35
7	Sony	10	-
7	Unilever	10	-

Spain		1993 %	1991 %
1	Coca-Cola	65	55
2	IBM	30	35
3	Daimler Benz	25	15
4	Repsol	20	-
5	British Airways	15	-
5	Ford	15	5
5	General Motors	15	-
8	BP	10	5
8	Barclays Bank	10	-
8	Marlboro	10	5

Source: MORI, © Copyright: Henrion, Ludlow & Schmidt, 1993

points, and improved their placings to three, four and five. Daimler Benz/Mercedes-Benz lost 25 percentage points and fell back from third place to seventh. Newcomers to the Austrian Top Ten were Shell, Esso, Sony and Unilever.

In the Benelux countries, Coca-Cola improved by 10 percentage points, reaching 40% of votes, while IBM lost 25 percentage points and slipped to place two behind Coca-Cola with only 35%. Shell improved from 25% to 35% and reached, together with IBM, place two. BP was the climber: a newcomer which didn't rank in the Top Ten two years ago, it reached 20% and third place. Two years previously, ICI could claim place four. This time it did not enter the Top Ten at all.

The interviewees' judgement in Spain, too, was internationally-oriented, with Repsol the only Spanish company in the listing, with 20% of the votes and in fourth place. Repsol was the number one climber. Incidentally, Coca-Cola built on its dominant position of recent years and reached 65%, more than the rest of the field combined, which was led by IBM with 30%. British companies did well in Spain. British Airways won, with 15%, place five and Barclays Bank, with 10%, place eighth equal. Both companies are active in Spain, and obviously the identities are seen as exemplary by Spanish managers. Similar to the British, Spanish managers defined corporate identity principally in terms of image and profile.

Comparison of the survey results 1989 to 1993

From the three studies, some general results are worthy of separate comparison. The largely external orientation of corporate identity understanding has not changed over the years although, since the first study, internal aspects such as 'expression of culture/values/philosophy' and 'internal picture/influence/staff behaviour' are increasingly in the minds of people responsible for corporate identity.

Throughout the three studies, customers, existing and potential, were cited as the most important target group. With the intensification of competition and the recession, companies concentrated more on the primary target groups and staff, whilst the significance of other target groups such as financial institutions, shareholders and the general public decreased somewhat.

Whilst the formulated corporate philosophy in 1989 was mostly to be found 'somewhere else' (35%) and 'in the minds of senior managers' (29%), it is now increasingly presented and transmitted through the annual report (30%) as well as in the strategic corporate plan (28%). Coca-Cola has, over the last years, steadily improved its position in the Top Ten, from 15 in 1989, through second place in the 1991 survey, to first place in 1993. The evaluation of Coca-Cola is strongly related to the definition of corporate identity as image, profile and public presentation.

In all three surveys, IBM attained a good rating, even when the Company was devalued by 10 percentage points from 1991 to 1993, thereby losing prime position. On this occasion, the goodwill developed through corporate identity in happier times stood the Company in good stead. Otherwise, the rating would surely have been worse. Daimler Benz/Mercedes-Benz held the most consistent position in the rating of exemplary corporate identities. In all three surveys the Company reached third place. Also relatively constant were both oil companies, Shell and BP.

Besides the big climber Coca-Cola, there were other companies, too, which in 1989 did not gain appreciation, but which, via the survey in 1991, gained a place in the 1993 Top Ten, especially McDonald's and Sony.

The biggest loser is surely Philips. In 1989 still at second place with only one percentage point difference from IBM, by 1991, then 1993, the Company occupied places 14 and 15 respectively. Here, too, the management mistakes and financial problems of the Company must have played a rôle in the evaluation.

Conclusion and outlook

The general situation in Europe and the related challenges for companies have already been mentioned. European managers had to adapt to the new conditions, and in this they gave corporate identity, as an instrument of strategic corporate leadership, a special significance, as the results of the study clearly prove.

The expectations which corporate identity must meet change with those which companies must meet. And those expectations and goals include all dimensions of a company's identity, from corporate culture and corporate behaviour to market presentation, from the products and services to communications and design. In all these areas, corporate identity is an instrument of differentiation and optimises potential and resources. The demands on corporate identity are pragmatic and have clear economic relevance.

Europe's leading managers consider that a thoroughly-planned and implemented corporate identity strategy is an effective marketing and management instrument and therefore a valuable investment in the future. However, cultural differences and barriers are seen as the main difficulty in developing an international corporate identity. There is no doubt that, to be internationally

successful, a corporate identity must have worldwide relevance, clear visual identity and high identification value. Clear, strong corporate design should add to market presence, differentiation and international recognition as an expression of positioning.

Any company wishing to achieve a certain target position must consider the cultural conditions, and, in this situation, an integrative, holistic corporate identity strategy increases the effectiveness of the corresponding measures.

The corporate philosophy must express values, orientation and practical measures so that managers and staff understand targets and are thereby motivated and can identify with the company's goals. Companies can only reach those goals if they actually transmit their corporate philosophies to the relevant target groups. Effective and essential potential lies in the area of staff motivation. Such potential should be consciously integrated into corporate identity activities.

Corporate identity can also help to ease the effects of recession. The potential here is valuable internally as well as externally, and especially in the long term. During a recession, which for many companies means structural change, all available resources and potential can then be effectively and efficiently coordinated and optimised, clearly proving the real relevance and value of corporate identity.

Methods and means for holistic corporate identity development

DR KLAUS SCHMIDT

From the study and from practice it has become clear that the demands on corporate identity to solve current economically or socially-related business problems are on the increase and, at the same time, the complexity of those problems is growing, too. In the developed countries, economic growth, high levels of personal wealth and ecological awareness have all led to changes in values. The changes are characterised by an emphasis on social values and an increasing need for self development. People consequently expect greater social responsibility from companies and a more active contribution from them towards solving social problems. In consequence, corporate identity concepts must match the increasing 'emancipation' of customers and employees: through democratisation of the leadership and decision-making processes, open information policies, dialogue-oriented communications and responsible behaviour towards society and the environment.

The results of the study prove that corporate identity must take into account all relevant influential factors – strategic, economic, cultural, social, communicative – and their inter-relationships in order to reach a holistic way of dealing with perception and effect. In practice, it is often difficult to deal with corporate identity in a comprehensive way in the context of various corporate functional structures and responsibilities. Work is often carried out on merely one-dimensional or isolated measures, or on single aspects of the identity, for example advertising, PR, logotype or product design. The vital inter-working of all relevant aspects through a holistic corporate identity strategy therefore does not happen.

There is a lack of experience and means of recognising and consciously directing the complexity and variety of all relevant corporate identity aspects. Insight is particularly lacking on the possibilities of influencing corporate culture and thereby the corporate behaviour. Behaviour, however, is an essential characteristic of identity. Corporate culture influences both individual and collective behaviour and is, in turn, expressed by it. Particularly in internationally-oriented corporate identity concepts, it is important to include the cultural aspects and behaviour dimensions. Multinational companies are shaped by cultural variety which can express itself in divergent patterns of communication, varied management methods and different estimations of values.

Through such demands, a series of additional aspects becomes relevant to corporate identity.

- The internationalisation of companies, markets and management structures makes it increasingly necessary to define values and goals which are acceptable to different cultures.
- Through ecological awareness and value changes, increased social, cultural and ethical demands are made on companies. This implies that acceptance of companies is now measured by meaning and values, goals and behaviour.
- Companies are valued for their factually-perceived business qualities and performance as well as for their subjectively-perceived social behaviour, internally as well as externally.
- There is an increased relevance in cultural aspects and multicultural conditions.
- It is expected that companies should be good citizens, carrying their social and ecological responsibility and being involved in the national or regional host culture.

The demands on corporate identity have thus become more differentiated and extensive. This requires a far more complex range of instruments, which allows the structuring, analysis, conceptualisation and development of identity in all essential areas.

An appropriate structure model for dealing with this situation has been developed by Henrion, Ludlow & Schmidt. It takes into account all relevant aspects of a company's identity and structures them into operational dimensions: culture, behaviour, products and services, communications and design.

By means of this model, individual aspects of identity can be structured and ordered in relation to the total identity. It thus becomes possible to trace the aspects back to their origins and to establish causal relationships. In this way, the interdependence between the perceptions and the effects of different aspects of a company's identity becomes comprehensible and clear. With the help of the structure model, corporate identity can be developed in a holistic way.

Structure model for holistic corporate identity development

Our model structures the individual aspects of a company's identity in line with their relevance to benefits and activities, with five operational dimensions:

- corporate culture
- corporate behaviour
- market conditions and strategies
- products and services
- communications and design

We do not consider the dimensions as separate, but as mutually-influencing parts of a whole, which are related by the interdependence of perception and effect.

Corporate culture

The culture dimension consists of all cultural factors, situations and aims of a company.

On the one hand it contains the mission, the corporate goals and corporate philosophy, together with the corporate principles and value systems which form the basis for reaching goals.

On the other hand the cultural surroundings of the company and the resulting mutual influences are also subsumed into the culture dimension. This means all cultural conditioning, for example the socio-economic environment, the historical and political conditions; the nationality, ethnic origin, education, arts, literature, music, language, religion, and so on.

Corporate behaviour

This dimension is defined as the sum total of those actions resulting from the corporate attitudes which influence the identity, whether planned in line with the company culture, occurring by chance or arbitrary.

Corporate behaviour is therefore the collective action of the company as a whole, or of its parts: from its combined communicative behaviour to the behaviour of the management, the relationship to the public, the environmental behaviour, the use of resources, and the social behaviour down to the location and relations to the host country. Behaviour in internal communications is also part of the dimension.

Market conditions and strategies

The market dimension contains all the conditions, goals and strategies which relate to the market or result from it: the target groups and marketing strategies, the market position and the competition, and also trade restrictions or the state of technological development.

Products and services

Besides products and services, this dimension also contains all related aspects from product design, ergonomic qualities and product benefits to price-performance relationships and customer service.

Environmental design, architecture, or interior design can be seen as part of this dimension, as for example with airlines, retail chains, hotels, restaurants, healthcare establishments, department stores or leisure parks.

Communications and design

This dimension consists of communications and design, which are seen as interactive influences on both information and behaviour, internally and externally. It is not restricted to visual or verbal communications, but includes content and subject matter.

The dimension contains, included within corporate design as a conceptual framework, the form and content of internal and external corporate communications, marketing communications, all below-the-line activities, product branding, architecture and interior design.

The five dimensions are interlinked in the holistic corporate identity structure, as shown in the figure below. The structure model facilitates recognition of the interrelationships in perception and effect. It supplies a working basis and the required areas of knowledge for the structural analysis of corporate identity. By analysis of causes and interdependences the model also allows insight into how effect can be structured. It offers an interactive structure as an ideal starting point for the control and meaningful influence of a company's identity.

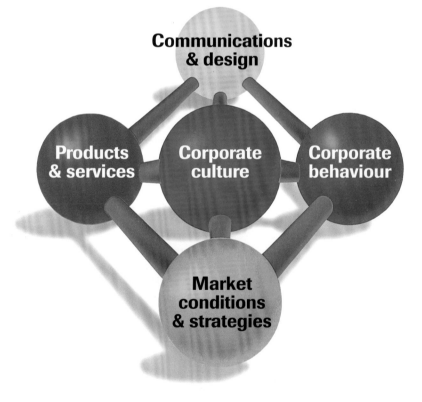

Process model of holistic corporate identity development

Based on our holistic corporate identity understanding and the structure model, we have conceptualised a fundamental process for a corporate identity development. The model shows how, from a given starting situation, through the status quo strengths and weaknesses analysis, a precise picture of the internal and external identity can be gained, a positioning strategy conceptualised and a catalogue of measures developed.

The holistic corporate identity process can be structured into four phases:

Phase 1: Given tasks and problem statement
Phase 2: Status quo and strengths and weaknesses analysis
Phase 3: Positioning strategy and recommendations on measures
Phase 4: Corporate identity measures

The structuring of the process by dimensions and phases facilitates division of the corporate identity development into individually comprehensible and manageable steps. In this way, the single phases and steps of work in the different levels of corporate identity development are controlled by the process model and brought together at strategically important points.

The methodology is designed to be an analysis, planning and interaction process, on the basis of which a holistic corporate identity can be structured, analysed, conceptualised and controlled.

Starting with the given task, a preliminary problem statement is formulated, in which the focus, the procedures and the scope of measures are structured and more closely described. Based on this, a status quo strengths and weaknesses analysis is carried out, which virtually acts as a stock-taking of the existing identity and creates a basis for the development of a strategic positioning goal. The positioning strategy then describes the desired target identity. By comparing existing and target identity, the scale of the need for action is made clear. Subsequently, recommendations for corporate identity measures, by which the target identity can be reached, are given. For the positioning strategy and for the recommendations, it is necessary to collaborate with those involved in the corporate identity development. The measures can then be structured in relation to the short, medium and long term and carried out accordingly.

Phase 1: Given tasks and problem statement

The given tasks for corporate identity projects are based on actual situations, as described in more detail in the first chapter of this book. Regarding the concrete actions, however, there is frequently no comprehensive view on, for example, the aspects and dimensions of identity which need to be taken into account, the target groups, disciplines, company departments and management and employee levels. The process model is of help in deciding on the anticipated efforts and the relevant measures during the analysis phase. On this basis, the dimensions and aspects to be taken into account by the analysis can be identified. In conjunction with those in charge of corporate identity within the company, the problem situation is established, and concrete propositions for procedures, for the emphases and scope of the strengths and weaknesses analysis are developed. By this a foundation for further action is created.

Process model of holistic corporate identity development

Phase 1 — Given situation/objectives

Phase 2

Status quo-/strengths-weaknesses-analysis

Corporate culture	Corporate behaviour	Market conditions & strategies	Products & services	Communication & design
• Corporate goals • Corporate philosophy • Corporate principles • Competence • Corporate guidelines • Cultural conditioning • Social & economical environment • Ecological environment • Nationality • Arts, literature, etc. • Historical & political background	• Management behaviour • Communicative behaviour • Internal communications • Public relations • Sponsoring • Environmental behaviour • Use of resources • Social behaviour • Specific location/host country conditions	• Market position • Competition • Marketing strategy • Market organisation • Target groups • Distribution • Trade barriers • Level of technological development	• Product strategy • Product benefits • Performance • Price/performance ratio • Product design • Ergonomics • Product competence • Unique selling proposition	• Corporate design • Marketing communications • Corporate communications • Internal communications • Environmental design • Architecture • Interior design • Branding • Packaging • Product presentation • Point of sale material • Shop design

Phase 3 — Positioning strategy, scope of action recommended

Phase 4

Corporate identity measures

Corporate culture	Corporate behaviour	Market conditions & strategies	Products & services	Communication & design
• Corporate goals • Corporate philosophy • Corporate principles • Competence • Corporate guidelines • Cultural conditioning • Social & economical environment • Ecological environment • Nationality • Arts, literature, etc. • Historical & political background	• Management behaviour • Communicative behaviour • Internal communications • Public relations • Sponsoring • Environmental behaviour • Use of resources • Social behaviour • Specific location/host country conditions	• Market position • Competition • Marketing strategy • Market organisation • Target groups • Distribution • Trade barriers • Level of technological development	• Product strategy • Product benefits • Performance • Price/performance ratio • Product design • Ergonomics • Product competence • Unique selling proposition	• Corporate design • Marketing communications • Corporate communications • Internal communications • Environmental design • Architecture • Interior design • Branding • Packaging • Product presentation • Point of sale material • Shop design

Phase 2: Status quo and strengths and weaknesses analysis

The corporate identity development is continued with an analysis and evaluation of the existing situation in the form of a status quo strengths and weaknesses analysis. This analysis is a stock-taking of corporate identity and includes all aspects and dimensions.

To facilitate the analysis, individual aspects are attributed to corresponding dimensions so that they can be seen in context and traced back to their original cause. It is important in this to analyse the reasons and to note interdependences and mutual influences.

Strengths and weaknesses can then be recognised, differentiated by dimension. Their importance for the complete corporate identity structure can be evaluated by comparing the individual dimensions. The actions, reactions and chains of influence between dimensions become comprehensible. Just as the problem situation varies, so the dimensions in the analysis need to be more or less extensively taken into account.

Even though the various investigation methods for the status quo strengths and weaknesses analysis are specific to the dimensions, the overall aim is to find results which transcend or link the dimensions. Particular investigation methods are especially suitable as measurements for specific dimensions or aspects. Qualitative inquiry methods are appropriate for management and target group interviews because extensive information can be obtained in an open, trustful atmosphere through focused questioning. Quantitative market and opinion research, on the other hand, is suitable for surveys of product acceptability and for motive and image surveys. Participatory observation, along with qualitative survey methods, is informative in the evaluation of behaviour and culture. Research on communications and corporate design can be carried out by expert judgment on the basis of general visual criteria related to content.

Desk research

As a first step, a company's existing documentation, investigations, market research findings and strategy papers are evaluated through desk research. The items of communication and corporate design are also subjected to examination and evaluation. As a rule, the relevant identity aspects of competitors are also incorporated into the desk research. Through desk research, basic information for better understanding of the company and its problem situation is obtained. Also, the existing situation is established, which includes the goals, strategies, strengths, weaknesses, resources and performance of the company. The insights gained are checked, given depth and added to through interviews and, if necessary, through focused market research. The communications of a company reach from corporate and marketing communications, through sponsoring activities to personnel marketing and human relations.

The elements, means and measures of all such internal and external communications are analysed and evaluated to draw out strengths and weaknesses and to identify appropriate action. Existing positioning aspects identified through desk research serve as criteria for the assessment of communications. In addition, generally relevant image and identity factors, as identified by our study, can be used for assessment. Besides analysis of the content and form of communications, an evaluation of the elements, means and objects of visual communications and corporate design is

---

Relevant information for the desk research

- Historic development
- Corporate philosophy
- Corporate culture
- Corporate principles
- Corporate guidelines
- Competence
- Corporate structure
- Legal structure
- Market position
- Competition
- Marketing organisation
- Marketing strategy
- Target groups
- Competitive situation
- Employees' attitudes
- Market partners' attitudes
- Public opinion
- Corporate communications internally and externally
- Marketing communications
- Product presentation
- Corporate design
- Human resources policy
- Socio-cultural environment
- Regional cultural conditions
- Specific location/host country conditions
- Potential environmental conflicts

carried out. These include identity elements such as symbols and logotypes, stationery, forms, brochures, product presentation, packaging, audio-visual items, 3-dimensional design, interior design, shop design, office furnishing, workplace design, production equipment, architecture and the environmental surroundings of corporate buildings and sites. Besides using positioning characteristics or identity and image factors as criteria to judge content, visual criteria are valuable for assessing the means and items of visual communications and corporate design. Nevertheless, there have

been examples of corporate identity projects where the results and insights gained from desk research were sufficient to argue the case for further corporate identity measures or steps towards them.

For example, the existing documentation, strategic papers or investigations can yield so much information that the goals for the desired target identity, the positioning strategy and the recommendations for measures can be developed from them. As a rule, it is recommended to involve the people affected.

Identity and image factors	Examples of relevant positioning aspects	Identity and image factors	Examples of relevant positioning aspects
Corporate goals	short-term – visionary communicated – confidential tactical – strategic	Financial solidity	financially sound – unsound modest – dominant risk-averse – risk-willing
Corporate culture	restrictive – tolerant factual – personal conservative – progressive	Investment attractiveness	high return – low return safe – risky unfathomable – transparent
Social competence	social – unsocial individualistic – collective non-transparent – transparent	Product quality	quantity – quality continuous – fluctuating standardised – specific
Management quality	successful – unsuccessful staff-function – line-function bureaucratic – lean	Brand identities	weak – strong masculine – feminine popular – elitist
Human resources quality	cooperative – individual adapted – initiative-taking pragmatic – theoretical	Innovation	imitator – innovator technology oriented – customer oriented occasional – constant
Environmental responsibility	responsible – irresponsible minimal – comprehensive opportunist – programmatic	Communications	reserved – open relevant – abstract intelligible – unintelligible
Market position	leader – follower product-oriented – customer-oriented consolidating – expanding	Visual identity	inconspicuous – prominent classic – dated abstract – relevant

Source: Institut für angewandte Psychologie, Prof. Dr H. Erke

Formal visual criteria

Information contents
- Content
- Symbol function
- Associations
- Relevance, modernity

Impact
- Appeal
- Signal quality
- Prominence in surroundings
- Recognition value

Associated qualities / psychological qualities
- Image associations
- Aesthetic quality
- Pleasantness
- Feelings conveyed

Originality
- Unmistakable
- To the point
- Unambiguous
- Independent of fashion trends

Practicality
- Spectrum of application
- Reproducibility
- Consistency through all applications

Management and target group investigations

For management and target group investigations, qualitative interviews for free exploration on the basis of an interview guideline have proved productive and motivational. In these interviews, decision makers and opinion leaders within the company are questioned, as are, if necessary, external target groups such as actual or potential clients, market partners, investors or representatives of the press.

The interviews are important as qualitative primary research in two respects: firstly, they are invaluable in gaining information and, secondly, they are a fundamental means of involving people, thus ensuring motivation and acceptance of the measures and contents of an identity programme.

The structure of the interview guide and the questions reflect the holistic view of corporate identity and take all dimensions into account. The weighting of the responses depends on the emphases of the given task. Depending on the interviewee's position and responsibility within the company, questions on values, attitudes, motivation and atmosphere, or even strategic direction, create focal points within the interviews. Relevant themes are, for example:

- the way a company sees itself
- how it presumes others see it
- internal communications
- competence
- market presentation
- resources
- cooperation
- the corporate climate
- the behaviour of the leadership

The subject of future-oriented ideas and opinions on corporate goals is raised, as with, for example:

- strategies
- potential
- aspects which could be improved
- obstacles
- chances
- willingness

The management and target group investigations can also be carried out in the form of workshops or as group discussions. However, these methods are not so critical, profitable and motivational as individual qualitative interviews, although they can be adequate for partial enquiries or in certain situations. Individual aspects of a company's identity can be evaluated through semantic differentials related to the positioning. This is especially useful for discussing how the company is seen by others, in the target group interviews.

For surveying the existing situation internally, staff views can be established by means of a standardised questionnaire, but this will give very little feedback on goals, strategies and potential. Staff questioning is more useful for the determining of atmosphere or climate and therefore is especially valuable for checking changes relative to the achievement of goals and for gauging the development of corporate culture and behaviour.

During these investigations, as well as information being gathered, a preliminary explanation of the 'theme' is developed and shared during the interviews. This is an important part of the identity process, which increases acceptance and prevents the 'not-invented-here' syndrome.

The results of interviews are evaluated qualitatively. They mirror the subjective opinions of those interviewed. In the interviews, information on goals and strategies, potential and resources, atmosphere and moods, attitudes and patterns of behaviour, is obtained. Through this, the

---

Sample structure of questionnaire for internal interviews

General
- If you were to interpret your company as a personality, how would you describe this personality?
- What in your opinion are the strengths and weaknesses of your company?

Corporate culture
- Every company has a culture (working atmosphere). How would you describe this culture (atmosphere) in your company?
- Do you know the objectives and strategies of your company?
- Do you perceive your company as an attractive employer?

Corporate behaviour
- What is your opinion on the company's social and environmental behaviour?
- How do you judge cooperation between different fields of activity and departments in your company?
- What abilities and qualities of staff/management are important for the success of the company in your opinion?

Market condition and strategies
- What are the characteristic differences between the company and its competitors?

- Which image factors determine the perception of the company with target groups in your opinion?
- What aspects could be enhanced to improve the presence in the market?

Products and services
- How do you rate quality and performance of your company?
- What is the status of quality with regard to services provided by the different fields of activity/departments?
- What could be done to improve performance in your opinion?

Communications and design
- Are corporate values expressed and communicated internally? Which aspects could be improved in your opinion?
- Does the way in which corporate values are expressed and communicated externally correspond to the corporate values? What could be done to improve this?
- What do you think of the visual appearance of your company? Which qualities should it communicate?

Conclusion
- What do you personally expect from the development of a corporate identity?

Source: © 1994 Henrion, Ludlow & Schmidt

investigations also serve to verify and validate the information gained by desk research on official statements and strategies, by comparing them with individual opinions and interpretations. Thus, differences and deficiencies between expectations and reality become clear. In addition to the interviews, it can be meaningful to carry out quantitative market and opinion research, for example in the area of image and product acceptability.

Participatory observation

Image and identity, as well as quality of service, are largely characterised by subjective perceptions, impressions and moods. Even when known facts draw a positive picture of the company, in spite of that the 'atmosphere' can still sometimes be bad. For this kind of differentiation and assessment, participatory observation has proved to be, besides interviews, an appropriate method of research.

Depending on the aims, it allows, especially in the field of corporate behaviour and corporate culture, detection of interesting descriptions of actual situations and recognition of deficiencies and overlapping interdependences. On top of that, participatory observation can contribute an evaluation of performance which is virtually an expert opinion. So the behaviour towards the client, as an important part of the service performance, can be effectively checked by this.

Phase 3: Positioning strategy and recommendations on measures

Positioning strategy

On the basis of the knowledge gained through the status quo strengths and weaknesses analysis, a positioning strategy can be developed. This is the description of the desired identity, of how the company understands itself, how it wants to be understood, how it behaves and how it wants to be seen. A position which differentiates the company from competitors is described, developed out of the way the company understands itself. Status, mission, goals, competence and values are shown in the form of a target positioning.

In the status quo strengths and weaknesses analysis, the corporate identity aspects are differentiated according to their dimensions, and structural overlappings are investigated. In the positioning strategy the desired corporate identity is again described holistically. First it is shown under the headings of dimensions, aspects and goals, weighted in accordance with their position and contribution to the total identity, then condensed into a comprehensive target positioning. Afterwards, the individual positioning statements are explained relative to actions. The positioning strategy must be developed in close cooperation with management and opinion leaders within the company. It should be relevant to daily action and become a living element in the work of all staff. The implementation of the positioning is at the same time the aim and the programme of the corporate identity. By way of illustration, excerpts from a target positioning are shown in the table on page 45. The positioning brings the way the company understands itself and its goals to the attention of staff, customers, market partners and the public, together with its behaviour and, for example, its handling of natural resources. So the positioning defines how the company wants to be seen from inside and outside, which market position it wants to adopt, how it is differentiated from its competitors and what it expects from its employees. In this way, the positioning creates criteria by which to judge corporate identity measures.

Recommendations on measures

Using the positioning strategy, by comparing the target identity and the existing identity, the necessity of developing a corporate identity can be established. It quickly becomes clear which aspects need to be worked on, where existing aspects will be retained and where a necessity for action exists. Corporate identity development is a process, and the various interdependent aspects must correspond to a programme of measures in which component targets and subject matter are aligned and measured against a comprehensive positioning strategy.

The development of a corporate identity must be controlled and the intended changes must be assessable and measurable. One common measure is the corporate identity audit, which is the checking of what has been achieved and the measuring and assessing of changes in the light of the target identity described in the positioning strategy. Corporate identity

Model of positioning differential

	4	3	2	1	0	1	2	3	4	
product oriented	·	·	·	·	•	·	·	·	·	customer oriented
standardised	·	·	·	·	•	·	·	·	·	specific
short-term	·	·	·	·	•	·	·	·	·	visionary
risk-averse	·	·	·	·	•	·	·	·	·	risk-willing
leader	·	·	·	·	•	·	·	·	·	follower
modest	·	·	·	·	•	·	·	·	·	dominant
conservative	·	·	·	·	•	·	·	·	·	progressive
irresponsible	·	·	·	·	•	·	·	·	·	responsible
bureaucratic	·	·	·	·	•	·	·	·	·	'lean'
unfathomable	·	·	·	·	•	·	·	·	·	transparent
reserved	·	·	·	·	•	·	·	·	·	open
popular	·	·	·	·	•	·	·	·	·	elitist
imitator	·	·	·	·	•	·	·	·	·	innovator
quantity	·	·	·	·	•	·	·	·	·	quality
classic	·	·	·	·	•	·	·	·	·	dated
inconspicuous	·	·	·	·	•	·	·	·	·	prominent
tactical	·	·	·	·	•	·	·	·	·	strategic
successful	·	·	·	·	•	·	·	·	·	unsuccessful

measures are always bound up with concrete goals, such as increase in recognition and acceptance or improvement of specific image and identity aspects, environmental behaviour or attraction of shareholders. It is possible to measure the changes through an audit using investigation methods as described in the status quo strengths and weaknesses analysis. The method chosen should be that which is particularly appropriate for the aspects or dimensions in question. Semantic differentials and positioning maps are also effective ways of presenting the status quo as well as changes in relation to the target identity. The positioning aspects or the image and identity characteristics set the appropriate assessment parameters.

Development of a corporate identity must be holistic if it is to be efficient and if lasting success is to be achieved. Not all dimensions have to be dealt with at the same time, but they must be considered as interrelated in perception and effect. The recommendations on measures are also divided into the five-dimensional view of a holistic corporate identity and are explained with reference to the aims. In turn, the aims of the individual dimensions are assembled together via the positioning strategy. So by the working through of individual measures, a contribution is always made to the holistic corporate identity. An excerpt from a catalogue of recommendations is given in in the table on pages 46/47.

Phase 4: Corporate identity measures

The measures, and therefore the programme, for the development of a corporate identity can be divided into dimensions and individual measures, structured to be short or long term and broken down into manageable, affordable steps. Consequently, it is possible to work on different measures in parallel and, for example, the corporate vision can be further developed out of the target positioning, the leadership principles can be worked through, the product offer optimised and, through communications or also the corporate design, the desired identity achieved. The programme for the development of a corporate identity is worked out on the basis of the holistic positioning strategy. The different measures can be carried out by different disciplines, such as marketing, product design or personnel management. Other additional tasks can be handled by interdisciplinary working groups of communications experts, business administrators and designers. Holistic corporate identity thinking is important here also for the rationalisation

Realisation of the target positioning i.e. the development of the corporate identity requires measures in all five dimensions:	Corporate culture	Corporate behaviour
• corporate culture • corporate behaviour • market condition and strategies • products and services • communications and design	**Objectives** • Implementation of the positioning in the company • Action relevant interpretation of the positioning for the individual fields of activity • Realisation of the strategic concept **Scope** • Corporate mission • Targets and strategies • Defined values • Structure and cooperation • Competence and services • Attitude towards staff • Expectations of staff • Attitude to and dealing with conflict potentials • Attitude towards client • Attitude towards the public **Measures** • Development of corporate guidelines • Information events • Social events • Workshops on 'corporate culture' • Seminars on 'teamwork and management'	**Objectives** • Improvement of management conduct • Improvement of communications • Improvement of ability to apply strategy **Scope** • Management style • Employee support • Teamwork • Mutual understanding **Measures** • Development of corporate guidelines • Development of individual communications abilities • Staff development concepts • Requirement profiles for applicants • Criteria for support and promotion of employees • Creation of specialists and management career options • Requirement profiles for employees and managers • Agreement of targets • Systematic management training • Coaching of board of directors

and concentration of efforts and means. The various disciplines can be steered and controlled by the corporate identity target positioning. A holistically-developed corporate identity can make an essential contribution towards corporate success, if all relevant dimensions and aspects of identity are taken into account. The focus can vary widely, and the relevance of different measures will depend on the particular corporate situation. The relevant benefit aspects of holistic corporate identity are as follows:

- Strategic positioning
- Expression of competence, performance and quality
- Positioning and differentiation
- Clarity and presence
- Structuring and visualisation
- Expression of change or continuity
- Goodwill and synergy
- Product branding
- Marketing communications
- Internal communications
- Rationalisation and efficiency
- Acceptance, identification and motivation
- Corporate culture

Market conditions and strategies	Products and services	Communications and design
Objectives • Exhaust differentiation potential • Support of globalisation • Representation of group affiliation	**Objectives** • Development of product and service range • TQM • Exhaust synergy potentials	**Objectives** • Enhancement of market presence • Development of dialogue with target groups • Development of self-portrayal in accordance with the positioning
Scope • Performance in the market • Differentiation against competitors • Distribution structure • Communication of positioning aspects	**Scope** • Quality awareness • Service awareness • Customer orientation • Innovation • Research	**Scope** • Information and communication about the company performance: processes, conflicts, success • Development of communicative abilities of managers and employees • Development of corporate design
Measures • Development of objective differentiation aspects • Development of subjective differentiation aspects • Strategy workshops • Portfolio analysis • Creation of identification symbols • Brand development • Competitor analysis • Marketing plan • Organisation reviews	**Measures** • TQM measures • Development of unconventional products and problem solving systems • Development of customer orientation • Analysis of services offered to customer (costs/benefits) • Establishment of targets for R&D • Innovation support programme	**Measures** • Development of a communications programme • Development of internal communications structures • Presence of management • Development of public relations • Development of corporate design • Development of information logistics • Technical, logistical optimisation of the design process through the use of DTP

Source: © 1994 Henrion, Ludlow & Schmidt

Dr Klaus Schmidt

*Managing Partner of
Henrion, Ludlow &
Schmidt, London.*

*Born 1946 in Salzgitter,
Germany. Studied
graphic design at the
Staatliche Hochschule
für Bildende Künste
(HfBK) in Braunschweig
(Brunswick). 1973-76
interdisciplinary diploma
studies in experimental
environmental design,
also at the HfBK
in Braunschweig.
1976-77 research
assistant at the
Institut für angewandte
Psychologie at the
University of
Braunschweig.
Then freelance
consultant and designer.
1978-80 project leader
for corporate identity,
HDA International,
London.
Since 1981, Managing
Partner of Henrion,
Ludlow & Schmidt,
a leading, world-
renowned consulting
firm in corporate
identity.*

In the following chapter, a series of corporate case studies are introduced, which have different triggers and emphases for corporate identity development. Fascinating parallels and certain contradictions exist, but all have in common the consistency of a holistic approach or the interdependence of relevant aspects and dimensions of corporate identity. When the cultural behaviour, the market conditions and strategies, the products and services and the communications and design are understood as interconnected dimensions, it becomes possible to develop an economically, socially and culturally successful company identity. Then, corporate identity becomes a management tool with strong performance potential, which contributes to reaching the desired target positioning in the market, differentiating from competition, creating visual identity and market presence, overcoming cultural differences, developing a culture to support corporate goals and acting according to the social and economic challenges of the time.

ABB Asea Brown Boveri is one of the world's leading companies in power generation, transmission and distribution of electrical energy as well as industrial and building systems and rail transportation. ABB was created in 1987 through the merger of the Swedish ASEA and the Swiss BBC Brown Boveri companies, the biggest merger to date in this industry sector. The Company's head offices are in Zürich, it is active in more than 140 countries and has 1,000 companies worldwide, with a total of more than 200,000 employees. Group turnover is around $30 billion.

Introduction

A key marketing challenge for ABB Asea Brown Boveri since operations began in 1988 has been to establish and continuously increase the awareness and understanding of ABB as a global leader in the field of electrical engineering.

A related challenge is to coordinate the building of such a corporate global image within a highly decentralised group of some 1,000 companies worldwide. Effectively managing the link between its global and local needs is as much a key factor in ABB's communications success as it is to the Group's business success.

Bruce Kaukas enlarges on these themes, describing ABB's culture and its rôle in forming and communicating aims and values. The need for a unifying identity is made clear, as are the communications goals set for the organisation, both locally and globally, which are implemented by 'Country Communications', 'Business Area Communications' and by Corporate Communications in Zurich.

In representing ABB's far-reaching capabilities, the corporate identity helps to act out its declared policy of 'think global, act local'.

Global brand/local customers: The challenge of corporate identity in the 90s

ABB is the result of a merger between two electrical engineering companies – ASEA AB of Sweden and BBC Brown Boveri Ltd of Switzerland.

Both of these companies, established during the 19th century, were among the first electrical engineering firms to generate and supply electricity to the citizens of their respective nations. For more than one hundred years, both were cornerstones of the economies of Sweden and Switzerland, and both were among the first to export their expertise. Each, sometimes as competitors, saw the necessity of exporting their technologies given the relatively limited size of home markets. Therefore a strong and profitable tradition of working in foreign markets existed in both company managements before the merger.

ASEA

BBC
BROWN BOVERI

*Logotypes of the
parent companies
of ABB.*

Percy Barnevik, President and CEO of ASEA since 1980, conceived of the merger as a way to create a company with the necessary global economies of scale to become a major player in the increasingly open and competitive global electrical engineering markets. It was understood that while ASEA's and BBC's customers would continue to demand to be served locally, they would increasingly have access to, and demand, the best products and services the world had to offer. The approach was to 'think global, act local' – operate domestically but with access to the best global resources.

However, the merger still left ABB to a large extent dependent on Western European markets. Shortly afterwards, therefore, ABB began a programme of acquisitions and investments to build its presence in North America. A third, ongoing phase of expansion and local investment is presently underway in Eastern Europe and Asia.

The result is a globally operating, multi-domestic company with three major legs in an expanded Europe, the Americas, and in the Asia/Pacific region.

Global messages in a decentralised organisation

ABB is comprised of four industrial Business Segments and a Financial Services Segment. These Segments further subdivide their activities into 45 global Business Areas, 1,000 companies, and 5,000 individual profit centres. In order to coordinate efforts of individual businesses and take advantage of global technological and financial resources, as well as efficiently provide turn-key project capabilities to customers, ABB operates with a 'matrix' system of organisation. In brief, this means that every company head (the average size profit unit in ABB is 200 employees) has two supervisors – a business

area (gas turbines or robotics, for example) head, with strategic responsibility for the production, sale, and service of such equipment worldwide, who may be located in another country or continent, and a country head, who leads all ABB businesses within that country. This system is designed to maximise cross-border communication and cooperation.

The emphasis, however, is on the local customer being served locally by these local profit centres and largely autonomous companies. Marketing individual products is left to the profit centres, companies, and country organisations. Marketing/communications programmes are not questioned or interfered with unless they mis-represent the Company, fail to acknowledge the size and scope of the organisation, or do not take advantage of the considerable synergies available within the Group. However, each local unit is expected to contribute to ABB's global image by incorporating a number of key messages into its communications activities.

The key global messages

ABB's image-building activities must always accurately reflect true strengths and characteristics about the way ABB operates and how it benefits customers and the communities and countries in which it does business. All external advertising, media, promotion, public affairs, sponsoring, trade fairs, as well as important internal efforts, are based on accuracy and a low-key presentation of facts.

As a company with very long-term customer relationships, projects and product guarantees that extend over decades, and a responsi-bility in power production upon which sometimes entire cities or states depend, nothing short of absolute accuracy will do.

At the same time the Company is justly proud of its products and people, and does not hesitate to communicate its strengths.

It is intended that all audiences of corporate as well as local communications programmes understand three primary reasons why ABB can supply better products and systems tailored to their needs:

1. ABB is multi-domestic. The organisation combines local management and close customer contact with the capability to draw on worldwide financial, management and technological resources. It is the first true 'multinational' in its industries – the eight-person Executive Committee, for instance, is comprised of five nationalities. ABB is committed to becoming 'local' as fast as possible, all over the world. Being local also means being a good corporate citizen in terms of protecting the environment and supporting local communities where Company facilities are located.

2. The Company is technology-driven – a world leader in electrical engineering markets with more than a century of experience in critical technologies. ABB spends 8 per cent of its revenues on research and development to maintain and extend its technological edge. The Company is also proud of the environmental benefits its products offer.

3. ABB is totally focused on satisfying the customer and anticipating the increased market and environmental demands of that customer. Customers now expect more than top quality at a competitive price. They need a business partner who has an intimate understanding of their business, who can anticipate changing needs and shifting markets, and who can deliver fast, innovative, total system solutions that help them achieve their business goals.

Responsibilities within a decentralised Group

For all of the very considerable advantages ABB's structure offers, it also presents considerable challenges with respect to global brand management. The definition and scope of communications tasks at all levels within the Group – what is communicated and who communicates with whom – is described in ABB's internal 'Mission, Values and Policies' guidelines. This document, first developed shortly after the merger to 'form the basis of ABB's culture and identity', was extensively discussed and prepared by the top 200 managers in the Group, and has been carefully reviewed and updated by an expanded group of managers periodically since that time. It provides the guidelines needed to work together in order to make ABB successful.

A key function of the very small staff of ABB Corporate Communications in Zurich is to help all marketing/communications representatives within the organisation communicate a clear, uniform, strong, and accurate image of ABB to customers and other key audiences around the world. Key management principles, messages, and goals are disseminated throughout the organisation to be integrated into local and country communications programmes. Corporate Communications also actively builds the ABB brand externally by communicating directly to international target audiences.

It is the responsibility of the Group corporate communications function to clearly explain ABB's missions, values, and goals as a world leader in its markets. A clear and accurate description of what makes ABB unique has been and continues to be the basis for a strong global brand umbrella that assists both new market entry and continued success.

The ABB Way

- Entrepreneurial drive – all employees are expected to act as if every customer is their personal customer. ABB offers the opportunity to take charge, personally.

- 'Hands on' attitude – get personally involved in problems and ways to find solutions.

- Speed – a special sense of urgency in getting things done is felt at every ABB operation and in every department. A 'business as usual' attitude is discouraged.

- Teamwork – use the Company resources available to find the best customer solution as fast as possible.

- Lean organisation – with fewer employees taking full responsibility for their work, the customer benefits from fewer levels of management and clearer accountability.

Source: © 1994 Henrion, Ludlow & Schmidt

*Central design
element of the
visual identity is
the logotype.*

Elements of ABB's culture, how employees approach their tasks and do business, are also important to convey to target audiences in order to clearly differentiate the Company from its competition.

The basis for fostering and spreading these and other elements of ABB's culture is the simple but important notion that every manager is personally responsible for communicating with his or her employees.

The message is communicate, communicate, and over-communicate with your team. First and foremost – discuss specific business problems and challenges to make processes or products more efficiently with a focus on customer needs now or in the future. But in addition, involve employees in discussions about other related ABB businesses, competitive challenges worldwide as well as locally, and the general business climate in which ABB operates. Group, country, and

business area publications and videos provide a selective stream of information to fuel these discussions. ABB executives devote an unusually large amount of their time – President and CEO Percy Barnevik is the best example – visiting facilities and engaging in discussions with employees at all levels to learn about specific local problems and successes as well as to communicate Company values.

Group Communications periodically measures how ABB is perceived by customers and trade groups, business and financial leaders, government decision-makers, journalists, etc. Competitor communications activities are of course also monitored and reviewed. ABB faces long-established competitors with considerable financial resources in its markets, so it is important to understand how, why, and in what markets they are spending money to most efficiently position themselves in the marketplace.

Guidelines within the matrix

Guidelines are provided to the communications professionals throughout ABB to assist them in attaining short- and long-term communications goals. For example, in the fall of each year, an international media report discussing and updating ABB's corporate brand strategy, media plans and creative executions, is sent to the country, segment and business area communication managers. At the same time, these counterparts forward and exchange their communications/media plans so that economies of scale can be achieved and a uniformity of image assured. This is not as easy to accomplish as stated, given the variety of markets and countries in which ABB operates, but open communication is always regarded as the foundation for achieving success.

Coordinating and assuring that no conflicts existed between the way in which ABB was being described locally and the Company's global marketing goals was more difficult several years ago than it is now. When ABB was first established, and particularly following acquisitions, a number of companies used ABB's emphasis on entrepreneurialism as a rationale for creating their own names, logos, design parameters, and to exhibit at major trade fairs separately and independently from any other ABB companies.

Some time and persuasion was at first required to convince these 'entrepreneurs' that being under the ABB umbrella brought far more benefit than setting up separate and confusing-to-the-customer operations outside of it.

Communications responsibilities

Within the ABB matrix, communications managers in country and business areas have very different responsibilities. The country communications managers focus on building the ABB image within their countries through media and advertising programmes aimed at nationally-focused business and economic publications, newspapers and journals. They primarily target government ministries and officials, business and financial communities, academics and opinion leaders. Within the described parameters, they are entirely independent in carrying out their local programmes.

Corporate Communications in Zurich works with these country communicators to best inform their audiences about ABB's strengths and local presence. Local conditions are reflected through and combined with key corporate messages to provide a consistent image.

These country communicators use various communications disciplines, including media relations activities, exhibitions planning, internal communications, and organising customer events and advertising, to achieve written yearly communications objectives.

Identification works over a wide variety of applications.

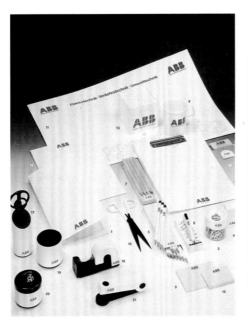

They are the builders of ABB's image in each market. These individuals help to ensure that each ABB company within their country borders follows the few and clear communication guidelines that have been set for everyone. They also act as a resource for the various ABB companies by providing material, training and guidance where needed. Country communications assignments can be very challenging – a new communications head in a new country management in

Segment programme are complementary and mutually supportive. The Segment and Business Area marketing/communications representatives coordinate their activities with the Group and most importantly with each country, where customer needs, ABB's level of awareness, and the competitive climate, require local involvement. As might be expected, disagreement and lively discussions between Segment or Business Area communications managers and country

Advertisements from the international campaign.

Eastern Europe or Asia often starts with no office, much less a desk, but with considerable autonomy, and works from the ground up helping management to create awareness of ABB's commitments to local employment and training of local management.

Within the ABB Segments and Business Areas, individual products and systems are the chief focus. The Power Generation Segment communications people, for example, communicate to their existing and potential customers and audiences primarily through international trade media and regional/international trade fairs and events. An image programme for Power Generation in business publications is also being used to reach decision-makers not always covered by the trade press. Careful coordination with Group communications ensures that key messages within the corporate image campaign and the

communications managers working with local salesmen, take place. Advertising content, frequency, or media selection are usual points of debate, but, perhaps surprisingly, serious conflicts seldom occur. It is expected that all parties openly exchange market information and work together to solve issues in favour of the ABB Group and not a particular local entity or business area.

The Design Management System

The ABB Design Management System (DMS) provides graphic standards and guidelines to ensure all 1,000 entities within the Group present ABB in a uniform, easily recognisable fashion. This system provides a clear graphic system for ABB in applications ranging from business cards and stationery to signage, advertising, and product identification.

The central design element, as it is for most companies, is the logo. The red ABB logo – a combination of the A of ASEA and BB of Brown Boveri – represented a new enterprise emerging from the combination of not just two companies but two, and later many more, cultures. The Country, Segment and Business Area Communications managers are responsible for monitoring these standards within their specific scope of activity. The DMS guidelines are intended to strike

products under that designation. A company that performs well and also attains a high level of general awareness acquires credibility. Its name becomes a brand that has a value that is shared by all of its products and services. ABB's largest competitors, particularly those in Japan, the United States, Sweden, and Germany, are acutely conscious of the value of their brand names, and consistently place extensive image campaigns in international media. ABB has had a modest but continuous

the right balance between providing a strong identity without being too restrictive for ABB's entrepreneurs. Finding the many creative possibilities within the system are stressed rather than having it perceived as 'edict from above'.

The global brand in international media

In addition to, or in spite of, its decentralised structure, with a heavy emphasis on being local at all times for local customers, ABB recognises the value of global branding. Research repeatedly shows that decision-makers asked to rank the factors which influenced choice of suppliers, indicate that general awareness of a company and its perceived performance are closely linked. A global brand 'umbrella' eases market entry and aids in continued success for those

and successful image programme in the international business press and other media since 1988. The objective then and now is to establish and reinforce ABB as a brand name that represents a leader in electrical engineering. The attributes of technological leadership, customer focus, and 'the art of being local worldwide' have been consistently stressed in this continuously evolving, award-winning programme.

This international campaign provides an umbrella for national image programmes where they exist, and in newer or smaller markets, provides the only brand support to trade press advertising for specific products. The corporate campaign and complementary activities (over 40 products ranging from corporate marketing brochures, a video programme, and access to worldwide customer research, are available from Group

Bruce Kaukas

*Vice President,
Communications,
ABB Asea Brown
Boveri Ltd.*

*Joined ABB in 1989.
As head of communi-
cations and marketing
his responsibilities
include positioning
the corporate brand
and developing
strategic marketing
communications
programmes.*

*Mr Kaukas has more
than 20 years' experi-
ence in marketing/
communications
in the electrical
engineering, aero-
space, and electronic
communications
industries. Prior to
joining ABB he
directed the global
brand identification
and marketing/
communications
function at
The Singer Company
in the USA.*

communications to local communicators)
all contribute to increasing the ABB brand
awareness in key markets among decision-
makers. ABB is aware that its rivals continue
to raise the stakes in a very competitive
environment. They, as well as ABB, are aware
that while every customer is local, they look
for and expect the best from around the globe.

More change and more competition

ABB is an organisation which recognises that
change is constant in business, and the
uncertainties arising from change present
opportunities rather than threats. As
described, the marketing/communications
structure within the Group is a flexible and
dynamic one which encourages individual
business autonomy while continuing to build
a strong global brand image. The marketing/
communications messages are a direct
expression of an evolving corporate culture
that was created to better anticipate
and capitalise on new opportunities in an
ever more competitive and demanding
international business climate.

*Ford is one of the
largest business
corporations in the
world. But despite
its size, it is still
significantly
influenced by the Ford
family. Founded in
1903 by Henry Ford I,
the Company today
manufactures private
and commercial
vehicles and, largely
unknown, operates
in financial services.
Ford decided at an
early stage to extend
its activities to
Europe. The first
European production
site opened in
Manchester in 1911,
but it was not until
1976 that the
European subsidiaries,
which by then
numbered 66, were
brought under the
umbrella of 'Ford
of Europe'. European
turnover in 1993
was £20 billion
(not including the
Jaguar Group).*

Introduction

Ford employs more than half a million people worldwide, 83,000 in Europe.
It was in part the vision of the Ford family which led to the establishment of Ford
of Europe, one of the first truly European companies.

Ian Slater tells the story of the genesis and development of Ford in Europe which
paralleled the growth of the identity itself, an identity which had to cope with
the need for the restructuring and cultural reorientation of the Company under
competitive pressure within the automotive industry. This facilitated pan-European
cooperation between various production sites and distribution organisations,
eventually leading to joint research centres and product development.

The development of Ford's internal communications through the Ford
Communications Network (FCN) is also described. In this way, Ford of Europe
promotes company unity across sites and over borders and cultural barriers.

The Ford Motor Company reached its ninetieth birthday in the summer of 1993. The depressed state of much of the world automotive industry meant that celebrations were somewhat muted. Though there were signs of slow but steady recovery in the North American market, Europe was in the midst of a freefall in sales volumes that was unprecedented in its severity – in the order of 17 per cent, year over year.

Understandably, therefore, the thoughts of company insiders were focused not so much on the considerable achievements of the past nine decades, but much more on the challenge of the next one and, in particular, what kind of enterprise Ford would need to become, and how its identity and culture would need to adapt, in order to ensure that it prospered into its second century. Ford is, by any standards, a huge and complex industrial organisation. It is the world's fourth largest corporation, and the second largest producer of cars and trucks. Some 325,000 employees in Ford factories, offices and laboratories serve the automotive and financial services needs of customers in more than 200 countries and territories worldwide.

Henry Ford's signature.

Ford is one of the best known companies in the world, and its corporate identity has been shaped by many and diverse influences over the years, and continues to evolve.

A global player in several business areas

Though it has always been most closely identified with the automotive business, Ford is fast becoming a global player in the financial services industry. In 1982, earnings from the Ford Financial Services Group topped $1 billion for the first time. This second core business comprises four subsidiaries: Ford Credit, The Associates, First Nationwide Bank and US Leasing. Ford also is engaged in a number of other businesses, including electronics, glass, electrical and fuel handling products, plastics, climate control systems, automotive service and replacement parts, vehicle leasing and rental, and land development.

Substantial though these businesses are, however, Ford's identity is and will be closely tied to the automotive business for the foreseeable future. Indeed, the name 'Ford' is almost synonymous with 'car'. Henry Ford was 'the man who put the world on wheels', and the company which bears his name will always retain his reputation for providing millions of people with affordable technology to enhance their personal freedom.

The strongest corporate identities are able to transcend national and even cultural barriers. Ford's has indeed been helped by its close identification with one of the true founding fathers of the automotive industry. This influence is strongly felt internally.

In strictly logical terms, it seems absurd to suggest that an organisation which employs directly the best part of half a million people can have a family feel to it. Nonetheless

it is the case that, within Ford, there is a remarkable sense of belonging, and this is an important aspect of its culture which distinguishes Ford from some of the more anonymous large corporations.

Personal influences on corporate design

Corporate design aspects apparently also reflect Henry Ford's presence. It helps, of course, that the Ford oval is one of one of the best known corporate trademarks the world over, and this mark remains an important part of Ford's corporate identity. It has the distinction of what seems to be the Ford signature, which gives it a personality lacking in many corporate logos. Its air of permanence is slightly misleading, however, because the Oval took a long time to evolve into the form we recognise so well.

When the Ford Motor Company was founded in June 1903, it needed a trademark. It was then that Henry Ford's engineer, blessed with the rather romantic name of Childe Harold Wills, revisited an earlier hobby. He had trained as a commercial artist and, in his youth, he had earned money by printing visiting cards. Wills still had his old printing press in the attic of his home and, using the script typeface he had used for his visiting cards, he developed a stylised version of the words 'Ford Motor Company'. Most people assumed that, because Wills had used script lettering, the eventual trademark was derived from Henry Ford's personal signature, but this was not the case. The myth grew all the same, and has influenced Ford's identity ever since. So Wills' trademark was used in the Company's communications from the first year of its life, but it was not until the following year, 1904, that the script first appeared on vehicles. In 1909, a Ford script trademark much closer to the one we know today was registered. The definitive design was then created by

1903

1907

1909

1912

1927

combining the script with the oval. Its success over rival designs was assured when Henry Ford took a sudden dislike to an alternative trademark, which was used at the time in advertising and also in dealer identification. This was something completely different – a triangular shape with wings attached. Coloured in dark blue or even in orange, it carried the motto: 'Ford – The Universal Car'. Ford explained its symbolism in 1912 in an elaborate expression of corporate identity: 'From oldest Egypt comes the Winged Pyramid, a happy combination of sacred scarab wings – symbolising speed, lightness, grace – and the Royal Pyramid – typifying strength, stability, permanence'.

However, Henry Ford's dislike of it meant that the Ford Oval prevailed and it was in 1927 that the new Model A became the first Ford car to use the script within the oval as a radiator badge. The oval badge was then used on a succession of Ford cars until the late 1950s and, since 1976, the oval has been used on each new European model, beginning with the Mark IV Taunus/Cortina.

So for much of Ford's ninety-year existence, the blue Oval has been the principal visual element of its corporate identity. Another mainstay of the identity has been Ford's international manufacturing philosophy, which in many markets, particularly the UK and Germany, has contributed strongly to national perceptions. From its earliest years, that philosophy has been to produce Ford's cars where it sells them. This is a philosophy about which the Company's managers remain as sincere as ever, so it will continue to be a leitmotif in the identity of Ford within Europe.

The establishment of Ford in Europe

Ford started producing cars in Europe in 1911, only eight years after the Company was formed, having established its first

factory outside the USA at Trafford Park in Manchester. The use of as high a proportion of 'local content' as possible has been a Ford commitment from these earliest days, and it was a pattern that was repeated as a chain of Ford plants appeared across Europe during the subsequent decades. Thus, similar factories quickly followed, in France, Ireland, Denmark and Germany.

Ford also committed itself from the outset to being in the forefront of manufacturing technology, a commitment which also has been an important aspect of its reputation and identity. In 1914, Trafford Park became the first automotive plant in Europe to assemble cars on a moving production line, a process which Ford had innovated in Detroit only a year before. Similarly, the factories which opened in Cologne and Dagenham in 1931 represented the state of the car manu-facturing art, though their first years of production were marred by the ravages of the economic depression. The way in which the Company has developed an integrated pan-European organisation has been a major influence on its corporate identity during the latter part of the twentieth century. This had its roots in the vision of the Company's founder, but the Depression and the World War which followed it were to frustrate Henry Ford's dream of creating an integrated European manufacturing and sales operation. He had planned to create a network of factories and national offices across Europe, coordinated by a European Central Office.

It was Henry Ford II who took upon himself the task of realising the dream. First, with the cessation of hostilities, he arranged an extensive tour involving eight European countries. He was to create his own vision of a more integrated Europe earlier and more clearly than many Europeans did. His visits to Britain and Germany confirmed that, if Ford were to maintain its independent develop-ment of the two main companies there, then

Today

this would simply be a formula for chronic under-achievement. Mr Ford realised that it made little sense to have British and German Ford products which were engineered and developed separately, with different bodies, engines and transmissions, yet intended to meet broadly similar customer requirements and tastes.

European consolidation and identification

As the years passed, he became increasingly impatient about finding new ways of doing business in Europe. German and British managers began to work in each other's factories. Then, in 1967, he made the crucial decision.

The Ford Transit was the first vehicle to emerge from Ford of Europe's combined vehicle operations.

The Common Market was working well, and it seemed inevitable that the United Kingdom could not remain outside it for much longer. Not only that, but he could envisage the further expansion of the Common Market into a broader economic community, embracing other countries, notably Spain and Portugal.

So Ford of Europe was established as a formal business entity. With a central coordinating office, it would work towards the development of a common vehicle programme for Europe and, in the process, create a model of what economists would call specialisation and exchange within a common market. The Ford Transit was the first vehicle to be developed within this vision, a product which has since become a generic term for medium-sized commercial vehicles in much of Europe, and thus one of Ford's most successful-ever products.

A stream of European products has followed them over the past quarter of a century, out of Ford's manufacturing and product development operations spread over seven countries. The geographical spread of these operations across the Continent, without undue dependence on a single production base or market, has given Ford in Europe an identity of its own within Ford's global operations. Ford's European managers still take pride in telling people that, despite the organisation's American parentage, it can claim to be the most European of all the manufacturers. Most of its competitors have been, more or less, 'national champions', with heavy reliance on a particular market or host government. Even General Motors, whose European operations are perhaps most like Ford's, did not establish its GM Europe until the late 1980s.

Ford of Europe had become a cohesive and successful operation. Over the years, its imports of either materials or built-up vehicles have been extremely limited, meaning that Ford of Europe has been more or less self-sufficient in terms of production, research and product development. Today, Ford of Europe has 24 major factories in Britain, Germany, Spain, Belgium, France, Portugal and Hungary; it also has two huge complementary R&D facilities in Dunton (Essex) and Merkenich (Cologne).

This adds up to a vast industrial complex which employs directly 83,000 people in some twenty different countries. Its culture has developed considerably over the past two decades, never more so than in recent years, when further progress has been made towards an integrated organisation. In fact, it was an external threat to Ford's business which forced the Company's leaders to define its culture for the first time.

The Japanese threat

Complacency is always the biggest danger to successful businesses, and the automotive industry is no exception. Western manufacturers were rather slow, at first, to understand and then respond to the great competitive challenge that was being posed by the Japanese and other Asian producers. Having been preoccupied with this challenge over the past decade or so, Ford managers feel that they now understand its nature and magnitude better than most. There are still signs that the industry as a whole has yet to come to terms with this challenge completely.

The Japanese approach is really a question of a different philosophy, involving a lower degree of commitment to the local European economy, and especially to its technology and engineering base. The real battle, both in Europe and the US, is over whether the indigenous industry can prevail through maintaining its 'core competences' – if not, the bleak prospect is that these competences will be lost for ever, something which has already happened in many other industries.

In 1950, Ford was pleased to make welcome a young Japanese engineer called Eiji Toyoda, as he began a three-week pilgrimage to our Rouge Plant in Detroit. We were to find out later what a good learner he was, and it's easy to forget now that the potential Japanese challenge to the bastions of the West's automotive industry seemed barely credible in those days. It was only after the second oil crisis that we really began to wake up to the fact that the Japanese were determined to conquer the automotive world and, worse still, they were a long way towards their strategic objectives. We woke up to this just in time.

Now, it was our teams who were travelling to Japan to find out how they managed to do business so effectively. Ford's 25 per cent ownership of Mazda gave us an inside track on this which, at the time, probably just meant that we were more aware than some of our competitors of the size of the challenge. We have been running scared ever since, which is the way everyone in the international automotive industry needs to be, now and in the future. We do not intend to get complacent again. The Japanese had simply leap-frogged the Western manufacturers, particularly in basic manufacturing productivity. Not only was there a significant productivity gap, but that gap was growing rapidly, to an extent that it did not take a top consultant to realise that the Western manufacturers were facing extinction unless they could first stop the productivity gap deteriorating further, and then close it quickly.

A cultural response

Clearly the 'business as usual' option was not a real choice. Ford had to find, urgently, new ways of doing business which would transform its competitiveness. One theoretical possibility was to adopt the approach of trying to become more Japanese than the Japanese themselves; in other words, trying to graft a Japanese cultural approach on to our existing business. Many of the factors underpinning the success of the Japanese, were based on practices such as 'just-in-time' delivery systems which were originally Western ideas. Similarly, so-called lean production techniques could be introduced into Western companies just as they were being applied within Japanese ones. However, it was recognised that much of the Japanese success was also attributable to their own manufacturing culture. This was easy to caricature in terms of massed ranks of workers doing group exercises before shifts while singing the company song, but their approach worked for them.

At that time, the Japanese were also doing a more effective and systematic job of satisfying their customers. Ford's response was not to try to become more Japanese than the Japanese themselves. Rather, it was to examine critically its own culture, and introduce a process of managed change which would be sufficiently radical to transform the Company into a world-class competitor.

Mission, Values and Guiding Principles

Ford's top management team was committed absolutely to this culture change. In 1983, they articulated Ford's 'Mission, Values and Guiding Principles' (MVGP) as a clear statement of intent regarding corporate mission and ethics against which their future performance could be measured. Though Ford had been manufacturing vehicles for eight decades until this point, it was the first time that the corporate culture had been defined and, because corporate mission statements since have become commonplace, it is easy to under-estimate the importance of this call to arms. The MVGP statement recognised that: '...our people are the source of our strength... involvement and teamwork are core human values'. This represented a revolutionary change in thinking in the historical context of the automotive industry. Traditionally, rigid hierarchies and narrow specialisation at all organisational levels had created a 'chimney mentality', with individual

managers blocking flows of information and protecting what they perceived as their own interests.

It had become manifestly clear that these old ways no longer worked. The corporate culture would have to change, and the perceptions of all the stakeholders in the business, whether employees, shareholders, dealers, or suppliers, would change too. The implications for corporate culture and identity would be far-reaching. So much so, that it was recognised that the change process would take a long time to implement, probably in the order of twenty years. This was no 'quick fix'. Making the transition, from being an autocratic top-down organisation to one that gives its people authority and promotes teamwork, is not an easy thing to achieve. For one thing, people had become accustomed to having narrowly-defined responsibilities, and not thinking outside their own specific task. For another, managers tended to browbeat their subordinates, and asked for their opinions only rarely. They tended to dictate their orders, because they were treated that way when they joined the business – the old culture was self-perpetuating, and was therefore not susceptible to gradual change. This was not an operating environment in which people were keen to demonstrate initiative, to share ideas, or to trust each other. In extremis, it develops into an 'it's someone else's problem' mentality when things go wrong.

An enormous, untapped resource

The more the change process was considered, the more it became obvious that the Ford workforce represented an enormous and largely untapped resource of energy and ideas. In addition to tapping that resource, it would be necessary to develop and communicate a consistency of purpose for Ford's global business and a common focus for employees. As Ford's CEO at the time, Don Petersen, noted: 'People find inherent satisfaction in doing a job well. They will strive for excellence if they are allowed to'. Therefore, much management effort during the 1980s was focused on creating a less compartmentalised, less bureaucratic organisation structure; one in which team-work would be the norm, with the emphasis most strongly on anticipating and being responsive to the needs and expectations of our customers. Of course, in recent years, many large companies have been trying to do much the same thing. Ford's intention was to approach this challenge in a more effective, perhaps different, way from anyone else in our industry.

Perhaps the most important guiding principle was the need to establish and then to maintain trust and credibility at all organisational levels in what management was communicating internally. Ford's most senior executives embraced now-familiar concepts such as participative management, teamwork, employee involvement and open communications. This would involve a never-ending commitment to a radically different way of working together. So, as part of the culture change process, there has been a particularly strong emphasis within Ford on improving internal communications, as a means of mobilising the entire organisation to meet the competitive challenge ahead. The objective, in essence, was to create a pre-vailing 'all for one, and one for all' mentality.

The leading edge of internal communications

It was not simply attitudes towards internal communications that would have to change. Ford intended to set leadership standards in employee communications and, to achieve this, the long-established existing internal communications media needed to be augmented, using the latest electronic communications technology. Some ten years ago, Ford had begun to use satellite technology for simultaneous communication of new product launches to the media in North America. The senior Vice-President responsible for External Affairs asked aloud whether we should consider using this technology to communicate with our own employees.

When the formal proposal was presented to the Board, it's said that the only question raised was whether this new internal communications medium would indeed practise genuinely open communications. The response was that, yes, this would be 'the freedom of the press inside the Ford Motor Company'. This was the informal charter for the Ford Communications Network (FCN), one of the first and most ambitious corporate initiatives in what was to become known as business television. Good news and bad news would be treated consistently, and openness would be the norm. It would be information for its own sake, covering anything that should be of interest to employees in their working lives. Anything that might be perceived as propaganda was to be kept out – the whole initiative would rest on its being credible as a source of accurate and objective information. FCN was to be a statement and demonstration of Ford's Mission, Values and Guiding Principles. Today, in Ford's North American Automotive Operations, FCN transmits a daily television news programme by satellite to some 300 locations. Employees also receive a continuous teletext service, including both locally and nationally generated news, covering everything from explanations of corporate strategy to stories about individual employees' anniversaries. FCN was seen as a significant contributor to the dramatic improvement in the Company's fortunes which took place in the mid-to-late 1980s.

The challenge of European cultural complexity

Given the success of this new communications medium in North America, it was natural that Ford of Europe management should consider building a similar network to link their European operations, using similar technology, but adapting the style and content to the more complex local broadcasting environment and corporate culture. Within Ford of Europe communications needs are in many respects more complex and challenging than in other parts of the corporation. Some of this complexity relates most obviously to language and culture differences between European countries, which create potential barriers to inhibit effective communication within an international corporation.

Through the FCN telephone and satellite network, employees can receive Company news within hours. With other, more traditional, technologies, this would have taken days, if not weeks. But this news service is not just one-way. It is being used more and more for live question and answer programmes; staff can question management directly about corporate strategy and performance.

The operating charter, based on open and consistent internal communications, was identical to that upon which the US Network operated from the beginning. Employees receive a continuous teletext service, including both local and national news, complemented by regular studio-based news programmes. They are encouraged to take the time to watch FCN on television monitors situated in each workplace, in areas where employees find it convenient but unobtrusive to watch. From its earliest days, audience research has confirmed that employees welcome FCN as a new and effective source of information about their industry, their Company and their place of work. FCN compares favourably as an information source with its complementary (and long-established) internal newspapers and with the external media.

Employees particularly welcome the speed and accuracy of the information received from FCN, meaning that they are no longer likely to hear of significant developments first through the external media or through the grapevine. Having first installed the Network in the UK, it has now been extended to Ford's facilities in Spain, Belgium and France, broadcasting in local languages in each case. Installation within Ford's German plants and offices is at the planning stage, and should be nearing completion by the end of 1994. In total, this represents a substantial commitment to open communications within Ford of Europe at a time when the industry is undergoing one of the most difficult periods in its history.

The aim: to be competitive globally

Substantial restructuring has been taking place throughout the automotive industry, as individual companies have striven to improve their basic competitiveness in the face of falling demand. When Ford announced its own programme to its workforce a year ago, the emphasis was not on cost reduction for its own sake, but rather on making the entire organisation more responsive to its customers by giving individual employees more responsibility and authority, by streamlining the management structure and by reducing bureaucracy. Above all, it was explained carefully to employees that Ford of Europe must ensure that it was fully competitive on a global basis, not just on a

TV screens can be found in canteens and rest rooms, so that staff can follow the programmes during their breaks. Visitors can also benefit from FCN, gaining information on the latest news from Ford and the motor industry.

European basis. In the future, being the best in Europe would merely be a good consolation prize, because there would be no hiding place from the full rigour of competition within the international automotive industry. For Ford's European operations, achieving global standards of competitiveness is an objective which represents a moving target for all areas of the business. Most obviously, this objective can be interpreted in terms of achieving world class levels of cost performance. However, it is more important still to achieve it in terms of total customer satisfaction. Of course, there are few if any companies in our business which set out to achieve anything less than completely satisfying their customers. The successful companies will be those which manage to make this dedication a part of their corporate identity, as perceived by customers and potential customers alike. That is why, for example, Ford has put considerable effort into communicating internally its message, Everything We Do Is Driven By You, as an expression of a corporate commitment to achieving excellence in customer satisfaction.

The importance of the product aspect of identity

Product style, performance and quality is clearly a leading aspect of a car manu-

facturer's corporate identity. In this context, the launch of the Mondeo, Ford's world car which had been developed by an international team based in Europe, took on even more importance. At the Geneva International Motor Show in March 1993, Ford announced that it would begin exporting the Mondeo from Europe to Japan during the following year. In announcing this, it was recognised that the news probably would be much more significant to our own employees than it would to our external audiences.

Similarly, the announcement that Mondeo had been awarded the prestigious European Car Of The Year 1994 title by a panel of top automotive journalists was, to Ford's

Product style, performance and quality are the most important factors in a car manufacturer's corporate identity.

Ian Slater

*Director
Communications
Small/Medium
Vehicle Centre
Ford Automotive
Operations, Brent-
wood, Great Britain.*

*1975 graduated in
economics from
Edinburgh University,
then worked in
marketing rôles for
British Gas and
Unilever, and lectured
in economics.
Has worked since
1980 for Ford of
Europe, at its
Brentwood head
office.
He has led the
development of the
Ford Communications
Network (FCN).
Previous rôles at Ford
include handling
European product
public relations
activities,
government relations
co-ordination, and
economic forecasting.*

European employees, external recognition of the positive changes which had been taking place within their organisation. Europe has been labelled 'the automotive battleground of the 1990s'. Certainly, the outlook for all manufacturers is one of unremitting toil, with more Japanese transplants coming on stream and chronic excess capacity. However, Ford of Europe management, and employees alike, know that, by producing a stream of world-class products like Mondeo, they will have nothing to fear from the best that the competition has to offer from anywhere in the world. So the Mondeo is the statement of a broader strategic objective on the part of Ford of Europe. When Ford US begins to manufacture the Mondeo in North America in 1994, it will be proof that Europe

can lead the way in the vehicle industry. There is a lot at stake: in 1992, Europe produced 17.7 million vehicles, equivalent to 37 per cent of the world's total, and more than either Japan or North America.

We will continue to work with determination to make Ford of Europe a world-class, globally competitive operation. This process has already involved some tough decisions and some satisfying discoveries.

As it progresses, it will enhance Ford's corporate identity in all the countries in which it sells its products. As Ford's centenary comes within sight, that identity will play its part in building an organisation that can prosper into its second century.

Footnote
The Ford Contour and Mercury Mystique, sister models to the Ford Mondeo, have now been launched successfully in North America. Ford's 'world car' is being sold in 76 countries (including Japan), and the millionth car came off the line at Kansas City in May 1995.

The work of the Hanover-based Henriettenstiftung, a large social welfare foundation in north Germany, includes the care of the sick and elderly as well as training in these areas. The 'Stiftung' (foundation) has 13 hospitals and specialist sections with 638 beds, old people's homes with more than 520 places and institutions for training and education for more than 300 people. The Henrietten-stiftung employs 1,600 people, spread over 80 different disciplines. The turn-over in 1993 was DM 135 million.

Henriettenstiftung

Introduction

A charitable institution in the process of change – the reducing number of religious workers together with the increasing number of employees, the broadening of activities, the distinctions between professions and the fluctuations of staff brought about by increased mobility: all these things are radically new for the Henriettenstiftung ('Henrietta foundation'). How can identity be maintained through such circumstances? How can the Christian idea of 'love thy neighbour' be related to a professional approach to competence?

Pastor Wolfgang Helbig describes the new strategic direction of the identity and the changes in the Henriettenstiftung, from the traditional values of the Christian welfare work ethic to an acceptable model for providing modern healthcare and social services.

Corporate concepts have been developed, which interpret the corporate philosophy in ways relevant to business behaviour. They address essential questions relating to daily work, giving comments and information.

Corporate identity, as a strategic management tool, was applied without reservation to this charitable institution. The target and philosophy might be different from those of a normal business, but corporate identity has proved equally appropriate in forming the corporate culture and developing the identity of the organisation.

The 'company' Henriettenstiftung

Founded by the Hanoverian Queen Marie in 1860, the Henriettenstiftung (stiftung = foundation) represents one of the largest religious charitable institutions in northern Germany. Its core is a community of deaconesses, whose traditional work in Germany is with the sick and poor, but its various up-to-date medical and care facilities have transformed it into a large-scale modern centre.

If you only considered the hospital and presumed that each patient was visited on average by four relatives and friends a week, this means that, numerically, approximately a third of the population of Hanover, the capital city of Lower Saxony, would be in contact with the Henriettenstiftung every year.

Again and again, the Henriettenstiftung has secured new territory for its work. Hanover is a world medical centre but, even so, the Henriettenstiftung was the first there to open clinics or departments for the following disciplines:

- eye diseases
- radiology
- nuclear medicine
- intensive medicine
- medical rehabilitation and geriatrics (a 'Bundesmodellklinik'– federal model clinic)
- psychosomatics.

The situation is the same for our educational and vocational training:

- specialised institute for medical rehabilitation and geriatrics (the first such foundation in Germany)
- school for the care of the elderly
- specialised vocational training for anaesthesia and intensive care
- refresher courses

Within the work of caring for the elderly, we try to create new possibilities with offers of integrated holistic care for elderly people in various circumstances.

From our roots

The Henriettenstiftung was brought to life as a religious institution. Queen Marie of Hanover gives the reasons for the foundation in the charter: 'Since the reawakening of religious life in our dear evangelical church, with deaconesses caring for the sick and the poor (= the old), and with other such establishments already doing holy work in other places, it has been our heartfelt desire to found a house for deaconesses to serve our Hanoverian country.' The heavy language of those days is again in evidence when a

definition of 'deaconess teaching' is given, which speaks of the spiritual structure of the foundation. Within the training of deaconesses, there was clearly a good amount of corporate identity thinking. The training gave the community of the Mutterhaus ('mother house'), which lived, believed and worked together, the set daily order:

'Out of the preaching of God's word and the administering of the sacraments, the community of sisters, and the Mutterhaus, lives. Without this service, the sisters' other, far-reaching purpose is not conceivable and not possible.'

The starting position for our corporate identity work

Today, the number of deaconesses belonging to the Henriettenstiftung is steadily decreasing, whereas the overall staff numbers are rising. This situation has been dictated by the expansion of our activities, shortening of working hours and divergence of professions. Additionally, the increasing mobility of the labour market and the consequently increased staff turnover, have shaped the personnel structure of the Henriettenstiftung.

How could the identity of the Henriettenstiftung be protected in the light of these developments? How could it be conveyed in a credible way? The process of secularisation and the weakening of the church's influence, felt in so many areas of life and work, gave this question even more point for us. How had the expectations of patients and customers towards the Henriettenstiftung developed? How had the image which staff have of the house changed? What was the first impression and what was at the core? Was the reputation based on the Mutterhaus, or on the religious foundation, the renowned hospital, the well-known centres for the elderly, the affiliated schools, or was it based simply on our being the most important employer in this field offering the most interesting job? Or was it formed through the spirit of Christian neighbourly love, the level of professional competence, the working atmosphere? In any case, we knew that an uncoordinated inward and outward picture, disparate expectations and contradictory aims could not safeguard the identity of the foundation, nor guarantee work satisfaction and success. The position of the foundation in the public perception was certain to be affected if its religious character decreased.

However, apart from the fame of the doctors and the equipment levels in the clinics, the caring reputation of the hospital of the Henriettenstiftung counted for a great deal. This made it vividly clear that the personal aspect of caring for the sick and elderly is regarded as an outstanding feature of charitable work, and that there are specific popular expectations of this from a religious establishment. Internally, similar conclusions were drawn. We aimed to recognise clearly, in our own house, what was special about hospital and geriatric care in religious, as compared to secular, institutions. We sought the particular, and therefore the typical, in the Henriettenstiftung.

We therefore began to think, over twenty years ago, how to intensively involve new members of staff in the mission of the Henriettenstiftung which we had developed. The heart of the problem was how to present the traditional aims and values in a positive and engaging way in the context of changed times.

The corporate culture as expression of our own perception

At the outset it was clear that this task could not only, and certainly not in the first place, be fulfilled by our board. A corporate philosophy developed by the leading body

In the corporate philosophy, tradition, values and standards as well as practical information are linked to a system of targets.

Corporate mission		
Traditional target aspects	**Ethical moral values**	**Science, technology, environment, market**
Jesus Christ to Christians is maker and provider of standards of neighbourly love In nursing, serving the sick = serving God	To be there for the sufferer (the fellow who is in need)	Competitiveness/efficiency, progressiveness
His life is an example of brotherliness/ sisterliness	To help him physically, spiritually, mentally (therefore holistic)	'To do the utmost possible'
He compels us to do merciful work	To respect and protect his dignity	Security, closeness
He invokes reintegration and social rehabilitation	To protect his life. Not to abandon him in dying	Openness, approachability, trustworthiness
Traditional representation in hospitals run by the church, monasteries, bishops, towns and cities, holy orders, sisterhoods, parishes, organisations	'The care for the sick comes before and above all other duties'	Economy, social responsibility
		Competition, guarantee

Source: Author

only sets the rules for the activities and aims of an institution. Its promulgation and realisation need a permanent implementation process and the active participation of everyone. The Henriettenstiftung, in all its complexity, had therefore to face the effort required to develop its corporate identity further. We were always aware that, in the development of a corporate philosophy, the historical characteristics of the institution were going to play a major rôle along with the various present-day considerations. In the first instance, the traditional aspects were emphasised, as they represent our inheritance. For example: 'He who serves the sufferer, serves God and obeys the most noble commandment.' From such aspects – protection of life, of human dignity, total care and devotion – derive the ethical and moral values and standards, as well as the motivation, of our leaders.

In a second step, we analysed the environment, the market, the conditions and developing trends in the medical, care and economic aspects (for example, demand and competition situation) and set the knowledge gained against aspects of our aims and values. What we strive for in medicine, gerontology, care, vocational training, spiritual welfare, social work and health policy, what seems economically feasible, what is religiously meaningful: all these things precondition our actions. This must be taken into account in creating our system of goals.

After preparatory work in 1973, and above all in 1985 to 1987, we initiated workshop groups in 1987 to develop outlines for a corporate philosophy. The fulsome theological language of the old texts had to be transformed into a generally approachable form of expression; themes and contents had to be checked, to be newly assembled and applied. By the time the first text of the philosophy was printed (it is now in its fourth edition), over two hundred members of staff from all professions, grades and levels of responsibility had participated in its creation – from head of care service to administrative employee, from cleaner to cleric, from senior consultant

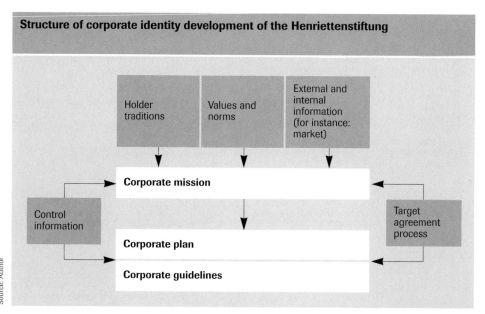

Structure of corporate identity development of the Henriettenstiftung

Source: Author

to nurse of the elderly. We therefore well understand that the development of a corporate philosophy is a dynamic process, which takes into account both changing contexts and prerequisites, and changes in our own self-perception. Our corporate philosophy is based on the Christian character of our institution and interprets this against the background of today's social and economical situation, within which the foundation must operate. Based on the corporate philosophy which we had now fixed in guidelines, further corporate concepts and leadership principles were then worked out.

Corporate concepts, which are essential rules for the entire work of the foundation in its most important areas of activity, were to be formulated. Their purpose is to form a guiding process with respect to the achievement of results within tolerances, to achieve a standard for the future. Feedback ensures that the processes are self-regulating. Deviations cannot be stopped, but they can be kept in check. The corporate concepts must be known to all leading staff, must guide their actions towards goals, must be soundly structured and must be consistently held. For example, they refer to how we define the performance of our hospital. As an example to illustrate this, we have a rule which encourages us increasingly toward caring for risky pregnancies rather than resorting to abortion. In such decisions, the statements of the corporate philosophy are mirrored: 'We regard as important the idea that each human being is an individual personality, created and loved by God. We wish to respect this individuality...' 'We protect the right of the weaker to live'. A further example of this acted-out corporate philosophy is that the subject of death should not become taboo. Death and dying are part of life just as are pregnancy and birth. To accept this, to be beside and to care for people in their varied walks of life, with all their fears and anxieties, is expressive of our roots and

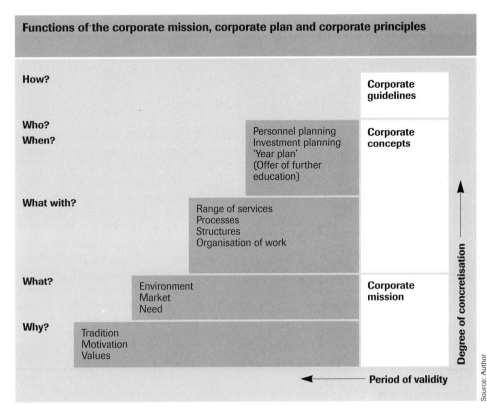

our perceptions of ourselves as Christians. In addition, the corporate concepts contain the formulation of conceptual and structural principles in personnel matters, such as concepts for vocational training, performance assessment and organisation of labour. Then there is an outline of the hospital care regime and the pastoral service for the benefit of patients and staff. Leadership guidelines help us to think more deeply into the relevance of our everyday work. In this, it is crucial how the leadership style is typified within the purview of our corporate philosophy.

A new chapter begins with the corporate identity consultancy

Since 1989, we have worked with external consultants. Through collaborating with them, we wanted to gain a proper perspective on

Corporate identity development stages

- Status quo analysis

- Self-perception of the foundation

- Communications research

- Management and expert interviews

- Positioning strategy/targets

- Criteria for content

- Optical-formal criteria

the insights and measures developed internally, to be able to evaluate them critically, to detect shortcomings and to obtain new stimuli.

Positioning

Based on the corporate philosophy, corporate concepts and leadership principles already worked out by the Henriettenstiftung, the consultants firstly developed a target positioning that presented the self-perception and requirements in a structured way. This positioning represented a consolidation of many different papers and documents on the self-perception of the foundation as well as interpreting and fixing them in action-relevant statements. The positioning, internally, serves to orientate staff and, externally, differentiates the foundation from other public social institutions. It is divided into three areas: foundation, employees and community of deaconesses. Within the foundation, there are members of staff who act from a range of different motivations. Comparable expectations are required of all of them. The staff of the Henriettenstiftung

- gain strength and hope for their service from faith and from appreciation of their performance;
- bring the whole self as well as their skills into their tasks;
- through constant reflection on their actions, recognise their own limitations and potential;
- accept the tension between subordination and self-realisation;
- practise openness in interaction with each other, and acceptance of personalities with all their strengths and weaknesses;
- in their relationships with others, presume the unity of body, soul and spirit.

The foundation has clearly defined its target relationship with the public and the state. It wants not only to practise individual attention

and care, but also

- to stand up in public for the Christian view of humanity;
- to identify social discrimination and unhealthy living conditions;
- to practise an open, pro-active information policy;
- to communicate and cooperate actively with various target groups.

The foundation operates as a business: the foundation must do so economically. Nevertheless, one can see a specific positioning arising from the traditions of our origins:

- the relationship between humanitarian and business priorities;
- the latitude given by particular religious values;
- a cooperative way of working, based on dialogue.

Staff and target group interviews

After the target identity goals were produced in the form of this positioning strategy, requirements and reality had to be compared before we could move forward to implementation. We gained invaluable insights by carrying out a survey in which the existing situation was established and the targeted position was checked.

This was done by qualitative interviews with staff and external target groups. It was possible to determine the present self-perceptions through the things which staff said, then to identify the current image of the Henriettenstiftung through external opinions. Both of these were then set against the target identity described in the positioning in order to assess the requirement for action. Subsequently, the content of the positioning strategy was reworked with the help of the knowledge gained in the interviews and distilled into the following positioning aspects. They reduce the positioning statement to a few concentrated focal points which are readily grasped:

- spiritual welfare – caring
- cooperative – all-embracing – innovative
- open – communicative
- responsible – aware
- peace – security – familiarity
- vitality – growth
- quality – competence
- rational – economical
- human scale
- Christian – cultural – social

A corporate identity based on these aspects enables the foundation to develop and strengthen its inherent culture, esprit-de-corps and internal attitudes. At the same time, it conveys those attitudes, together with our competence and ability to perform, to staff, the general public and customers, serving as a link between inward identification and outward presentation.

Research on communications

As the central instruments for conveying the organisation's identity, the various communications of the Henriettenstiftung were subjected to thorough analysis. The Henriettenstiftung and its departments communicate externally in various ways with the public, with patients and their relatives, with doctors and social institutions, state authorities and clerical institutions, as well as internally with staff and amongst the various parts of the foundation. The communications include many different elements, means and measures, ranging from corporate symbols to stationery, publications, internal newsletters, events and seminars. Assessment of the visual communications was made by criteria relating to content (the positioning aspects

What contribution can corporate design make?

Corporate design is the visual expression of the values, competence and potential towards employees, the general public and target groups. It should:

- carry and express the positioning

- express the independence and interdependence of the individual divisions of the foundation

- present the offer and range of services professionally

- increase the degree of knowledge of the Henriettenstiftung

- ensure differentiation from similar organisations

- build a strategic visual framework for internal and external means of communication

Source: © 1994 Henrion, Ludlow & Schmidt

mentioned above were used for this) and by general visual criteria. An important aspect of these researches was the discussions on the relevance of a consistent and attractive corporate design for the Henriettenstiftung. In the interpretation of the positioning, one of the practical tasks consisted of the creation of elements and means of corporate design to achieve a visual identity which met requirements and targets. A programme of standards, systems, colours and materials was developed and documented for sites, equipment and signs for buildings and environments, so that implementation could be consistent even during subsequent replacement, renovation, rebuilding and new building. In addition, information logistics were developed for the whole area of internal and external communications. The basis for

The layout system for printed communication is derived from the mark.

this was a matrix in which the target groups of the Henriettenstiftung were related to the content of information, means and measures. Such logistics make it economically possible to achieve synergetic communications, aimed accurately at our targets.

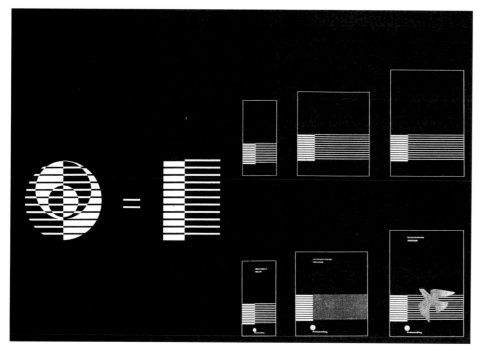

The implementation of corporate design

As an outward sign of change, the first thing to be developed was a new mark or symbol. The chosen device expresses that, even in changed circumstances, the foundation still deals with traditional religious values and ethical goals. It can be interpreted as showing open arms which rescue and protect, or as an abstract description of three circles which are independent, but which have a centre. In relation to the positioning, the symbol can be interpreted in the following ways:

• from a multitude of elements comes one whole

• caring and comprehensive
• open, integrating and striving
• gathering around a centre
• light and shade
• rational and constructive.

In a further stage, various brochures for patients and staff of the Henriettenstiftung emerged. The brochures were consistently designed with the help of a layout system based on the corporate design, and using the new logotype. The staff newspaper, 'Blätter (pages) aus der Henriettenstiftung', was redesigned following the same style. Further implementation of the corporate design included stationery such as letters, memos and so on, which include the new symbol. Form and certificate design was reworked based on the design criteria. To enhance the links between the individual establishments and the public, and to improve their function, a new orientation and information system was introduced. Today the foundation presents itself in a professional manner towards the public and has been able to increase its level of recognition significantly.

Experiences and outlook

Looking at the project in retrospect, it can be seen that corporate identity as a strategic management instrument can also be used in relation to our own type of 'company', the 'diakonischen Stiftung'. Of course, the goals and philosophy of the Henriettenstiftung are different from those of profit-making corporations but corporate identity, as a management instrument for the development of corporate culture, is just as valuable and effective.

It is confirmed that, to grasp the complexity and interrelationships of facts, areas and levels with each other, it is not enough to look at single aspects. Instead, a holistic viewpoint is necessary, which requires an interdisciplinary approach. For this, a structural model is necessary, which takes into account all aspects influencing the corporate existence, structures them into operational dimensions and makes interdependences obvious. The development of the corporate identity of the Henriettenstiftung can be organised into three dimensions:

Brochures for patients and staff, stationery and a staff newsletter have been developed on the basis of the layout system.

- corporate philosophy (design/communication/culture)
- corporate concepts (market/product/services)
- principles of leadership (behaviour).

The corporate philosophy finds its internal and external expression through design and communications which aim to provide targeted information, as well as influencing the perceptions and behaviour of all internal and external target groups.

The desired positioning of the Henriettenstiftung is still in the process of being achieved and in some areas is naturally more advanced than in others. The positioning represents both the basis and the goal for all communications, from the development of our corporate philosophy to corporate concepts and principles of leadership.

In this way, the foundation presents itself professionally in the marketplace and towards the public, enhances the level of recognition, differentiates from other comparable institutions, expresses the desired positioning through the corporate design, conveys the spectrum of its expertise and acts internally and externally according to the agreed goals. For the future, it remains important that staff cooperate in the process of negotiating targets within the corporate philosophy. The ongoing development of communications in line with the positioning, in terms of both scope and depth, must take this into account.

Especially in the field of healthcare, whose accelerating development can only be partially glimpsed, reactions must be fast. The ability to change within a clearly defined frame of action is of paramount importance. For us, this means on the one hand specific

Pastor
Wolfgang Helbig

Principal of the
Henriettenstiftung,
Hanover, Germany

Born 1932 in Forst,
Germany. After
studying theology in
Göttingen, Heidel-
berg, Basel and
Birmingham, was
appointed as a priest
in Helsinki, Finland.
Subsequently Pastor
in Hildesheim, and
later in Hameln
(Hamlin). Senior
Chaplain to the
Bishop of Hanover.

Since 1971 principal
of the Henrietten-
stiftung.

expertise and professionalism, on the other hand human motivation and an awareness of our attachment to the values and sources of Christian service. This is increasingly possible through corporate concepts which are already partly formulated – for example, the performance spectrum for the hospital, the care concept for elderly people, vocational training, assessment, workforce organisation, pastoral service – or which still have to be partly realised. In the near future, we would like to give special attention to the principles of leadership. In such behaviour-oriented activities the wheels turn full circle again and again and the results become part of the corporate culture, which is the corporate philosophy practised and implemented daily.

Bibliography
W. Helbig: 'Krankenhausphilosophie – Leitbilder/Führungskonzepte und -richtlinien'
In: 'Leitung und Leistung im Krankenhaus', Symposium der Bertelsmann Stiftung,
24-25 September 1991, Gütersloh 1993, S.127-154

IBM is the world's largest information technology company. IBM's history started in 1914 when Thomas J Watson Sr joined the Computing-Tabulating-Recording Company, becoming President in 1915 and adopting the name International Business Machines in 1924.

IBM divides the globe into four principal geographic areas and operates in over 140 countries worldwide. In 1994, worldwide turnover was $64 billion, 85% of that being generated outside the US. In the same year, IBM employed over 200,000 people.

Introduction

IBM's corporate identity has often been cited as exemplary. The stable, monolithic nature of what had been achieved in terms of behaviour and visual coordination of products, promotion and architecture, perhaps obscured the daily effort needed to maintain this status quo. However, the continuity of the basic beliefs of the founder was always clear.

But even such a secure identity has to respond to global market changes, and IBM found themselves in the teeth of a recession and feeling the cold winds of competition as the race to get innovations to market was joined by all sorts of outsiders.

IBM's culture is described here, together with the circumstances which led to changes in the way the corporate identity was applied, to deliberate fragmentation and then back to uniformity for the sake of brand strength. The development of IBM's corporate vision and principles is explained in the context of change management. The rôle of the identity in balancing change with continuity is the principal theme.

A basic philosophy wins through

In 1963, Thomas J Watson Jr, Chairman of the Board of International Business Machines Corporation, wrote of the Corporation's 'basic beliefs':
'... I believe that if an organisation is to meet the challenges of a changing world, it must be prepared to change everything about itself except those beliefs ...'

The words were contained in an innocuous-looking but potent little book called *A business and its beliefs: the ideas that helped build IBM* and, while it would be manifestly untrue to say that IBM has changed 'everything' except its basic beliefs, IBM has virtually transformed itself in recent years, and the story of its corporate identity is inseparable from those beliefs and the Corporation's fortunes.

A BUSINESS
AND ITS BELIEFS
THE IDEAS
THAT HELPED
BUILD IBM

When Thomas J Watson Jr wrote that book, IBM had been growing strongly for many years and was continuing to do so. From 1,200 people in 1914, the Corporation had grown to 125,000 in 1963; profits had grown from $500,000 to $200,000,000, shareholders from 800 to 225,000. And this unbroken pattern continued for over twenty more years. Revenue peaked in 1990 at $68 billion, employees in 1986 at 407,080. For all that time, the Corporation had a secure, monolithic identity, which was reflected in popular images of white-shirted salesmen, immaculately-designed and innovatory products like the 'golf ball' typewriter, and landmark office buildings such as the one in La Gaude in France, designed by Marcel Breuer. This was the long-lasting era when it was said that 'nobody got sacked for buying IBM'.

The IBM culture

This success was undoubtedly largely due to the strength of the IBM culture and its effect on everything the Corporation did. IBM knew itself well, and it knew how to present that self. The culture, in turn, grew from the basic beliefs, which came directly from the very top of the Corporation through all the levels, being installed and reinforced by induction, training and a myriad of internal communications measures, formal and informal.

Above all, the fact that IBM's beliefs were (and are) acted-out and made manifest in all dimensions and aspects of the Corporation's daily life, made the culture a self-renewing resource. Within IBM, therefore, it was only possible to act in an IBM way, a way which was a tangible expression of the basic beliefs. The strength of those beliefs became even clearer when the Corporation had to respond to dramatic changes in global market conditions, which will be explained later.

The beliefs are very simple:

- respect for the individual
- pursuit of excellence
- best customer service.

And there are countless examples of their application in practice.

Respect for the individual

IBM has always sought to bring out the best in people, believing that success depends on doing just that. Principles such as full employment, promotion from within, community involvement and the 'Open door' policy, where employees are allowed access to managers at all levels, all helped to shape the attitudes and behaviour of IBM employees, again reinforcing the internal culture and communicating those attitudes to the outside world. IBM recruited, and kept, the best people, then developed them to help them to achieve their full potential, which is clearly in the best interests of both individual and Corporation. IBM has also led the way in providing outstanding working conditions and employee benefits, in most cases being far in advance of local legislation on these matters.

Although, particularly within the sales force, IBM developed a reputation for a high degree of standardisation in the presentation of the 'IBM way', the Corporation has always recognised a need for what Thomas J Watson Jr called 'wild ducks', who would not be bound by convention and who would be seeking out new and unexplored places. As he said: 'you can make wild ducks tame, but you can never make tame ducks wild again'. There is no doubt that the culture of IBM even pervaded the private life of many employees. Indeed 'family days', when spouses, partners and children are brought into Corporation locations, still survive. Corporation songs, or rather the performance of Corporation songs, have not survived, perhaps thankfully. IBM's strong stance on ethical issues has always been a central pillar of its way of doing business, and all individual employees are given guidance and instruction on this aspect. The impact of these various measures is, in sum total, very considerable, both internally and externally, and has been a principal building block of IBM's identity.

Pursuit of excellence

Everything which IBM does, it aims to do excellently. So this, like the other two beliefs, is an all-pervading aspirational value which affects everybody, everything and every activity, from product innovation and performance to presentation and customer service. It is particularly clearly expressed in the broad area of design, which IBM has, since the war, used as a primary tool in the areas of working environment, product benefits and appeal, and promotion. IBM has always sought to work with those designers, or architects, whose work represents, by its general acceptance and distinction, the best currently available.

IBM's adoption of design as a major aspect of corporate expression developed from Thomas J Watson Jr's friendship with the American industrial designer Eliot Noyes, whom he met during the Second World War. In a way, this very personal genesis of the Corporation's 'face' is a reflection of its emphasis on the individual. It was also the start of a process which resulted in one of the global classics of design management, for IBM stuck to its basic beliefs in this area, too, and produced a total oeuvre which has been quoted and illustrated as an example of best practice over and over again. A stream of classic and coordinated products, such as the 'golfball' electric typewriter, was etched into the public consciousness. A combination

of elegance, restraint and confident, yet understated stylishness gave IBM products an 'inevitable' look which befitted their status. These were products which brought the benefits of leading-edge technology into the office in a way which users could relate to.

The corporate design style, including the logotype which could be regarded as the kernel of IBM's visual expression, was designed by the American Paul Rand in the 1950s and has been consistently used ever since, becoming a true 'mark of excellence', fit to stand beside those of Mercedes-Benz and Shell, for example. Application of the corporate design elements, although documented and legislated through the usual guidelines, is heavily dependent on sympathetic treatment by first-class designers. This is why IBM's promotional material has always maintained an ideal balance between consistency and a variety appropriate to the target audience or function.

Design, or the commissioning of design, has also been used to express IBM's corporate social responsibility of investing in the community, or of being a 'good citizen' in the host country or region. This means that, in France, the 'best' French architects were used for IBM's buildings, in Germany, the best German architects were used, and so on. The practice of the basic beliefs is there-fore seen to interact with other corporate principles, in this case that which also dictates that IBM in the UK, for example, is led largely by British nationals.

Best customer service

Respect for the individual and the pursuit of excellence are both major influences on how the customer perceives IBM, but the central position of the customer in IBM's conscious-ness is reflected in the strength of this belief. Thomas J Watson Jr considered it to be the

Evolution of the universally-known IBM logotype, designed by Paul Rand, to the present 8-bar version.

key element in IBM's reputation and that an advertisement which simply said 'IBM Means Service' in bold type was, in his opinion, the best that the Corporation had ever run! IBM's sales force, with its famous training regime and rigorous selection procedures, has always been at the sharp end of the Corporation's customer service efforts. The behaviour of IBM's salesmen was the human representation of the corporate culture. The closeness of IBM to its customers was indeed a key to the Corporation's success, and there are many examples which show the extraordinary lengths to which IBM has often gone to meet special demands and thereby prove its capability and customer commitment. That commitment has never been in doubt, but more recent events have proved that this aspect needs constant reappraisal, readjustment and even renewal.

Global market developments

It had for long been the case that what the sales force had to sell (the product) was excellent, probably the best, that the style of everything was immaculate, that the salesman's appearance and manner were irreproachable and that IBM's corporate reputation, the thing which summed up all the Corporation's experience, activities and culture, was second to none.

However, by the late 1980s, developments in global markets, in user demands and in competition were putting great pressures on IBM and the recession, of course, was also taking its toll. This manifested itself very clearly in the figures. Revenues fell. IBM responded. The worldwide workforce was reduced by 100,000 between 1986 and 1992.

Ten out of 40 manufacturing plants were closed. Other economies were made. These moves were unprecedented in the history of the Corporation and were a severe jolt to the culture. And, of course, IBM's reputation – as an employer, as a caretaker of share-holder funds and as a supplier – reflected the realities of the situation. How had this happened? Had the basic beliefs somehow failed? Or had they become fossilised and inappropriate? Had they been misinterpreted in today's changed conditions? Or was some other factor involved, because surely respect for the individual, the pursuit of excellence and best customer service could never be out of fashion.

To appreciate the situation, some under-standing of those global changes is necessary. Fundamentally, IBM had been slow in responding to the way in which advancing technology was being applied to serve customer needs. The needs having been identified and served by others, IBM did not have the appropriate products

Above: IBM 513 reproducing punch, c. 1960.

Right: early IBM electromagnetic typewriter.

Far right: IBM tabulator, c. 1914.

to compete. In particular, IBM was late in entering the small, desk-top computer market (although eventually defining the product as the 'Personal Computer' or 'PC') and could not offer open systems, software, related services or integration skills. At the same time, hardware was becoming more and more of a commodity, which led to dramatically increased competition from other producers, especially those with a low cost base.

IBM's identity was not altogether helpful in this situation. Where an impression of flexibility was clearly needed, a monolithic aloofness was the perceived attribute. Where computers were becoming more user-friendly and colourful, IBM appeared almost mono-chromatic, not helped by the 'white shirt' ethos. Above all, the Corporation's identity was affected by the change in its fortunes. Whereas superiority had, to some, seemed an IBM birthright ('I am, therefore IBM'), this was now seen to be not the case. The monolith was not quite so secure, and was now encircled by newer competitors such as Apple, who just seemed more in keeping with the times, quicker, more innovative, more fleet of foot. The recession did not help, either – not in a total sense, nor in being able to attribute effects to causes. It struck sooner and with more severity in the UK than in many other places, and it was to be IBM UK which showed new directions for the Corporation in dealing with its difficulties.

Autonomy versus brand strength

A new degree of devolution and empower-ment led to IBM attempting to transform into a number of 'baby blues', rather than be one 'big blue'. In this process, there came to be a new degree of autonomy in certain areas of operation and in aspects of the identity. Of course, products were still designed in the US, but in promotion, more freedom was now allowed. The basic corporate design elements, principally the logotype, remained unchanged, but application was more flexible. However, this resulted in a myriad of variations on the Corporation's identity worldwide.

In the Corporation's communications, the logotype was used in a variety of ways. Straplines and other devices were attached to it, resulting in a loss of consistency. Surveys showed that the messages being given out by IBM were becoming confused, and that the result of this was a diminution of IBM's brand strength. Clearly, although autonomy and freedom of action was necessary in many ways, the Corporation could not accept the enfeeblement of its brand values, built up over so many decades. Since the arrival of Louis Gerstner, in April 1993, IBM has therefore been moving back to a 'one company, one brand' ideal, and this is being worked on and promoted both internally and externally.

Communications has been put at the top of the agenda and new executives have been brought into the Corporation and given responsibility for advertising, brand image and communications, and public relations. In 1994, IBM took the radical step, having reviewed its advertising policy, of appointing one agency to handle all of its advertising worldwide. The agency will be responsible for brand management and, ultimately, for all external promotional communications. At the same time, work is currently under way to internalise the brand through cultural

Above: IBM 'Thinkpad' personal laptop computer.

Far left: IBM 'Golfball' typewriter.

The first structure created atom-by-atom , spelling out 'IBM'.

Restructuring for customer focus

Renewed focus on the customer is now evident throughout the organisation, from the basic structure outwards. IBM is still divided into four principal geographic areas – United States; Europe, Middle East and Africa; Asia, Pacific and Far East; Latin America – but is now also focused on what are termed 'Industry verticals'. There are 14 of these, such as finance, health and transportation, and they are further subdivided into segments – in the case of finance, the subdivisions are retail banking, wholesale banking and financial services. Industries are allocated to geographic areas, which are in turn designated as 'centres of excellence'. Thus, for example, IBM France is the centre of excellence for petroleum in Europe. So, while one country will have responsibility for the total global expertise of IBM in any given industry or segment, each and every country will also be able to draw on that resource where necessary. Those who work within IBM have been part of a cultural change which is again

development which encourages employees to act and work in those ways which bear out the brand attributes of technological leadership, responsiveness, expertise, quality and value for money. In essence, this represents a significant investment in re-establishing a strong, single identity. The products and services themselves have been a critical element in what is a massive restructuring programme to transform IBM from a general computer corporation to one which is solutions-led. The customer is truly king, and can now choose all sorts of permutations and options. Changes in manufacturing process make this possible, but it is the customer who calls the shots.

IBM's office complex at La Gaude, France, designed by Marcel Breuer.

led by the customer's demands. The culture has become more extrovert, more outward-looking than before. Informality and directness have become the norm, together with a recognition of the absolute necessity for fast response. This is the result of IBM reacting to the circumstances in which it found itself. In such an atmosphere, the uniformity of the white shirt could not survive and, thus, the outward manifestations become expressive of the Corporation's transformation.

At the core of the changes, be they structural, activity-based or in the area of communications, are IBM's efforts to redefine itself to enable it to prosper in present and future conditions without losing sight of its origins and without being untrue to its beliefs. IBM, after all, is still IBM and nobody, inside or outside the Corporation, would believe in it any longer if it abandoned its principles and tried to appear to be something else.

The basic beliefs endorsed

The basic beliefs have never been in question. Even if 'respect for the individual' took something of a knocking because of substantial personnel reductions, IBM has not been untrue to its roots. In fact, the beliefs are constantly being refreshed and applied in new areas of interpretation. So, when IBM funds care programmes for children and the elderly in the US, it is helping its own employees' children and parents, as well as those of others – a true respect for the individual. Other ways in which IBM respects the individual include support of education programmes, community programmes and disaster relief – and, ultimately, environmental policies and programmes, because that affects the air we all breathe or the water we all drink. Pursuit of excellence continues, at a most basic level, because of the need to innovate and be competitive. The motivation towards excellence is so deeply rooted within

IBM that it is almost second nature. What has been attended to is the focusing of excellence onto areas of customer need and demand. Best customer service is still regarded as the key to success, but it has been completely reinterpreted for today's conditions, and the Corporation has been restructured with the specific aim of embracing customers as part of the development process.
A customer is no longer regarded just as someone who buys what emerges at the end of the product development process, but as someone whose needs are represented and taken account of from A to Z, from product inception to point of purchase and beyond.

An outward-looking organisation

In fact, this intermeshing theme continues throughout IBM's structure and business operations. This is absolutely dictated by the rapid advancement of technology, the costs of product development, the demands of

A 'virtual reality' picture of Dresden Cathedral, produced by IBM as an aid to the reconstruction process.

*The information for
this chapter came
from interviews with
personnel in the
Corporate
Communications and
Property Design and
Management
departments at IBM
UK's headquarters in
North Harbour during
the summer of 1994,
together with material
supplied by IBM.
IBM has checked and
approved the content.*

customers and global competition. In 10 years, IBM has moved from being a self-contained and self-sufficient corporation with an inward-looking bias, to being an outward-looking organisation which positively seeks out new ideas and approaches that mesh with its own talents and strengths. IBM now has more than 20,000 business partnerships worldwide and more than 500 equity alliances with agents, dealers, distributors, software firms, services companies and manufacturers. This hardly fits with the description of an isolated monolith or a lonely dinosaur, and it indicates just how radical and far-reaching IBM's transformation has been. The basic beliefs, however, remain firm, but IBM has redefined its vision and principles to make them relevant and practical to the present global situation, the Corporation's aims and its day-to-day activities. In other words, the vision and principles are there to give direction and guidance which is credible, clearly understood and relevant to the issues which employees face every day.

IBM's vision

IBM's mission is to be the world's most successful and important information technology corporation. Successful in helping our customers apply technology to solve their problems, and successful in introducing this extraordinary technology to new customers. Important, because we will continue to be the basic resource of much of what is invented in this industry.

IBM's principles

- The marketplace is the driving force behind everything we do.
- At our core, we are a technology corporation with an overriding commitment to quality.
- Our primary measures of success are customer satisfaction and shareholder value.
- We operate as an entrepreneurial organisation with a minimum of bureaucracy and a never-ending focus on productivity.
- We never lose sight of our strategic vision.
- We think and act with a sense of urgency.
- Outstanding, dedicated people make it all happen, particularly when they work together as a team.
- We are sensitive to the needs of all employees and to the communities in which we operate.

IBM's identity was clearly both a strength and a weakness through the difficulties of recession and transformation. On the one hand, the image of sheer size and professionalism, of quality and consistency, of global reach and local responsibility gave confidence that IBM could overcome its problems. On the other hand, complacency, bureaucracy, inflexibility and aloofness were traits which threatened the Corporation's survival. Thomas J Watson Jr wrote that 'the basic philosophy, spirit and drive of an organisation have far more to do with its relative achievements than do technological or economic resources, organisational structure, innovation and timing.' During the most recent crisis, some within IBM might have argued about the relative position of 'timing', and wished also that the basic beliefs had included some reference to attitudes to change.

But, true to Watson's words, IBM has been prepared to change almost everything about itself except its basic beliefs and has gained respect and credibility in the process. Its identity has proved to be both resilient and adaptable. IBM is not the Corporation it was. If it was, it would not be here at all.

INSEAD is one of
the world's most
international and
respected business
schools. Each year,
over 3,000 executives
from more than
60 countries attend
its programmes. There
are 84 permanent
faculty members
representing 22
different nationalities.
In addition, there are
15,000 alumni, more
than 8,000 of whom
have graduated from
the MBA programme.
INSEAD retains
regular and close
contact with alumni.

INSEAD is located
65 km south of Paris,
near to the Forest
of Fontainebleau. It
is privately funded
and non-profit-making,
receiving support
from many inter-
national businesses,
individuals and
organisations.

Introduction

In the fourth decade of its existence, INSEAD was a successful, respected organisation at the forefront of the international business school scene. It attracted participants from around the world, had forged deep and lasting links with industry and had a board of directors and a number of advisory councils whose members included many captains of industry.

Ludo Van der Heyden explains the recognition of the need to create an integrating corporate identity for INSEAD, in the light of the many individual aspirations, cultures and interests represented within the body of the organisation. Recognising the need for a beneficial, consolidated image towards its target market while respecting its essential nature, a balance was sought, both in the process and in the end result.

Corporate identity has helped INSEAD to achieve a new self-understanding through redefinition of its purpose and mission, then to communicate this internally and externally.

An identity of cultural heterogeneity

Practising what is preached is perhaps one of the most challenging of all the aspects of being a business school. By definition, there is a large number of highly spirited people working at INSEAD, representing a wide range of cultures, experience and interests – people who are expected to, and do, develop their own unique, often divergent, hypotheses on the very structure of economic and business life so as constantly to challenge the boundaries of conventional wisdom. Individuals who will provide the managers who come here, some on the MBA programme at considerable personal financial sacrifice, with the latest in management attitudes and processes, stretch and extend their managerial aperture of mind, hone their skills and sustain their interest.

This heterogenous environment thrives on discussion and confrontation. But INSEAD is built on a deep-felt democratic foundation; so reaching consensus is essential and routed in our *raison d'être*. There is no place for any autocratic or dogmatic tendencies, which would undermine the intricate fabric of our structure and working methods.

A corporate identity programme, as a consequence, was therefore an initiative requiring the most delicate of approaches. Perhaps the detours and diversions that would befall us along the way were underestimated, but not having gone through an internal exercise of this kind before, this was to be expected.

Students come from all parts of the world, representing a rich cultural background.

There was at least widespread recognition that a corporate identity programme was necessary. Initial enthusiasm ran high. Everyone believed, at least on a superficial level, that everything that their department or core activity produced and printed differed slightly from that produced by others. Seen together, it was easy to suspect an internal and external touch of chaos. There was a more substantive phenomenon. Although the INSEAD brand was strong, no clear agreement existed on what the school stood for, nor were there any guidelines on what, or how, it should communicate. Every department gave its own interpretation of the school's essence through the communications elements which it controlled.

In reality there was not that much divergence in the interpretations. Most of the individuals closely associated with the school share a passion for its existence; yet without clear

definition or communications parameters it certainly seemed as though they were working for somewhat differing INSEADs. The school, favouring entrepreneurship and initiative as it does, did not actively discourage this.

At the end of the 1980s, INSEAD's thirtieth anniversary had just passed and competition in core markets was increasing. Many European universities and colleges, particularly in the British Isles, had sprouted business schools and were offering MBA programmes. Corporate identity had become a recognised and well practised, though often maligned, business tool. INSEAD knew that we had much to be proud of but also realised that it simply did not come across adequately. True, the school's reputation was very good, but it was felt that, while reputations have to be earned, they must also be sustained and perceived to be justified on first impact. A major media profile of INSEAD in an American international magazine, which raised visibility together with the involvement of design firms in some courses, heightened awareness of the problem.

People spoke highly of INSEAD. When they visited the campus they almost invariably went away impressed. But what of those people who were first exposed to us through written and visual material? Would this convincingly reflect the INSEAD reality? And, in any event, how would that reality be defined? This question had never been systematically looked at.

Scope and organisation of the programme

Calling in consultants to help, in itself, demonstrated a recognition of the need to undertake the task properly. Many members of INSEAD's faculty are consultants to industry and sit on the boards of management of multinational corporations. However, we are an academic institute where substance takes precedence over form, where the visual does not immediately impress. Additionally, none of our staff was a designer. Design, however, was not the central issue. Yes, we recognised that our current 'logo' looked old. But on what basis would anyone commission any designer to develop a new one? How would they draw up a brief and what would it say?

Consultants were needed to bring in their professional design skills but also to provide a more objective view of one institute, validate the various aspects of our organisation, expose what made us behave the way we do, feel the way we do and communicate as disparately as we did. A task force was established to select and work with the consultants and to establish all criteria throughout the process.

While every care was taken to have a cross-section of departments and sections represented, virtually all the members were from the administration. Few, if any, were faculty members . This proved to be a mistake. It is faculty which boasts some of our strongest personalities. They were only present through the administrators of the programmes on which they teach. That having been said, faculty had expressed little interest in an exercise for which neither their agenda nor innate sense of accomplishment had much time. Many also felt that to try and represent just such a body of diverse and strong individuals would be a thankless and unrewarding mantle to adopt anyway. Faculty were happy to play a counselling rôle in the process.

An additional challenge proved to be the interaction of our affiliated centres, including the Euro-Asia Centre, into the process. They have a distinct mission but share INSEAD's campus in different buildings and use fully INSEAD's faculty. Their representation on the task force was informal and should, arguably, have been stronger as the corporate identity process established the actual relationship of the centres to INSEAD itself.

INSEAD in essence

A strong corporate identity is as much a competitive tool as its articulation can be a culturally and behaviourally harnessing process. Using it to consolidate our market position remained at the forefront of our minds while it was recognised that this could only be done effectively once the inside core of the school had been adequately defined.

In 1959 we had started with an adventure, a credo, an applied, fundamentally European orientation based upon an American model. INSEAD was an ideal. Today INSEAD is an institute, an example for Europe, has a growing faculty and has earned widespread recognition. This having been said, our market was diverse, rapidly evolving, more competitive and clearly segmented than ever. So what are our core activities?

The MBA originated in the USA and its perception outside the USA was initially driven by the exposure Harvard had gained for its MBA programme around the world. Yet the MBA offer has been diluted and confused by the proliferation of new courses under the same name offered in many countries. While an MBA had once been a 'passport', it was fast becoming just a qualification. Retention of full 'passport status' for our own MBA programme was an objective that kept resurfacing. After all, the INSEAD MBA programme was one of the first to have been home-grown in Europe, and it stands out noticeably when one compares the truly international aspect it provides in preparation for a multinational career. We were committed to furthering our academic excellence with a newly

The campus atmosphere is conducive to creative thought and study.

developed PhD programme seen by many at its inception as an expensive risk. Now, we have 38 people of 21 nationalities enrolled, but at the time of the corporate identity exercise, this programme was just being launched into what was, after all, a new market activity.

Of all the activities, executive education, composed of a variety of shorter programmes of two to six week duration, including the flagship Advanced Management Programme (AMP), was, perhaps, the most complex in communicational terms. Here, INSEAD, competes with other business schools, management consultants, training companies and course organisers. Sustaining and communicating real differentiation is far from easy.

The business school market is hallmarked by an unusual market characteristic. The purchase of a course constitutes a one-off purchase: there is seldom (except by corporate buyers in executive education) a repeat purchase for the same product. We always have to compete and 'brand loyalty' for us means recommendation for referral.

Culturally we are as varied as we are complex. It is impossible for any national culture to dominate here. With around 50 nationalities represented at any one time, everyone on campus is in a minority. Our predominant language is English yet it is by no means our only one. In addition, INSEAD is situated in a country other than the USA or the UK, which has a very well-defined culture of its own. The different spheres of specialisation of our resident staff not only in business disciplines but in terms of research, teaching and personal orientation makes the tapestry of interests rich and diverse.

This range of interests and varied cultural exposure is reflected in our individual behaviour. Our people are culturally sensitive

and attentive. As might be expected, listening well is part of our make-up. Our style is relatively discreet and reserved. Bragging is anathema and aggressive marketing techniques have never been adopted. Perhaps they weren't needed: anyway they would have seemed contrary to our spirit.

Our communications had never been elaborate and, being fully private, without government subsidies, we are constantly disciplined by limited financial resources and having to earn our living. Our faculty travels extensively and frequently meshes with industry on various projects, both individually and on behalf of the institute. MBA fairs are attended regularly in various capitals, our faculty and administration are interviewed exhaustively and case studies, research projects and our own promotional literature are disseminated to the outside world. There is worldwide press interest in the institute. The result is that INSEAD must communicate at many levels in many different places and always with a slightly different culturally tuned message.

Measuring perceptions

There was a need to know how we were perceived before we could manage those perceptions more effectively. So how did we go about this? With a specially designed questionnaire, the perceptions held by the individuals attending courses here at the time were researched.

Our satisfaction ratings were high. Most executive education participants, once having attended their programme, rated INSEAD better than expected. While it is more desirable that expectations should be exceeded rather than the other way round, this suggested that our programmes were perhaps under-communicated albeit still perceptually of a sufficiently high standard to attract the large number of applications received. 99% of MBA participants having come to INSEAD, said they would attend the course again and recommend it to others. The problem was that INSEAD was not sufficiently known among a larger public and consequently was probably not maximising its communication with its potential participant pool.

Very few other schools were mentioned as having been considered before coming to INSEAD. Therefore, in our view rightly, we were only categorised in a small group of alternatives by those we wanted to attract. Thus, the main attributes of INSEAD were perceived as *modern, professional, exciting, responsive and fresh*. It was also felt, however, that awareness of us was probably much lower than that of Harvard or other American Business Schools. Most Europeans attending perceived us to be a very international institute. By contrast, the Far Eastern attenders perceived us as more French – the location is acknowledged as being a predominant factor in shaping image for those people coming from another continent just as the fact of being in France, for many for the first time, has a compelling novelty value of its own. Through management interviews right across the campus, including the affiliated centres, it became possible to undertake a detailed analysis of international perceptions.

Most people voiced considerable pride in belonging to INSEAD and in fact they even expressed some surprise at their own success.

However, there was some residual concern that INSEAD was still, externally, 'not perceived as autonomous enough' and that it has 'not yet entirely fulfilled its European ambition'. Organisationally, it was recognised that there was 'lack of communication between faculty and the departments' and that the organisation 'had not taken enough time to think about itself'. It was also felt that arrogance and complacency could creep into the culture from time to time.

Redefining ourselves

First and foremost we recognise that INSEAD is a place. It is both a 'home' and a location. This is an important consideration in shaping how we are, how we behave and how we are perceived and certainly, in part, plays a rôle in having people choose to attend programmes here. All programmes are held on campus. Our staff was defined as *confident, positive, professional, varied, open;* our participants as *critical, demanding, enthusiastic* and *hopeful*. The interaction between the two groups lead to *renewal, stimulation* and *learning*.

Below left: a session of the International Council.

Below: The logotype on the INSEAD flag.

INSEAD

MBA Programme

INSEAD

Executive Education

INSEAD

Alumni Fund

*The logotype with
'activity signatures'.*

Our focus became an important consideration and it soon became apparent that we had no single overarching focus across our activities. Perspectives between applied business interests and theoretical viewpoints had almost polarised, yet all of them were essential elements for a business school like INSEAD to focus on.

Keeping these elements in equilibrium while ensuring that each of them grows and prospers is our on-going challenge. We strive for an equilibrium between academic and commercial interests, recognising that we need to retain our academic excellence while covering our costs with revenues and some voluntary funding; between theoretical and applied orientations, ensuring the freshness and substance of our models and their validity in real life; between personal and collective interests, where personal business interests outside INSEAD have to be reconciled with the welfare and reputation of the Institute; between expansionism and exclusivity and knowing where to limit our growth; between research and teaching emphases, expressed both in our budgets as well as our choice of staff; between the targeted priorities of the affiliated centres and their dependence on INSEAD faculty to provide most of their teaching resources; and finally between the interests of INSEAD to be promulgated through the Alumni Association and the members' own simple desire to remain in touch with class mates and other like-minded individuals.

In short we found INSEAD is an invaluable and fragile equilibrium of philosophies, methods, cultures, interests and generations. Coupled with the many nationalities represented here it makes *richness and diversity*, perhaps the most appropriate words. It drives the need for an identity that reflects the experience of being here: whether as a member of staff or attending a programme. *Enrichment through diversity*

seemed to best encapsulate this. Following the analysis, our core values in support of this are defined as *open, confident, humble, mature (established and lasting), visionary, responsive, honest, top quality, realistic, lively, balanced, non-institutional and fresh.* These values needed to be communicated in a consistent and integrated manner.

Communications framework and the revised visual identity

Through an analysis of the constituent factors that shape the perceptions people form of us, we established those that we could seek to improve.

We were quite happy with our human and behavioural facets. Our culture was pervasive and, though now more defined, was in constant evolution by virtue of a reflection of resident enquiring minds and a closeness to ever changing business problems. Our market approaches were successful. Our range of programmes was inter-dependent and well-balanced. The provision of a highly respected MBA with an academic content supports our executive education programmes, while they in turn add validity to the MBA programme. The PhD programme helps both by pushing us to the frontier of management knowledge. We found it was almost solely in the area of communications that our weaknesses lay. They had a content and style that needed to be co-ordinated and honed in terms of tone, and a visual face which needed to reflect our values. So design did have a rôle to play.

Exploring the design options

As would be expected many options were explored. Anything too colourful or new logos that were perceived as trendy were considered wholly inappropriate and were shied away from. Yet some bolder designs particularly appealed to some parts of INSEAD as much as they were derided by others.

A voting procedure was organised on the final design candidates. The solutions proposed had a scattered response and they were all design options that were considered too far removed from our sense of style, too open to subjective taste, to gain widespread support. Perhaps too many people were also involved in the decision making process. Consensus was not reached. Consequently, a return to the drawing board, literally, was needed twice.

The determination to hang on to our existing 'globe logo' (an outline globe with longitudinal and latitudinal lines with the name INSEAD in heavy black sans-script type in the middle) both to reflect the truth of our pluri-national make-up and because everyone had grown accustomed to it, presented a problem in its own right. There are not many ways of drawing globes that are either distinctive or memorable. They are either too literal and old-fashioned looking or too stylised and abstract: this made it difficult to find a version that would be distinct from those in use by several of the world's major telecommunications companies, for example.

We eventually agreed on an evolutionary solution. One which it was felt provided strong threads of continuity with our original logo yet did reflect those of our core values that could be represented visually. (In truth, no design alone can embrace all the core value attributes we had defined nor hope to undertake all the communications objectives by itself.) It is a solution that proved acceptable to everyone by virtue of its inoffensive essential nature. The eventual decision to use the original globe as a secondary, yet constant, 'decorative' device, but separate from the logo proved the ideal solution. The serif typography selected was elegant

and held in place by two horizontal lines. There is now a visual integrity to our mark symbolising, above all, our *academic standards*. We chose deep green as a colour. It reflected our *maturity, hope* and our lush green location in the forest of Fontainebleau. It was a distinctive colour, we felt, but not used by our competitors who mostly use blue or burgundy. While the INSEAD logotype is itself arguably relatively neutral, the use of photography as part of the brochure cover system provided enough opportunity to reinforce our *diversity and richness*, to reflect certain sub-activities and to keep hold of human interest in an academic environment.

To further throw together the different core activities under the INSEAD mantle, the INSEAD name was given the most prominent position and the new mark used as a prefix to all our own activities and programmes. All the activities are named or described typo-graphically in close proximity to the INSEAD word mark and there are easily understandable guidelines governing the use of it. We print much of our own material on campus in our

Printed material is widely distributed and now gives a consistent impression.

**Ludo Van der
Heyden**

*Ludo Van der Heyden
was Co-Dean of
INSEAD from 1990
to 1995 and in this
capacity led the
corporate identity
exercise for INSEAD.*

*A Belgian national,
he is Professor
of Operations
Management and
Operations Research,
a post he has held at
INSEAD since 1989.
Before coming to
INSEAD Professor
Van der Heyden held
full-time professor-
ships at Harvard and
Yale universities in
addition to a number
of international
visiting professorships.*

large print shop so compliance to the graphic manual presents no major difficulty. There is nonetheless a need to control the visual process and to reinforce it on occasion.

With constant and consistent use of these elements in all visual communication with the outside world, we were confident that our visibility would increase and our name and reputation would be remembered by, and represented by, a much larger number of people.

Conclusion

The exercise was, ultimately, a successful one. We cannot now imagine life without a sense of our shared values, as an institute visually reinforced by items such as brochures, signage, letterheads, sweat-shirts, folders and other materials which form part of daily working lives at INSEAD for our staff and participants and which travel the world telling our story.

Perhaps we underestimated the time required to achieve the result, the (often justified) divergent interests of individuals and groups, the sensitivities, emotional attachments to names and symbols and words, the difficulty

for outsiders to grasp our culture, the challenge of managing large groups of erudite and sometimes vocal people and the personal opinions. Certainly towards the end there was an almost desperate impatience to finally bring the exercise to a conclusion. But a small group who were committed to the success of the exercise never gave up. The decision to involve consultants, notwithstanding some disruptive changes in the creative half of the team, was vindicated. The objectivity was crucial and the specialist skills in handling the process provided a framework which helped to bring the project to a conclusion.

All the indications are that INSEAD is now perceived accurately. The programme was completed before the recession. Our course entries held up well during that time. Arguably this might have been the case in any event. It is nonetheless felt that our renewed statement of confidence in ourselves and the quality of the material reaching prospective attenders will have played some rôle in ensuring this encouraging performance.

We look forward to a future bolstered by our sense of self, our purpose and mission and the way we communicate them internally and externally.

Keller is a leading international ground engineering specialist providing the construction industry with an extensive range of technically advanced solutions to problems of ground behaviour. Keller's techniques are applicable to all sectors of the construction industry including industrial, commercial, housing, infrastructure and renovation projects. Until 1990, Keller was a division of the British engineering Group GKN plc. Keller acquired its independence as a result of a management buyout in May 1990. Keller Group plc was subsequently floated on the London Stock Exchange in April 1994. Keller has three principal operating subsidiaries in the United Kingdom, Germany and the United States, and works extensively in Europe, North America and the Middle and Far East. In 1994 the Company achieved a turnover of £195.6 million with a total of 1,928 employees.

Introduction

The transition to independence through a management buyout was supported by the corporate identity. Corporate identity was employed as an instrument for the repositioning and strengthening of the corporate profile in the transition from outsider in a large organisation to independent company.

Mike Moseley describes the development of the positioning strategy, the new self-perception, the market presence and the corporate design as a signal of a new start with a new name. The corporate identity gives credible presence for a complex international corporate structure and gave reassurance during the transitional phase. The Company was therefore able to present the image of a united, competent Group, with an international edge.

Corporate identity was a decisive factor in communicating the Company's goals and the common aims of its different parts. The corporate identity created presence and profile. It conveys capability and credibility and became a vital asset in expressing the value of the Company at the time of the flotation.

An identity for a management buyout

A management buyout is one of the classic triggers for consideration of corporate identity. If, as was the case with Keller, the buyout is from a larger, parent Group, then the transition to independence must be assisted by an identity which gives reassurance to customers, staff and the financial community that the strength which lay behind it is replaced by a new force of equal potential, determined to succeed in the marketplace. An opportunity is also created for repositioning and for an increase in profile.

The Keller Group is the result of a management buyout carried out in 1990. All of the corporate identity factors just mentioned were present in Keller's case, but the needs were amplified by the nature of business and the industry of which it formed a part.

Construction is an industry which has a particularly long-term perspective, and which is sensitive to macro-economic indicators and political decisions relating to infrastructure and other large undertakings. Within the industry, there are specialists like Keller to whom general construction companies turn when faced with particular situations which require expertise and experience.

A great deal of reliance is placed on the competence and professionalism of such organisations, and the assurance of their reputations and corporate standing are vital to those who place trust in their opinions and activities, often in relation to projects where financial risks are large, and where further, professional risks would be most unwelcome. Perceived stability and competence are vital.

A world leader, but a peripheral business

Keller is a leading international ground engineering Group. The holding company is UK-owned and operates through principal subsidiaries in the UK, Germany and the USA. Keller's business is the solution of soil and foundation problems for the construction industry, including industrial, commercial and housing projects, and infrastructure for dams, tunnels, transportation and water treatment. Keller also provides specialised geotechnical requirements arising from renovation of existing buildings and the environmental contracting market.

Prior to 1990, Keller was a division within the large UK-based engineering company GKN, and was known as 'GKN Foundations Division'. Its apparent lack of synergy with GKN's core activities (which are largely in the automotive and fastenings areas) is explained by the history of its creation and development. The Foundations Division was established to offer site investigation as an extension of the activities of GKN Reinforcements, which designed and supplied steel reinforcement for concrete. However, by the late 1980s GKN Foundations Division had grown, organically and by acquisitions, into a major international organisation in its specialised area of business. It had become a world leader in its own right, but remained a peripheral business, albeit a profitable one, within the GKN empire.

A credible presence

At this time, ideas of independence from GKN were beginning to be discussed, with a management buyout being the favoured option. Of course, in this event the GKN name would have to be relinquished and, since this would leave only the generic 'Foundations Division', consideration of the name became of prime importance. At the same time, the newly independent Group would need to establish a firm and credible presence to communicate stability behind its operations, in the way that the GKN presence had done for it previously. This was not so much a question of perceived professional competence as of perceived financial substance, because the GKN name provided an assurance of organisational and financial strength, important when large contracts were under discussion with potential customers.

Before explaining the way in which corporate identity was applied to this need, it is advantageous to understand more about the development and composition of GKN Foundations Division, because there were further complicating factors.

Development and growth

The Division had started to trade in its own right in the early 1960s following a merger with two other ground engineering companies. During the early 1970s GKN purchased Johann Keller of Germany, with whom the Foundations Division already had a business relationship. Johann Keller had a reputation for innovation, with several world-leading products, particular vibro-compaction equipment for stabilising poor ground conditions. Their basic identity was left untouched by the takeover and, in any case, the name GKN meant little or nothing in Germany, so there was no case for strongly expressing the new ownership. In addition, Johann Keller had substantial overseas business through a wide range of international contacts, with particular emphasis on the Middle East. It was therefore considered commercially unwise to disturb the status quo. However, access to Johann Keller's products was to be a significant factor in GKN Foundations Division's (and, subsequently, Keller's) success.

After organic growth through the late 70s, another strategic acquisition was made, this time in the USA. Establishment of a branch office in Florida, as a first step, was followed by acquisition of Hayward Baker Inc, an organisation well known and well established in the States in the field of specialty grouting. As in the case of Johann Keller, no change was made to the basic identity, because substantial goodwill could have been lost, thus negating the very reason for the purchase. Again, as in Germany with Johann Keller, no benefit was seen in promoting GKN. A further acquisition was Colcrete, a UK company also active in specialist grouting. Colcrete had an excellent name in this activity so, again, no basic changes were made although, by this time, all of the companies in the Division were, at least in their statutory names, prefixed by 'GKN. They were thus:

UK: GKN Keller Foundations
           GKN Colcrete
Germany: GKN Keller
USA: GKN Hayward Baker

By 1990, the Group employed around 1,200 people and had a combined turnover of some £90 million. The UK and US markets were buoyant, discussions were proceeding about independence from GKN, and thoughts turned to a name for the new entity.

However, as already hinted, simply to remove the letters 'GKN' was not an option as far as

the name of the newly-independent Group was concerned. There were also other elements of identity which were requiring serious attention, especially the fact that both Johann Keller and Hayward Baker considered that their existing identities were instrumental in carrying recognition value and goodwill. In the case of Johann Keller, this was said to extend to a considerable area of the globe and included their trademark, nicknamed the 'Keller bird'. There was clearly a great deal of cultural loyalty within the companies, although the UK company had a less coherent identity, so was more able and therefore more willing to accept change.

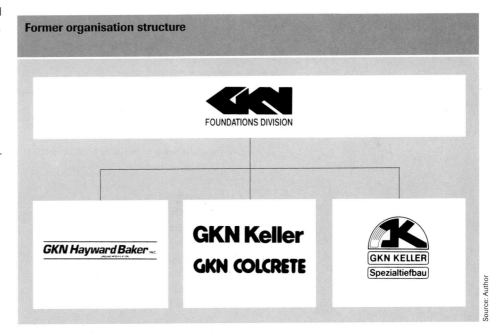

Former organisation structure

Source: Author

GKN Foundations Division decided to seek external consultancy help to assist them in assessing all relevant factors and formulating a new identity for their Group. In essence, the image of a cohesive, competent, world-leading, established Group of companies had to be conveyed before the management buyout. There was certainly an enthusiasm for independence, all parties clearly seeing the potential benefits, but the German company was extremely forthright in its views that its own management style and 'way of doing things' should be retained, which included the corporate design – the visible expression of their culture. The US company was a little less adamant, but held similar views. However, the need for a strong, credible and cohesive Group identity was agreed by all, even if the way of achieving it, given those constraints, was not clear.

The interview process

The consultants' work started with a programme of management interviews, which generally confirmed the strong views already mentioned. However, as is usually the case, those views were softened during the one-to-one interviewing process, with motives and concerns being discussed openly and in a positive atmosphere. The British-German structure of the consultancy firm was nicely matched to Keller's own structure and needs, and nuances of feeling and expression were consequently given proper consideration, something which is often neglected in projects which transcend European boundaries. Indeed, the British-German relationship is a complicated one, the unwary falling into the trap of assuming a too-close correlation of basic values, behaviour and culture. The truth is that, for all the superficial similarities, there are deep, hidden differences which, in a business situation where people must work in harmony to achieve potential synergies, can create difficulties and impede success. The corporate identity process, as applied in the case of Keller, can be of major assistance in overcoming these difficulties.

The consultants visited Hayward Baker's offices in the USA and carried out interviews there among staff and customers. Within Keller, the American-British relationship was

perceived as being closer than the German-British. Apart from language facility, it was cited that accountancy practices and standards were more compatible and that a similar flexibility of attitude prevailed. This latter was less the case with the German company, who were said also to have an 'engineering culture', where engineering excellence and innovation were the prime movers. It can be readily seen that, if the various national attributes could be combined and harnessed, the subsequent synergy would be invaluable in a global market context.

Target positioning statement

After the interview process and the gathering of information, the prerequisite for all further action had to be created – a statement of the target position for the new Group, which could be agreed, embraced, adopted and acted upon by all of the companies. Corporate communications being a new discipline to the managements of the Group and trading companies, such principles needed patient consideration before a statement was reached with which everyone could feel comfortable. In the end, the solution seemed modest enough, but it was a major step in clarifying the nature and aims of the organisation, primarily internally. The chosen statement was: 'A leading international Group of companies with the experience and technical expertise required to find the optimum solution to any ground modification problem. The Group is a problem-solver and offers that extra engineering edge'.

This was largely consistent with current perceptions of the Group. To ensure credibility, it was pointed out that the Group would have to behave in line with the statement, supporting it with an enthusiasm to discuss technical problems with clients and ensuring that its knowledge was at the leading edge. It was also decided that, if the Group was to maximise the potential which could result from its size, service range, technical expertise and current market goodwill, then it must have an integrated and consistent presentation in its market-places. This would result from a rational and easily comprehensible name structure and a common and consistently-used visual style, all based on the positioning statement.

Options for the name

In dropping the 'GKN' prefixes, and the 'GKN Foundations Division', three possible name and naming structure options were identified and evaluated.

Option 1 was to leave all of the trading company names exactly as they were, but prefix them with a new Group name and put them into a common visual style. This would have had the advantage of retaining names which were known in their markets, along with the goodwill. It would have involved minimal internal upheaval while strongly identifying the Group and signifying a fresh start. The disadvantages were mainly to do with the cost and time factors in introducing a completely new name, although it has to be said that these would have been some-what mitigated by linking the new name to the existing names. This option would also have facilitated the expression of further acquisitions.

Option 2, readily dismissed, was to re-name all companies with a completely new name. This would have given a strong indication of change, and would 'level out' perceptions of the Group, but would be expensive, also in terms of lost goodwill and recognition value.

Option 3 was, in principle, the same as option 2, except that it raised the suggestion of

using 'Keller' as the new name for all of the companies. The advantages of using the Keller name seemed very strong:

- It had considerable value in Germany and some international markets.
- It was somewhat known in the UK market.
- While unknown in the US market, it could be used to indicate a link with German technology, which would be a positive image factor.
- Launch and promotion costs would be relatively modest.
- The name was well known internally.
- 'Keller' had the potential to be an international brand, being short and universally pronounceable.

On the negative side, there was a chance that to change the name to Keller could be perceived as a German-led buyout of the Company, but all of the other considerations were positive.

Consistency and endorsement

However, the solution adopted combined a move to the name 'Keller' and a consistent visual style, with an endorsed approach where Hayward Baker in the US and Colcrete in the UK were allowed to keep their own names, prefixed by the Keller name in the latter case. The naming structure therefore became:

Keller Group plc (UK holding company)

Keller Ltd (UK trading company, trading as Keller Foundations and Keller Colcrete)

Keller Grundbau GmbH (German trading company & subsidiaries)

Hayward Baker Inc (US trading company & subsidiaries)

All companies were to be endorsed as being part of the Keller Group, which necessitated a strong visual expression of the name as an international brand for coordinated marketing purposes. A logotype approach was recommended, for the classic reason that a logotype contains, and is indivisible from, the word. It is therefore at the same time visible, recognisable and pronounceable, so capable of being communicated both visually and verbally. A symbol, on the other hand, must be actually, then conceptually, linked to a name before it gains any communications value.

The communications criteria for the Keller visual identity, and therefore the logotype, were that it should be consistent with the Company being:

- professional
- technology-oriented
- solid, large, substantial
- secure
- honest

Given these criteria as a prerequisite, together with consideration of the building-site environments where Keller staff and equipment would often be seen, led the way to a fairly robust approach to the whole corporate design.

A strongly-branded approach

Bold capital letters were selected for the name, which happily has a good letter-pattern. A series of cubes or diamonds was inter-twined with the initial 'K', giving associations of drilling, brilliance, accuracy or building blocks – entirely appropriate for the Company's activities. This attractive, forceful and memorable logotype has been particularly popular internally, and very effective externally in creating impact and memorability. The brilliant yellow colour

was chosen also because of its recognis-ability in building site environments and because the colour was already used by parts of the Group. Partnering it with a rich, dark blue gave it even more brilliance and differentiated it from the simple 'warning yellow' which is often used for earthmoving equipment. A strongly-branded approach for literature systems was devised. Keller do not produce a vast amount of literature in total, so strength and consistency were favoured over flexibility and subtlety, on the reasoning that if their marketing and promotional material was seen infrequently by potential customers, then a strongly consistent approach would be the only one which would optimise memorability.

A strong unifying effect

Because a name change was involved, implementation had to be carried out over a very short period of time. Budget limitations did not allow elaborate launch processes, but the concepts, and the reasons for them, were objectively explained to top management. A basic design manual was produced and distributed.

As a result of the demonstrably close correlation between the communications need of the Company with the proposed and agreed concepts, acceptance was immediate and enthusiastic. The combination of British holding company, German-derived name and independently-named US company was culturally comfortable and operationally practical. The visual expression of the Keller name, and its use as an endorsement in all situations had a strong unifying effect, with people actually wanting to use it.

Implementation and maintenance of the identity in the UK is the responsibility of the Sales Director, who places the design of all promotional material with a local agency.

The 'K' can be seen as a row of cubes or rhomboids, giving associations of drilling, brilliance, precision or building elements.

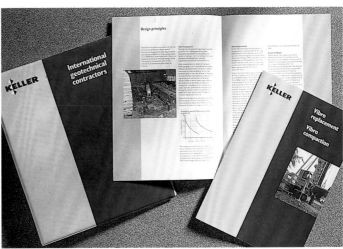

There are in-house design facilities in the German and US offices. Motivation and training of these resources was carried out prior to the launch of the identity.

Five years on from the management buyout and name change finds Keller operating in very different market circumstances. Keller joined the stock market in a successful flotation in May 1994. In total, the Group now employs over 1,900 people and has a turnover in excess of £190 million. It is active in the UK, Germany, USA, Austria, Bahrain, Canada, France, Hong Kong, Malaysia, Mexico, North Africa, Portugal, Saudi Arabia and the UAE.

In the UK, the Keller name has become well established, but the construction market has entered its deepest recession for 50 years. Despite a severe reduction in sales and fierce competition, Keller has remained profitable in the UK. In Germany, of course, the picture is entirely different, with the construction industry going flat out. Within six days of the fall of the Berlin wall, Keller gained their first contract in the 'Neue Bundesländer' and work in the former East Germany now accounts for over one quarter of total German-office turnover. Offices have been opened in

Leipzig and in the Slovak and Czech cities of Bratislava and Prague. A successful entry has been made into the French market. Hayward Baker in the USA has also been successful. Although the Keller name is still little known in the US market, it performs its internal task as Group identifier and unifier. International projects are often discussed internally as 'Keller Group' projects, and Keller is increasingly seen as an international identifier.

However, a careful approach has been adopted, which allows the market to decide for itself. If it should ever be seen as desirable that both Hayward Baker and Colcrete – or any future acquisition, for that matter – should be subsumed into the Group identity, then the system and building blocks to trade internationally as Keller already exist.

Facing new challenges and opportunities

The establishment of an independent, internationally-active and market-leading group has been achieved. Keller is now facing another challenge, one in which its identity will have to be portrayed to a quite different target audience. Keller's shares

A strongly branded appearance was developed for the various items of communication, with more emphasis on impact and consistency than on flexibility.

Mike Moseley

*Staff Director,
Business Develop-
ment, Keller Group plc.*

*Joined GKN as soils
engineer 1962,
Manager, Ground
Engineering for GKN
Foundations Ltd 1975,
1979-86 Director,
Ground Engineering
Division, GKN Keller
Foundations.
1986-87 Director,
GKN Colcrete Ltd.
1987-89 Deputy
Managing Director,
GKN Keller Ltd.
1989-91 Staff
Director, GKN
Foundations Division.
1991-93 President,
Hayward Baker
Environmental Inc,
USA. Since 1993
Staff Director,
Business Develop-
ment, Keller Group Ltd.*

*He is also Editor
of the book 'Ground
Improvement',
published by
Blackie Academic
& Professional.*

have been floated on the London stock market in 1994, bringing the Group into the limelight and under the gaze of analysts, institutional investors, other shareholders and the financial community in general. The perception of a single, unified Group with a coherent and consistent mission will become of paramount importance in the determination of its value. The identity has provided focus and credibility, and is a key step towards flotation. Keller's identity has helped to form and to portray the Group. In future, it will help the Group to face new challenges and opportunities as markets and market conditions change and develop. In Keller's terms, it is a foundation for success.

KLM Royal Dutch
Airlines is the world's
oldest commercial air
carrier, founded in
1919. The national
flag carrier of the
Netherlands takes
sixth place among the
more than 200 IATA
airlines, measured in
international traffic.
KLM operates from
Schiphol Airport, one
of Europe's most
efficient 'hubs'. KLM
stock is traded on
the Stock Exchanges
of Amsterdam, New
York, Brussels and
Frankfurt. The Dutch
government owns
38.2% of the stock.
KLM holds a
25% stake in North-
west Airlines, the
fourth largest
American airline.

KLM's headquarters
are in Amstelveen,
The Netherlands.
In 1994, the Company
employed 24,000
people worldwide
and had a turnover
of NLG 8.7 billion.

Introduction

KLM Royal Dutch Airlines (Koninklijke Luchtvaart Maatschappij) is the Dutch national flag carrier airline. It has pursued a consistent identity policy since the late 1950s.

Ies Hoogland, KLM's Corporate Identity Director, outlines the early history of what was the oldest airline still operating under the same brand name, then describes the reasons behind KLM's pioneering approach to identity in the face of huge growth in traffic and, therefore, in competition. Its expression through visual means ('house style' to KLM) and through culture, and through quality and service delivery, is also explained, as are the careful developments which have kept the identity abreast of the market. KLM is in no doubt as to the benefits it has obtained through its uniquely consistent, persistent, long-term approach to identity in terms of differentiation and positioning.

The story is brought up to date with hints of future developments and of the identity implications of KLM's alliance with the US airline, Northwest. The identity is shown to be still responsive to change, yet consistent at its core.

Building the KLM image

An airline lives through and from its identity. And, unlike many other kinds of company, an airline's identity is composed of everything except the hardware – its people and their behaviour, standards of service, history, national associations and so on. The hardware is common to most of the competition. They all fly more or less the same planes, they use more or less the same equipment and, quite often, their networks and fares are broadly comparable.

So it is the corporate identity which characterises an airline and which forms the basis of competitive differentiation. This is the story of the evolution of the identity of one airline, and the story shows the dependence of each aspect of identity on all others.

Marketing communications as a specific aspect of identity also forms a strong thread in this story. So much so that, ultimately, the two become synergetic and perceptually inseparable.

*'The Flying Dutchman',
a poster from 1920
by M. Güthschmidt.*

However, there is a particular characteristic of KLM's identity history which sets it apart from others in the sector, and that is the long-lived consistency of the basic elements and the careful, logical, but often innovative, development of the identity to respond to market changes and opportunities, and to stay ahead of the competition. KLM has always believed in the long-term value of its identity, a typically broad and strategic view, which is reflected in the history of the airline itself.

KLM is formed

Koninklijke Luchtvaart Maatschappij voor Nederland en Kolonien (Royal Dutch Airlines for the Netherlands and Colonies) was established on 7 October 1919, making it the oldest airline still operating under the same brand name.

The Dutch, travellers and traders for centuries, were enthusiastic about air transport and the commercial opportunities it presented, and the following years were marked by successive expansions in the network of the airline, whose name had now generally become abbreviated to KLM.

As public acceptance of air travel grew, so the route network and services expanded, but it was in the years following the Second World War that competition between airlines really heightened to an intensive pitch. Soaring passenger numbers gave tremendous impetus to growth and, in turn, passengers

demanded more and more in the way of destinations, frequency of flights and service. During the 1950s, then, KLM started to give more focused attention to what we termed 'house style', or visual identity, in order to encapsulate, communicate and differentiate KLM's competitive position.

The positioning

After extensive market research, a basic positioning statement was proposed by KLM's advertising agency of the time: 'The Reliable Airline, made by the careful, punctual Dutch'. Based on this, a recurrent pay-off, 'The Reliable Airline' was introduced and persistently retained for many years, even though it was criticised on a number of occasions. In 1984, however, KLM Deputy-President Jan de Soet confirmed and expanded on the theme and KLM's positioning was reformulated in four words: reliable, punctual, caring and friendly. Perhaps not surprisingly, worldwide market research has shown that 'reliability' is still one of the most important selection criteria for the passenger of the 1990s.

As a prerequisite, the positioning has always been supported and communicated by the behaviour. 'Behaviour' is one of the most important corporate identity instruments for any corporation, but even more so for service companies. An airline's reputation is based largely on the performance of its 'front line' staff in direct contact with the customer. A house style may be consistent and an

KLM logotype developments over the years, culminating in the 'Consistency Plus' version introduced in 1991.

advertising campaign may be brilliant, but the fact remains that a service company has only one raison d'être: it must live up to the constantly changing expectations of its customers.

This aspect has always received particular attention within KLM, with institutionalised training programmes and, latterly, adoption of concepts of quality. The inter-relationship between quality and identity is explained later.

The 'house style' is created

Like many visual identities at the time (the 1950s), KLM's had evolved over the years, changes occurring from time to time in response to various stimuli, both internal and external. The first KLM logotype – the 'finch' – dated from the birth of the airline. Although it was undeniably an attractive design, it had certain disadvantages. It was almost illegible and non-Dutch speakers could not then easily place the abbreviation 'KLM'. At this stage, the KLM house style, such as it was, was still being applied inconsistently and no fewer than ten different logotypes were used during the first thirty years.

The logotype eventually came to include the crown – the 'hat of the Queen' – and it was this element which was to prove particularly controversial when the time came to express the positioning visually. KLM decided to call in external help and, through their advertising agency, contacted a British consultant who

was pioneering the new discipline of design coordination as a means of focusing and strengthening the corporate image.

It should be mentioned that at this time, also, KLM had employed a firm of top international management consultants to examine and make recommendations on corporate structure, so this was a time of great self-examination and change for the airline, which was really setting its strategic agenda for many years to come. It was clearly not an easy time, for radical decisions had to be taken, and the early progress of the visual identity demonstrated the alternating internal pressures for conservation as opposed to change.

The first aspect which the consultant considered was the design of the KLM logo-type, or 'house mark' as we termed it. There was a clear need to rationalise this, but the Company was certainly not prepared for what was suggested. For both communicative and optical reasons, a geometric design was presented, in which the existing figurative crown was reduced to a bar, four dots and a cross. Apart from associations of technical competence, modernity and reliability, this design was demonstrated to be highly practical in terms of legibility – important when viewing it at speed or under conditions of poor visibility.

Despite its excellent qualities, it did not, however, receive quick approval. Tampering with the Queen's hat was a serious business and the Board had to come to terms with it.

Only when the potential benefits were seen to be inescapable (and perhaps when emotional barriers had been overcome) was the decision taken to proceed and, of course, time has proved the decision to have been a correct one.

Great attention was paid at the same time to coordination of all elements of the visual identity. The house typeface, for example, amplified the character. Specific shades of blue were stipulated for the first time and colour became an essential element of the house style. The significance of a corporate colour is often underestimated. It is a strategic means of communication, which can be applied to great effect in expressing emotions, style, personality, clarity, discipline and quality. This potential has been fully exploited in recent years.

In total, the exercise marked a significant pioneering step, paving the way to present understanding of corporate identity. In the context of the airline industry, it was something entirely new, and gave us a competitive edge through a means which others would eventually also employ, but never with greater success and never with greater conviction and consistency.

House style developments

At the beginning of the 1960s, the period of greatest growth, KLM therefore had a head start. Not only was the house style created, but it was documented and promoted internally through an innovative manual, which detailed all applications. In addition, an in-house team took responsibility for its implementation and the original consultant was retained to monitor the situation.

But time does not stand still, and KLM has never allowed external developments to get ahead of its corporate identity. Constant research and monitoring activities have led the way to both major and minor develop-ments. There have been changes aimed at simplification, and therefore strengthening, of the identity. The first of these concerned

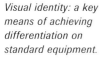

Visual identity: a key means of achieving differentiation on standard equipment.

removal of the light and dark blue stripes while freeing the logotype from its enclosing circle. This particularly affected aircraft livery, which was later further modified to include a light blue top for the fuselage, a change which made a significant contribution to the distinctiveness of the fleet, as well as emphasising 'blueness', a theme to which we will return. Other important developments included the creation of related, systematised sub-identities for the branding of services such as cargo operations, helicopter services, general aviation facilities and catering services, as well as for KLM's commuter airline, KLM Cityhopper. Each of these is distinguishable from, but clearly a part of, the core KLM identity. The basic positioning is thus reinforced, while perceptions of the range of competence are expanded. Through all of these developments, the logotype has remained unchanged. Over the 35 years of its existence, it has come to represent all that KLM stands for and it still accurately transmits the positioning, but more strongly than when it was introduced, for its long life has simply served to emphasise reliability, through consistency. Before finalising the history of the identity, a significant develop-ment in one major aspect must be explained, together with KLM's attitudes to integrated communications and to quality.

Marketing communications

In 1981, KLM took a giant step forward along the marketing communications track, when the management decided that the airline should present a uniform face through all of its communications worldwide including advertising. The Marketing Division was charged with developing a unified communications strategy, which could be applied worldwide. An advertising agency was commissioned to develop a core campaign whose basic message was that KLM was a reliable, no-nonsense airline,

which had the following strengths: all-round professionalism and expertise. In short: the positioning as KLM, The Reliable Airline, was to be reinforced.

Certain criteria were stipulated for the advertising concept. It had to:

- support one distinctive worldwide identity
- be in keeping with the house style
- allow for implementation in different cultures
- leave room for local creativity
- be credible
- be suitable for use over an extended period
- be suitable for use externally and internally
- focus on the brand

After submitting a wide variety of proposals, the agency eventually came up with a concept which was as obvious as it was ingenious: blue skies! The concept combined uniformity of copy and visuals – one worldwide identity – with flexibility. It could be used to put across a wide variety of messages in different countries.

There was a clear link between the campaign and the house style, especially in the use of blue. The minuscule plane and vapour trail, positioned between the question and answer of the dialogue, ensured there was always a clear reference to the airline, even if the support visual did not feature a plane. The pay-off was once again 'The Reliable Airline'. Today, this concept is still being used in national and international media campaigns. The Marketing and Communications Department is the driving force behind this so-called 'Umbrella Advertising', which allows KLM establishments worldwide to adapt the message to suit the requirements of the local market. In this way, the effect of the advertising campaigns is mutually enhanced, because the same basic concept is used in

Culture translates into service: a vital differentiating factor.

international and national advertisements. This is a prerequisite to achieving a prominent position in the market and in the mind of the customer.

When the concept was first introduced, there were fears that the rigid conceptual guidelines would have a suffocating effect on creativity. However, in practice it has repeatedly proved possible to add something new to the 'blueprint'. Distinctive new approaches have been conceived through creative cross-fertilisation between countries, underscoring the positive effects of a uniform global approach to marketing

KLM's corporate identity strategy and the suggestion that all activities in the fields of advertising, sales promotion, direct communication, sponsoring and public relations must be optimally geared to one another found strong acceptance. The Marketing Communications Department in concert with the Bureau of Public Relations started developing joint campaigns. They emphasised the importance of orchestration to establishments abroad, by providing workshops and training programmes for KLM staff involved in internal and external communication outside the Netherlands. The House Style Manual soon rubbed covers

KLM's famous 'blue skies' advertising has spanned the years and the globe.

and communications. Although KLM has recently implemented a policy of far-reaching decentralisation, this concept has played its part in maintaining a uniform global identity.

Integrated communications

In 1981, a marketing best-seller was published, entitled *Positioning: the Battle for your Mind*, written by Al Ries and Jack Trout. Its sub-title, *How to be seen and heard in the overcrowded market place*, makes it clear what this book is all about. The deluge of messages with which the public is inundated is so overwhelming, that only a few ever really hit home. The implied need for consistency and coordination in communications was entirely in tune with

with the Marketing Communication Manual, which not only stipulated design guidelines, but also outlined the strategic aspects involved in the orchestration of the communications mix. With the introduction of this 'orchestration' concept, the last cornerstone of the house style had been laid. All forms of mani-festation, from advertisements to annual reports, from TV commercials to corporate films, from cabin interiors to booking offices, had become facets of the positive image presented to customers and stakeholders; that of a reliable, punctual company offering caring, friendly service.

Quality as an aspect of identity

Quality has already been referred to and is another key aspect of KLM's identity, and much attention has been paid to delivering it over the years. Customers are constantly becoming more and more demanding. They compare, they shop around and then they choose. They want value for money. As former President Jan de Soet put it: 'Quality will determine our future. Without quality, it is doubtful whether we will have a future. Our own views on the subject are totally irrelevant; the only thing that counts is customer opinion.' A new internal communications campaign was launched at the beginning of the 1980s to motivate all KLM staff to improve quality generally. The campaign motto 'KLM is Continuous

Consistency Plus

While the 1980s saw a considerable improvement in consistency, owing primarily to the integration of the house style and the advertising concept, the 1990s started with a critical reassessment of the different modes of communication.

This became a 'tuning' exercise in which remaining inconsistencies were identified and steps were taken to eliminate them as far as possible. The exercise was given the name 'Consistency Plus', and its aims were to:

Quality', or KICK for short, underscores the necessity of a reliable, punctual product and caring, friendly service. The main goal of this internal campaign – which also features elements of the house style – is to deliver top quality. In 1985, KLM won the 'Passenger Service Award 1984' and the following year it was proclaimed 'Airline of the Year 1985' by the leading aviation magazine, *Air Transport World*. These awards became the theme of a new campaign, in which both external and internal communications were based on a single concept, whereby their effect was mutually enhanced. The drive to deliver top quality was continued into the 90s. Throughout the organisation, product and service improvement was based on the model outlined by the European Foundation for Quality Management, of which KLM was a founder member.

- increase the consistency of all design items, to support the positioning
- increase the number of graphic resources, so that messages could be communicated more efficiently
- gear the language of images to the demands of the 90s, without losing recognisability
- cut production costs.

KLM's in-house design studios worked in close cooperation with the airline's advertising agencies and KLM establishments abroad, with KLM's corporate identity consultant, now having acted for the Company for 35 years, as project supervisor. A variety of concepts was implemented on a trial basis in the United States, Europe and the Far East. Subsequently, the following modifications were proposed:

British Airways and 12 European Airlines introduce AirPlus.

This advertisement (not KLM's own) shows the high impact, legibility and recognisability of the identity in the context of the competition.

- The shades of blue would be adapted slightly to suit contemporary tastes.
- The preferred version of the logotype would be in a single colour which would simplify the production of advertising material and would cut costs considerably.
- The basic layout of brochures and publications was adapted to suit contemporary market conditions, and was geared to cost-saving, modern, desk-top publishing techniques.
- The wide range of sub-identity logotypes was rationalised.
- The range of special-offer advertisements was extended.

The Consistency Plus programme did not affect the basic concept of the house style, but effected subtle changes, simplifications and adaptations to suit contemporary tastes and conditions and cut production costs. Although the public will have hardly noticed the difference, 'renovations' of this sort are essential if the house style is to be kept up-to-date.

Monitoring corporate image

In order to gain insight into the state of KLM's corporate image a Market Monitor was launched in 1993. A market research bureau ran continuous telephone surveys in various European countries. KLM's corporate image was compared to the image of the respective local carrier on the basis of the following parameters: reliability, punctuality, efficiency, care, neatness, friendliness, comfort, fleet, prices, quality of food and drink, perks for frequent flyers, extent of the route network, and prestige. The Market Monitor will be extended in 1995 to include countries outside Europe as well. By combining the findings of the Market Monitor with data obtained via in-flight surveys and surveys run by the International Air Transport Association (IATA) in the Far East and on the North Atlantic routes, inconsistencies between corporate identity and corporate image can be quantified and remedied.

Corporate identity management

Effective corporate identity management requires discipline and control. Constant re-alignment of application in all fields is a necessity. Staff throughout the organisation must be alerted to the need to act in strict accordance with the stipulated guidelines, in order to present customers with the desired positive image. This requires rigid, centralised supervision and control by top management. At KLM, decisions concerning corporate identity management are taken by the Company President. He is the Chairman of the Corporate Design Group which also includes the Marketing Manager, on behalf of the Passenger Sales and Services Division, the director of the Cargo Division, the head of the Public Relations Department, and the managers of In-flight Catering and Tax-Free Services. The implementation of all proposals is supervised by the secretary of the Corporate Design Group, the Marketing Communications Director.

Consistency and persistency are thus seen to be essential elements determining the success of an effective corporate identity policy. However, one should not be oblivious to current market developments. KLM President Pieter Bouw considers organisational flexibility to be a vital aspect of the Company's capability to confront the challenge of its competitors in the future. Flexibility will therefore also be a key aspect of the house style and communications strategy, which will be developed to meet a variety of scenarios.

Partnerships and other challenges

The partnership of KLM with Northwest Airlines of the USA is thriving. In 1993 a 'Seal of Partnership' was created, establishing an initial link between the corporate identities of the two carriers and expressing the reality

and ideals of the collaboration both internally and externally. In the autumn of 1993 a joint global campaign was launched, introducing World Business Class. The work was supervised by one of the joint committees set up by KLM and Northwest to encourage collaboration and cultural understanding. At present, a marketing communications concept is being developed for this nascent global airline system, which will determine the shape of all future joint ventures. This 'format' should complement the house styles of the two carriers and any other partners. During the coming years, the segmentation of the market will become even more intricate.

Above: the 'Seal of Partnership' between KLM and Northwest, used on printed matter and on launch advertising.

KLM will constantly assess whether its identity is adequately suited to the new conditions. KLM staff involved in corporate identity will clearly have their hands full. The greatest challenge will be to increase the flexibility of the KLM identity without obliterating the accumulated goodwill and

Ies Hoogland

*Ies Hoogland joined
KLM Royal Dutch
Airlines in 1978
after five years'
experience at the
Lintas Advertising
Agency in Holland.
After having filled
various marketing
positions he was
responsible for
marketing
communications
worldwide from
1983 onwards.
On 1 February 1995,
Ies Hoogland was
appointed Director
Corporate Identity.*

image capital of 75 years, which represents
billions of guilders. KLM's identity story
is remarkable in its clear demonstration of
the value of long-term, strategic consideration
of all aspects. It is the compatibility of
this approach with our positioning as
'The Reliable Airline' which has given KLM
its outstandingly effective differentiation
over nearly four decades, and which provides
a firm foundation for an increasingly
uncertain future.

Bibliography
*G.I. Smit, R.C.J. Wunderink and I. Hoogland, 'The Image of KLM, 75 Years in Design and Promotion',
V+K Publishing/Inmerc, 1994, ISBN 90 6611 433 9 NU GI 921/656.*

Krups is located in Solingen, Germany and is a leading international brand in small electrical appliances. The product range includes appliances for the kitchen and the bathroom, the core areas being coffee and espresso making and food preparation.

Today within the Moulinex Group, Krups continues to operate with its own independent brand management, achieving a turnover of more than 500 million DM.

KRUPS

Introduction

At the beginning of the 90s, Krups found itself in a strategically critical situation. On the one hand, the Company could be viewed as the largest of the smaller international brands in electrical appliances. On the other hand, it could also be seen as the smallest of the largest. It was therefore imperative to define the future direction of the Company, and the result was integration into the French Moulinex Group from the beginning of 1991.

Anthony Lewis explains the market situation, linking it to changed consumer spending trends which particularly affect branded goods. Krups' response to the situation is described with reference to management of the brand identity – 'the corporate identity of a brand' – and to the cornerstones of Krups' positioning strategy. Corporate design is referred to as the visualisation of the positioning, and the highly successful pack redesign is featured.

This is the story of corporate identity's rôle in global brand management and marketing. Krups' corporate identity expresses the Company's competence and commitment towards its target audiences, and its regard for the customer as the focal point.

Brand management needs brand identity

Robert Krups GmbH & Co. KG started as a family firm founded by Robert Krups in 1846. In 1910, Krups made its first step into the consumer goods business with the manufacture of household scales. The entry into the market for small electrical appliances came over a hundred years after the Company's foundation, in 1955, with the introduction of electric coffee grinders in cooperation with the coffee company HAG. Manufacture of hand mixers in 1960 was followed by the development of the legendary 'Krups 3 Mix', the universal appliance for food preparation that has become a generic product, synonymous with functionality, quality and durability.

Today, the Krups brand is highly regarded and widely distributed in many countries. In Germany alone, a total of some 36 million Krups products are in use. Three out of four households own Krups products. More than 90% of men and women in Germany are aware of the Krups brand and no fewer than 15,000 specialist dealers stock Krups products. Krups is also recognised as a leading brand in the rest of Europe and in North America.

Krups' brand strength is built on a history of product innovation together with outstanding user benefits and distinctive design. Decades of delivering excellent quality have created huge confidence in the brand. The vision of the Company's founder is as valid today as it was 150 years ago: 'It has always been my special endeavour to manufacture all my products to the highest degree of technical perfection'. In order for Krups to remain competitive, this customer confidence must be constantly expanded and reinforced. To achieve this, the management of the brand must be increasingly sensitive to ever-quickening changes in the pattern of demand.

stagnation in Europe and the USA and the excess capacities resulting from this, as well as by increased imports from Asia. These factors all add up to a significant increase in competitive pressure.

Clear segmentation of the market according to price or quality is now a thing of the past. Differing values and living styles are leading to fragmentation of demand. Changes in personal values, bound up with a sharp recession in Germany in 1994, have resulted in a significant drop in overall consumption, characterised by an increasing rejection of so-called 'no-sense' products. Purchasing attitudes are also now being influenced by the concept of consciously reducing consumption, which has become known in Europe as the 'new modesty'.

This trend in consumer behaviour manifests itself as a greater self-consciousness in ways of spending money. Consumption becomes divided into 'needs' and 'wants'. The new customer credo declares: 'Buy brands cheaply, don't buy cheap brands'. This leads to new, freer attitudes to choosing where to buy. The customer can make rational purchases in a supermarket or hypermarket in the morning, then enjoy spending extravagantly in a designer shop in the afternoon. It is neither necessity which drives him to save nor excess which drives him to seek luxuries. The 'new' customer has a new-found independence and indulges in all forms of consumption, but he or she draws a sharp distinction between quality-oriented purchases which are mainly for pleasure, and the price-sensitive purchase of necessities.

It is here that the question of image – and brand values – arises. If the product or the brand values are not emotionally attractive to a potential purchaser, he or she will usually make a decision based on price. In fact, from a brand marketing point of view, there are only two types of product today – those

The Krups positioning

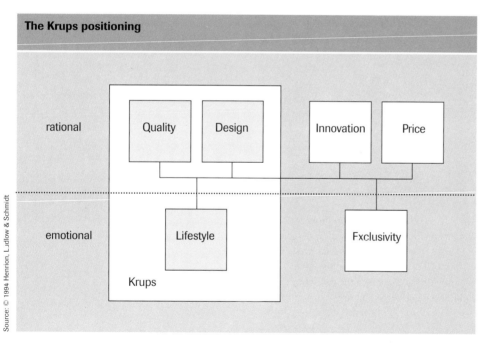

The challenge – restricted markets

What is the outlook for Krups in the 90s? The challenge can be summed up in two words: restricted markets. Like nearly all markets for consumer goods in the 90s, the small electrical appliance sector is characterised by changing consumer attitudes, by increasing similarity of product performance, by economic which do and those which do not stimulate the ego. The all-important question for the consumer is: Which product do I prefer? Consequently, the objective must be to become the most desired brand for the customer target group. To achieve this, competitive strength can only be derived from product and brand strengths. The values associated with the product must not, however, be confused with status value, because the time of pure status products seems to be passing and the trend is reverting to products which are straightforward to operate and which offer clearly-recognisable user benefits.

Meeting customer demands through individual customer marketing

So what does all this mean for Krups? It was quite clear to us that whoever wants to stimulate customers these days must, much more so than in the past, know what motivates them, how they live and what wants and needs they have. Changes in household and age structures, trends in living habits as well as shifts in purchasing and usage habits, must also be recognised very early in the brand management process and must serve as a basis for positioning, product development and communication.

Since individual needs are always subject to short-term change, only constant market research can reveal information about the characteristics of the consumers and their lifestyles, attitudes, motives and affinities. So Krups commissioned a study from a market research institute to establish just how different these 'new' consumers really are. The results indicated that the future potential for Krups lies substantially with the 'upper conservatives', the 'social climbers' and the so-called 'no-collar employees'. (These were the socio-economic targets defined for the German market.) The significant

characteristics of these groups are a striving for self-realisation, understatement, individualistic demands and an orientation towards trends. Brand-conscious and quality-oriented women form the common denominator of our target groups. They are adventurous, health and environment conscious, open to intelligent innovations, technically aware and receptive to functional styling. Despite the difficulty of assimilating the vast selection on offer, they expect even greater variety, especially of those products which display contemporary design and increased individuality.

For Krups, this means a realignment from 'mass marketing' to 'individual customer marketing', necessitating a strategic market segmentation based on the socio-cultural groupings and directed towards continual enhancement of the benefit to the individual customer. It follows that segmentation according to purely socio-demographic considerations is no longer enough.

Brand identity – the corporate identity of a brand

Today's customers are looking more than ever for emotional attachments to products and brands and therefore also for characteristics with which they can identify themselves. This provides a challenge for every brand within the small electrical appliance market and demanded a critical reassessment of the Krups brand and its entire manifestation in the eyes of the public, the objective being to formulate internationally harmonised, universal and precisely defined principles coupled with a clear and consistent visual identity. These are the preconditions for our success in the future.

Krups' overriding principle is therefore total customer orientation, achieved by continuously reviewing the criteria of the target group.

So we don't just offer something for everyone, but something special for particular people. Only in this way can products emerge which meet fresh needs and which open up attractive new niches in the market. The first step is then to ensure that the presentation of the Company or brand is entirely customer-oriented and sufficiently distinctive to be easily recognised by both internal and external target groups. Thus, for Krups, a strong, comprehensive corporate identity is of vital importance and an indispensable prerequisite for consolidating and developing the brand further. However, our position within the Moulinex Group is that of an independently conducted brand, so we refer to 'brand identity' rather than 'corporate identity'.

Brand identity for a brand is what corporate identity is for a company – a perceived self-image which embraces products, behaviour, communications and visual identity. Both companies and brands have similarities to people. Each person strives for his own identity. His effect on others is expressed, either consciously or unconsciously, by his appearance and manner, his demeanour and behaviour. A brand or company also has a personality, so we can speak in terms of brand personalities whose appearance and manner are experienced through their identity by the customer. The perceived

attributes of a brand constitute its character. A brand, just like a person, should give out charisma, messages and signals – or, in other words, create a positive impression and appear desirable.

Brand identity does not only strengthen the brand's appearance, but is essential for clear differentiation from the competition. Within the overcrowded area of branded goods, the brand identity must offer clear and long-term recognition. Brand identity is capable of building customer loyalty, even if the products are not clearly differentiated from competing products. At the same time, it helps to support the identification of the employees *with* the brand. Customers, trade partners and employees all expect clear and direct signals from the brand personality.

Realigning the Krups brand

Competition today is so intense that classical forms of publicity are no longer enough to communicate product advantages. It is important to present the relevant customer benefits in a more effective way than the competition and to make the brand stand out from the 'norm' of the segment. In the same way, just demonstrating the features of an appliance is no longer sufficient to create differentiation, because product quality and performance are taken for granted. Effective differentiation can only be produced by adding emotional benefits to the basic features and functional advantages of the product. We firmly believe that a brand's success is as dependent on effective differentiation as it is on the speed and responsiveness of new product development.

A high level of brand loyalty is the most important prerequisite for binding customers to the brand in the long term, so the brand identity must inspire a comprehensive feeling of trust in the quality of the product and the

Early mechanical scales and pioneer electrical appliances – coffee grinder and filter machine.

brand. Such trust can only be built up through the brand being true to its principles over a long period of time. Quite simply, continuity in the brand's principles safeguards the brand's values, both for the Company and for the customers.

Furthermore, a strategically managed brand identity makes it easier for products positioned in the upper half of the market to withstand price pressure from the cheaper segments. In this way, each and every product which corresponds to the brand profile endorses the competence of the brand by focusing brand image, quality, performance and price.

But brand management also means keeping the brand up to date. For Krups, brand identity is a strategic instrument of corporate management and is an expression of Krups' thinking, action and appearance, both internally and externally. The updating of the brand identity was the logical outcome of realigning brand strengths in relation to changed market conditions.

Quality, design and lifestyle – the three cornerstones of the positioning

It is a strategic corporate objective to strengthen the Krups brand identity, a brand which already enjoys a high degree of aware-ness of its competence in the core areas of coffee and espresso making and food preparation. The brand should confer a feeling of reassurance and offer the necessary persuasion to both trade and consumers at the point of purchase. It should express a particular manner, style of living and personality. Within its target socio-cultural groups, Krups should be regarded as the desired brand. The customer should be offered tangible, relevant added value over and above the basic technical value of the product.

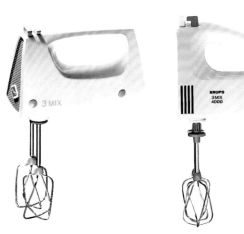

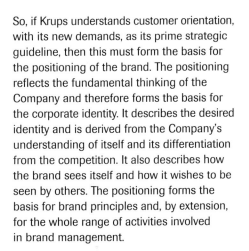

Evolution of the well-known 3 Mix appliance from the original model to the present version.

So, if Krups understands customer orientation, with its new demands, as its prime strategic guideline, then this must form the basis for the positioning of the brand. The positioning reflects the fundamental thinking of the Company and therefore forms the basis for the corporate identity. It describes the desired identity and is derived from the Company's understanding of itself and its differentiation from the competition. It also describes how the brand sees itself and how it wishes to be seen by others. The positioning forms the basis for brand principles and, by extension, for the whole range of activities involved in brand management.

The positioning

Krups is an international brand of German origin and stands for 'Quality made in Germany'. Through a quality strategy, the brand strives for the position of a leading supplier of small electrical appliances in the areas of coffee and espresso making and food preparation. The brand's core competence is in these product areas. The main markets are Europe and the USA.

The positioning is based on the three corner-stones of quality, design and lifestyle. Krups offers quality products with superior customer benefits and clearcut design, reflecting an elegant living style. The appearance of the brand and the corporate business style are determined by the positioning. The customer is the focal point of our corporate activity. We consistently orientate ourselves towards his or her needs and strive for the greatest possible customer satisfaction.We define quality as the sum of all the efforts we make to satisfy customer expectations.

Our customers are essentially women to whom brand image and high quality are important. The products are positioned in the upper half of the market and the top end of the entry level price bracket. We prefer to deal with specialist retailers and quality-oriented large outlets. Our publicity should assist in the pre-selling of our products and increase the desirability of the brand.

This positioning focuses on the statement 'Krups brings quality to life': quality products with superior customer benefits and clearcut design which reflect a modern lifestyle. In this respect, Krups places the three aspects – quality, design and lifestyle – at the very heart of its positioning.

Quality and environmental awareness – a comprehensive definition

Krups defines quality from the customer's viewpoint, so quality is not only a question of meeting functional standards such as the proverbial sturdiness and durability of our products, but is also the focusing of all Company activities on the customer. Quality is therefore the sum of all the product and service attributes which are provided to meet the expectations of the target groups. So how does that work in practice? Krups' Total Quality Management is based on small teams and on the constant optimisation of synergies resulting from internal quality orientation. An internal publication called 'Krups Principles of User Quality', which was

Krups Principles of User Quality (Excerpt)

- **State of the Technology**
  The purchaser of a new Krups branded product must not be able to identify any technique or technology which has already been superseded by a competitive brand. In the conceptual phase of a product project, it must be ensured that the product benefits of competitors have been researched and taken into account during product planning.

- **Functional Design**
  The design of Krups products should be uncomplicated, logical, systematic and clear. For the user, this means that function and operation of the product must be apparent from its design. The design must in principle be such that accidental incorrect operation of the appliance by the user is not possible.

- **Customer benefits**
  It is a further fundamental objective that each model in a product range should exhibit superior user benefits. No function may be included which confers no genuine user benefit. The packaging must not communicate any function or usage which the appliance is not able to deliver.

- **User satisfaction**
  We must ensure that the working and enjoyment criteria of the products meet the expectations of discerning customers, conform to claims and create a high level of user satisfaction. Instructions for use and recipe books must be formulated specifically with this in mind, whilst recipe books must take national habits and eating preferences into account.

- **Packaging**
  The smallest possible usage of material must be achieved in the construction of packaging. The smallest possible proportion of synthetic material will be permitted, consistent with the requirement of warehousing and transport. Paper and cardboard will be preferred for internal packaging elements.

New Krups product packaging showing consistency of approach on different packs.

developed to be in keeping with the brand positioning, forms the basic guideline for our Total Quality Management. The aim of the quality principles is to differentiate Krups from the competition in terms of the brand identity. The principles define the target groups' minimum requirements of a Krups branded product and thus form an invaluable guideline for all employees who are involved in the conceptualisation, development and manufacture of the products, as well as those who maintain and service them.

Krups is aware of its responsibility towards the environment. The use of environmentally-friendly and easily disposable materials, material consistency, environmental compatibility, banning of heavy metals, reduction in the use of Styrofoam in packaging to the necessary minimum, as well as the marking of plastic parts for recycling are all regarded as logical consequences of the positioning.

Innovation – a matter of course for a quality brand

Krups sees one of its most important challenges as being the continual enhancement of the user benefits of its products, in order to expand the market leadership it has enjoyed for many years in certain product areas. Krups sticks to the basic principle that no obsolescent technique or technology should be discernible in any of its products. In particular, top-of-the-range products should be characterised by technical sophistication and innovation. Innovative products are generated by the challenging of existing problem solutions and through regular consumer research. The constant transfer of technologies within the Moulinex Group encourages innovation, a process in which the European Research Centre of the Moulinex Group in Caen plays a central rôle.

1846

1956

1973

1988

KRUPS *1994*

*Example of a lifestyle
photograph to be
applied to packaging
or promotion.*

Corporate design – the visualisation of the positioning

Customers, trade partners and employees expect clear and direct signals regarding the brand personality, and the basis for this is consistent presentation of the brand. Along with the definition of the positioning and the development of the brand identity, the visual identity has been strengthened, creating the key elements necessary for brand recognition. The corporate design is one of the most important elements in the brand identity. It has to make the additional benefit of the brand visible. The uniqueness and unmistakability of the brand and the unique and unmistakable customer benefits – in fact, the brand identity – become tangible and ensure differentiation from the competition. A strong corporate design is really nothing less than the positioning made clearly visible. In order to retain the loyalty of customers in the long term, the corporate design must convey an all-embracing trust in the quality of the product and of the brand.

To achieve this, all the messages which originate from the brand and which are received by the customer must be consistent, so that their combined effect leads to a lasting impact. This must work worldwide, irrespective of whether it is the publicity, the packaging or the product itself that is communicating with the customer. To make this possible, the visual presentation must be universally comprehensible and be applied consistently, internationally. In this way, a consistently positive and recognisable brand message emerges, which is understandable as well as attractive.

However, Krups never follows short-term fashion trends, since the lifestyle scenes so often seen in advertising date quickly, become non-specific and, after a time, the target group to whom they are addressed becomes immune to them. Krups, on the other hand, should be identified by an original, independent visual language which is, maybe unconsciously, sought by the customer to express his or her own needs and desires.

To address this need, Krups undertook a fundamental redesign of its logotype, its packaging, and its entire range of printed matter for communications and business purposes, right down to its brand presentation at international exhibitions. The new visual presentation gives Krups an unmistakable appearance in the international context.

It distinguishes Krups quite clearly from the competition. The typeface of the rather ponderous logotype has been slimmed down. The name is now presented in a lighter script without unnecessary flourishes, more in keeping with the positioning. It now appears fresher, warmer and more elegant. Despite this, the continuity of the logotype design, known to consumers and the specialist trade for several decades, has been substantially preserved. Synergies will be generated through the continual and consistent use of the brand logotype on all products, publicity material and stationery.

Product packaging is one of the most important ways of communicating to the consumer. Apart from ensuring safe transportation of the product, it must give a positive impression in the shop window and at the point of sale. It must give out signals which visualise the positioning; it must highlight the main user benefits and express the differentiation from competitors. The newly-designed packaging, which incorporates a layout band portraying emotive, elegant still-life scenes coupled with a prominently-positioned logotype and red top, gives a generally lively, attractive impression and a high degree of recognition. In confirmation of this, it was established in market research of coffee machine packaging under competitive conditions, that favourable reactions to the new Krups packaging design, at 81%, were significantly higher than to the next contender, at 39%. The old Krups design registered only 14%. Krups' product design is based on a combination of high quality, innovative technology, clearcut shapes, user-oriented operation and real user benefits, with the main emphasis resting on the subjective, or emotional, experience of the product.

The designs aim to reflect contemporary living styles, and differentiate themselves from the competition through their aesthetic

qualities and their functionality. Because small electrical appliances in themselves are intrinsically complex, unnecessarily elaborate shapes and superfluous graphic decorations are avoided. The most clearcut design possible should convey the ideas of innovation and timelessness and a feeling of uniqueness.

It is not just the the packaging and product design, but also the various publications which play a special part in influencing the decision to purchase. Within the corporate design system, they serve to portray products and product benefits in the context of a lifestyle ambience. By the use of still-life

A filter coffee machine from the innovatory 'Azuro' range.

scenes rich in the ambience of an elegant living style, a pleasing and appealing environment is built up around the product and creates a subjective, aspirational relationship between Krups products and the quality of life depicted. If people are included in these scenes, they correspond to the target customer group, appearing casually elegant. The identification of the user with the Krups brand is promoted through this emotive presentation and through the simultaneous factual explanation of the unique selling proposition. The new corporate design has been consolidated internally into a Corporate Design Manual to ensure that, both nationally and internationally, all communications material corresponds to the image which has been defined as typically Krups. As Krups uses design strategically, the process of implementation under various conditions is made easier. And, as design is an integral part of our overall brand strategy, it ensures that our new positioning is made visible and tangible.

Our behaviour – a reflection of our positioning

A brand needs to be managed. We believe that brand positioning and brand manage

ment are of fundamental importance and therefore a matter for the Company's top management. To achieve continuity in brand activity, however, it is necessary to communicate the brand values to every employee, since the success of the Company is largely dependent on the attitude and involvement of those employees.

For this reason, Krups works on the basis of internal partnership. This stimulates motivation and the willingness to improve performance – and only motivated employees show commitment to the brand. For Krups, the maximisation of customer satisfaction is the result of partnership and collaboration throughout the whole organisation, directed towards the Company's market.

'Tempo Management': our answer to the competitive factor of 'time'

A substantial element of our brand identity consists of the so-called Krups 'Tempo Management'. At the heart of this is a number of small, simply-constituted, decentralised units which can use their know-how on the spot and facilitate quick decisions. In this way, corporate ideas and actions transfer them-

*Pages from Krups'
product programme
catalogue.*

Krups catalogues as produced for various national markets.

selves in the most direct way to the operative employees. This makes it possible to react quickly and efficiently to ever-changing requirements and conditions. Today we speak of 'time to market': when a decision has been made, it must be put into effect as quickly and efficiently as possible. By concentrating on the specialist trade and quality-oriented large outlets, Krups is able to remain true to the high standards set by its positioning. Complete marketing programmes are offered for each of the distribution channels: traditional specialist dealers, specialist chains, department stores and hypermarkets.

As an example, Krups was the first company in its segment to create and offer a tailored package for the specialist retailer, to take account of the specific advisory function which such outlets perform vis-à-vis their customers. We also offer to dealers an exclusive preview service for new products, in combination with advertising and sales promotion support. Our partnership package comprises product training for trade personnel, in-store demonstrations, point-of-sale merchandising, a window display service and joint advertising, plus a 48-hour

customer service for all repairs and spare parts. This latter service is guaranteed and Krups always maintains a stock of some 5,000 different spare parts. The supply of spare parts for appliances which have been withdrawn from the programme is maintained for a further seven years.

The aim is co-operative and professional collaboration which strengthens the competitive capability of the trade and therefore of Krups. In this sense, partnership means continual dialogue, mutual agreement and an exchange of opinions on important questions. Krups is always open to suggestions and constructive criticism from its partners in the trade.

The new alignment of the brand identity – a first assessment

Following the publication of the Krups Corporate Design Manual in mid-1994, the process of change began, with the objective of achieving an internationally-strengthened brand presentation in keeping with the new positioning. The implementation of the new

Anthony Lewis

*Brand Director,
responsible for brand
management and
international consumer
marketing at Krups.*

*Born 1951 in Sheffield,
UK. 1972 B.Sc. in
Management Sciences,
Manchester University.
Then joined Stanley
Tools, Sheffield as
management trainee.
Marketing and Export
Manager, Garden Tools
Division. Sales and
Marketing Manager,
Stanley Werke, Velbert,
Germany. 1982 Product
Line Marketing
Manager at Stanley's
European Headquarters.
1984 joined Krups in
Solingen, Germany,
as Group Product
Manager for coffee
makers, espresso
makers etc. Currently
Brand Director
responsible for brand
management and
international consumer
marketing for the
Krups brand within
the Moulinex Group.*

brand identity is a dynamic process which
provides a challenge for Krups management
and employees alike. The newly-developed
positioning and the visual identity now
form the basic guideline for Krups' global
brand management.

This does not imply a restriction of entrepreneurial freedom in the various national
markets. Rather, the brand identity should
be understood as the framework for local,
country-specific marketing which is in
line with the brand positioning, but which
benefits from cross-border synergies made
possible by a strategic, coordinated
approach.

Three million passenger journeys are made on the London Underground system on each average working day. In an average year, therefore, over 750 million journeys are made. The Company had a turn-over of £642 million in 1993 and employed more than 20,000 staff. The system has nearly 4,000 passenger carriages and over 250 stations. The network, of 245 route miles, is so extensive that it would take 24 hours to reach all stations. London Underground trains cover more than 30 million miles each year and are therefore a vital lifeline for the seven million people in the London metropolis.

Introduction

London Underground is the oldest underground system in the world and, with three million passenger journeys each day, it is also one of the busiest.

Paul Moss and Jeff Mills explain the Underground's function and meaning for London, including its architectural and cultural heritage. Investment problems and the effects on staff are explained, together with operational and service delivery problems, and public dissatisfaction leading to a negative profile.

The authors also describe how the needs of passengers – customers – provided the direction for the reorientation of the system and its staff towards being the provider of an acceptable public service.

London Underground is developing its identity in a consistent manner, from improving passenger information to enhancing the efficiency of equipment and staff, with the proviso that planning is dictated and restricted by budget conditions set by Government.

Corporate identity –
a pragmatic approach

On the evening of 18 November 1987, a small fire in some rubbish beneath an escalator at King's Cross Underground station grew into an inferno which killed thirty-one people.

It was, literally, a shock to the system and the changes which this tragedy set in motion had a major effect on all facets of London Underground's activities, including the way in which the corporate identity was considered and implemented.

The fire seemed to confirm the negative perceptions held by many people. It focused thinking primarily, of course, on the causes, but also on ways of improving the system and, then, ways of ensuring public understanding and acceptance of what was being done.

The new management, installed after the fire, had no doubt about the enormity of the task, and realised that communications and image were going to be vital in relation to various target audiences, including customers, political masters and opinion formers. Judgement of management's success would be based on their perceptions.

History

However, corporate identity (although not called by that name) had been a carefully-valued asset for much of the Underground's past. To understand the situation both before and after the fire, some of the history of the organisation needs to be related, from its inception to the present political and economic situation. The culture and identity of the Underground have displayed remarkable continuity, despite vicissitudes, which is especially notable in a country where system-oriented thinking usually takes second place to individual enterprise.

Station architecture from the 30s.

A brief mention of the importance of urban railway systems is also relevant. Transport is one of the biggest issues facing humanity in the 1990s and into the next century. Growth of car ownership and crowded skies, with

attendant environmental and traffic problems, have led to the resurgence of the railway as an efficient, environmentally-friendly form of transport. All around the world, in developed and developing countries, plans and schemes for railway improvement and new-building are in progress. Particularly in urban areas, railway systems offer a capacity, speed and efficiency which cars and buses cannot easily match. Construction costs, especially where tunnelling is involved, are extremely high, but that has not deterred city authorities worldwide, who are desperate to solve traffic congestion and pollution problems, from investing in this once-neglected form of transport. Among many newer systems, some older ones pay the price for having been pioneers.

London Underground's origins go further back in time than those of any other underground railway system. The first section of underground line was opened in 1863. Other independent lines followed until, just after the turn of the century, the basis of the present central London area system was in place. There was much argument between individual railways such as the Metropolitan Railway, the District Railway, the City and South London Railway and the Central London Railway but, gradually, a grouping emerged.

The grouping – called the Underground Group – began to develop common fare structures and interchange facilities. In 1907, it took a momentous step – momentous in hindsight. It appointed a young man named Frank Pick to look after publicity. Pick eventually became General Manager of the whole of London Transport, a position which he held until his death in the early 1940s, and was to be a hugely formative influence on the culture, identity and appearance of the system. That one man should be so influential is not unique, but very unusual in this context. Public and commercial pressure to improve the coordination of transport in London led to the Government taking all of London's transport companies into public ownership by the formation, in 1933, of the London Passenger Transport Board. This incorporated the Underground system, buses, trams and trolley-buses, with the aim of coordinating many disparate interests into a coherent transport system to serve a city which was, by then, the world's most populous, with around ten million inhabitants.

From the beginning, Pick and his Chairman, Lord Ashfield, set high-minded principles for the organisation, principles which sound pompous to modern ears, but which set the cultural tone. Pick said 'The [London Transport] Board's undertaking is a declaration of faith that its task is worthwhile and that its labours shall eventually contribute their appointed share to the transformation of our urban civilisation into some fine flower of accomplishment'. This kind of civic-oriented thinking fixed the cultural framework for the organisation's activities for at least the next two decades with every aspect of identity, including staff motivation, service quality, communications and design, playing its part in building up a total picture of a large, coherent, caring, service-minded organisation. Visual matters were accorded particular attention, with the design of stations, rolling stock, information, promotional material and other items now being regarded as classics individually and as a whole. For Pick, every aspect and detail counted. This, indeed, was a remarkable model of a multi-disciplinary corporate identity system.

After the Second World War the organisation was increasingly subject to the whims of its political masters. Major extensions of the Underground system were carried out in the immediate post-war years, most of them to plans which had been drawn up in the 30s. But the public-spirited thinking which had governed then seemed to take a back seat

to political wrangling. The visual manifestations, which had been so exemplary, now expressed the feelings of the time: there was a depressing reliance on past glories, a harking back to precedents but without the conviction and quality which came from the former principles and the culture.

As this is exclusively a story about London Underground and its corporate identity rather than London Transport as a whole, we should pause at this point and, so to speak, dispose of the buses. (Trams, incidentally, were removed from the picture in the early 1950s when they were abolished, to the regret of many people.)

Pick's (and the Government of the day's) vision had been concerned with a coordinated transport system for London, a vision which survived until the Thatcher years. In 1984, as part of the Government's drive for greater efficiency and accountability, a new holding company, London Regional Transport (LRT) was formed, with two quite separate main subsidiary operating companies, London Underground Ltd and London Buses Ltd. Since then, although cooperation is clearly necessary, the two companies have been run separately and subjected to many different criteria. London Buses have been forced to give up their monopoly situation, whereas London Underground, by its nature, has remained intact. However, this degree of autonomy has had also significant effects on considerations of corporate identity, especially internally.

During the 1960s and 70s the cultural capital of London Underground, and its expression in bricks, mortar and other artifacts, was being rapidly spent. There were bright spots, such as the opening of the Victoria Line in 1969, but generally these decades were a particularly bleak period during which funding problems and political see-sawing took its toll. It was only by the early 80s that,

Station signing from the 30s.

In the 60s and 70s, the cultural capital and the actual infrastructure of the Underground were both neglected.

the decay of the Underground system having become so obvious, the Government directed cash towards the problem and launched an ambitious Station Modernisation Programme. And it was through this programme that consideration of identity, at first by visible means, began to be readdressed.

The first priority was the passenger information system, including the fixed signing. The importance of ensuring passenger acceptance of the system by providing good information was recognised and, since the sign system represented the major part of such information, and was also closely linked to the Station Modernisation Programme, it was singled out for improvement. Consultants were commissioned by the Department of Architecture and Design, who had full responsibility for all design within London Transport. The architects were, by then, at loggerheads with the Department of Signals and Electrical Engineering, and the Operations Department who, between them, had been responsible for all aspects of signing.

The architects, as part of the Station Modernisation Programme, had started to depart from precedent in the design of signs, whereupon the other two departments accused them of not sticking to standards. As there were no properly-documented and adopted standards, they found it difficult to sustain their objections, but much bad feeling was created, with consequent delay. The consulting process was also lengthened by the prevailing political atmosphere, proposals being constantly challenged by the electrical engineers and operators, who felt that the consultants were acting in the interests of the architects alone.

New beginnings

Shortly after the creation of London Regional Transport, with London Underground as an

autonomous subsidiary, as described above, the consultants' work on information systems was reviewed, and a decision was taken that, because wider questions of identity were involved, the project should not continue to be driven by the Department of Architecture and Design, but by the Marketing and Development Department. This sideways move broadened the potential scope of the work and also took it out of the engineering arena, where the culture was clearly resistant to change and, therefore, to improvement. The basic visual identity elements – the famous roundel mark, the 'Johnston' typeface and the various colours – having been strengthened and rationalised, the process of designing other applications began, starting with publicity information such as posters and leaflets, and continuing with stationery.

It would be marvellous to be able to say that all of this work was done according to a clear corporate mission but, at this relatively early stage, the organisation was racked with the pain of restructuring, and was in no position to stand back and take an objective view. Although having the firm backing of the Managing Director, the programme proceeded on an ad-hoc basis as funds were made available and as needs in individual areas became pressing. The coordination which was beginning to be apparent in some applications was impressive, but the consultants decided that, with the potential scale and comprehensiveness of the complete identity task becoming clear, communications guidelines were going to be a necessity in order to ensure future consistency, and to help in the task of internal communication and motivation of the value of corporate identity to London Underground.

The qualities which it was decided that the organisation should seek to project were based on the results of extensive market research, the key words being efficiency, enjoyment, safety, competence, friendliness and reliability. The following quotation concerns the aims for the kind of corporate identity which would project those qualities, and is taken from a motivational booklet produced at the time.

'The corporate identity should be simple because simple things are easier and quicker to communicate, don't date and are more economical. It should be direct and consistent to express strong management control and increase customer confidence. Our corporate identity must be lasting, not fashionable. It should be open and approachable, not authoritarian. And, of course, quality must be apparent in everything, which is partly achieved through correct implementation'. Contrast this with Frank Pick's statement quoted earlier. Pick's was not a statement specifically about corporate identity, but the difference in tone between his highly-principled ideals and the present-day pragmatism of the quotation above is reflective of the respective eras and their priorities.

It is outside the scope of this article to trace the detailed history of which department has been responsible for corporate identity at any given point but, early in 1987, the design aspects came within the purview of a new design management structure which consisted of a Design Manager, a Corporate Identity Manager and an Environments Manager. This new element contributed greatly, both at the conceptual and implementations ends of the programme.

The Design Manager was given overall responsibility for all design matters within London Underground, including the visual identity. The Corporate Identity Manager was given responsibility for day-to-day development and implementation of the corporate identity programme, and became the principal point of contact with the consultants. The Environments Manager

was responsible for carrying through the principles into station environments. However, before the incumbents had time to become acclimatised to the situation, disaster struck in the form of the King's Cross fire.

Following the shock and then the investigations, the Chairman of London Regional Transport and the Managing Director of London Underground offered their resignations. The new Managing Director – Denis Tunnicliffe – and his team immediately set about their tasks of internal culture change and external confidence rebuilding, and the corporate identity programme was refocused and given fresh impetus to play its part in the management of change. The Company Plan, which was written shortly afterwards, contained motivational and communications aims which were remarkably similar to the identity criteria already in existence. Safety, naturally, moved to the top priority, so implementation of aspects of the signing concept, vital to safe escape in emergency, became a top priority also.

Dealing with autonomy

One particular aspect of the restructuring caused, and sometimes continues to cause, problems in relation to identity, and that is the status of the individual lines, such as the Northern, Bakerloo, Jubilee and so forth. In the push for effectiveness and accountability, the lines were given an unprecedented degree of autonomy within the system. However, it is not possible, on the one hand, to demand accountability of individual performance and, on the other, to deny some freedom of action to produce that performance, and this resulted in (a) an expressed desire for separate line identities over and above those provided by name and colour-coding and (b) some tendencies towards weakening of visual coordination because of individual choices of agencies or

The basic elements of the corporate design – the 'roundel', the 'Johnston' typeface and the house colours – were rationalised and strengthened.

equipment. At one stage, this led to a small number of lines inventing their own logo-types. Much as anyone involved in corporate identity can understand the desire for a rallying mark to encourage internal esprit-de-corps and to announce a presence to external audiences, this tendency to individualism could only be seen as antipathetic to percep-tions of the Underground as a coherent system and, thus, detrimental to its image. Therefore, individual logotypes or symbols were restricted to internal use only. Acceptance of this, and other restrictions, has been limited by the presence of a degree of scepticism or lack of conviction that it really matters. After all, line managers have to keep the trains running, deal with everyday emergencies and be accountable not only to their bosses, but also to local communities along their lines.

Internal communication of corporate values and how they are expressed through corporate identity has been the way of countering this, together with a rapidly-growing set of corporate identity standards, which will be referred to later. Video programmes, with accompanying printed material, have been produced to inform and to motivate. Events, both large and small, have been held and addressed to various groups and levels within the organisation. All have been consistent in promoting the integrity of the network, the spirit of the Company Plan and the relevance of the corporate identity in achieving the 'decently modern metro', which is the target, in ensuring customer acceptance while work is in progress and in communicating the desired characteristics.

There is still much effort involved from day to day in 'selling' the need for consistency to line management – indeed, sometimes also to individual station management – but, because of the clearly apparent improvement achieved by corporate design policies, the need is now more readily accepted.

Design of stations and trains

The same communications principles which were formulated in relation to the corporate identity have been applied with equal success to environments and products. In contrast to the early Station Modernisation Programme work, where decoration with pattern, illustration and lively colours was pursued at the expense of coherence, station design and décor is now controlled by a set of guidelines which encourage a move towards calmer, less fashionable but clearer environments, where prominence is given to information rather than extraneous decorative elements. Appropriateness of materials (which, as well as looking good, must conform to Underground's strict rules on fire resistance) with elegance of detailing are now the emphasis.

The products which furnish the stations, such as sign hardware, litter bins, ticket gates and security booths, have also been given careful design attention in a strategy which aims to achieve a corporate character throughout all manifestations. Many of the items are branded with the corporate mark to give a strong message of authorship, ownership and commitment, both internally and externally. The 'Stars of the Show' – the trains themselves – have also come in for treatment. There are many different shapes and two basic sizes of trains on London Underground, due to historical development and to the fact that there are two distinctly-different sizes of tunnel. Unifying the trains through a common livery as part of the corporate identity programme thus became an issue. For many years, London Under-ground's trains had been unpainted aluminium, but factors such as ageing of the material and the increased graffiti menace combined with the corporate identity programme to demand a painted solution. Within a railway company, strong feelings are created by the question of what colour to paint the trains. The solution eventually adopted was the result of a long process of discussion and struggle between consultants with design management on the one hand, and engineers on the other. At best, it is an acceptable compromise with which the

Corporate identity and marketing

The relationship of corporate identity to design is, in all of these manifestations, quite clearly expressed, but what of the relationship to marketing in a public transport system?

organisation feels comfortable and is happy to implement system-wide. For the consultants and design managers, it did not represent an ideal solution, but it does illustrate the realities of corporate design implementation within a large and complex public undertaking. New trains are being delivered to parts of the system but more impact has been created, so far, by refurbishments of the interiors of older trains according to principles laid down in a set of train interiors guidelines. As with the station environments, the aim is for simplicity, clarity and high quality rather than a stimulating décor. The improvement has been, in most cases, startling and trains built in the 60s, for example, have been given a new lease of life which will extend their careers will into the next century.

The Marketing Department of London Underground has, as was mentioned earlier, been involved in the corporate identity work from very early days, acting as a prime mover in increasing its scope. Since the system is so well-used (indeed over-used for journeys to and from work), much of the marketing effort goes towards persuading off-peak travellers such as shoppers and sightseers that they should use the Underground in preference to other forms of transport. As well as contributing to a better journey experience, the corporate identity supports the projection of corporate character through a distinctive tone-of-voice. It helps to confirm to customers that they are in a well-ordered and well-managed environment. It also provides a bedrock for promotional activities, which must vary to appeal to different target

The signposting, the ticket machines and the collectors' booths, amongst many other things, are part of a design strategy which aims to create a distinctive station character throughout the network.

audiences. Creative work carried out by advertising agencies and design groups is governed by guidelines and by the corporate identity criteria. Although this has caused some stresses, based on agencies' perceived needs for freedom of creative expression, promotional material is a cornerstone of the identity and must play its part in creating the total impression.

Train livery is based on the house colours.

They provide rules on the basic elements of the identity and on their detailed application. At present, there are eleven volumes:

- roundel standards
- colour standards for identity and information
- stationery standards
- publicity standards
- journey planner and line diagram standards
- engineering vehicle livery standards
- road vehicle livery standards
- written communications standards
- station works guidelines
- sign manual
- heritage signing handbook

These are added to as priorities and resources allow. The biggest limitation to progress is funding. It is not the case that funds are always tight, but that they can be turned on or off at very short notice, due to the effect of government decisions. At the time of writing, the organisation is experiencing a period of restraint, which has followed a contrasting period of high investment. In such circumstances, it is very difficult to plan a coherent programme and to maintain credibility for corporate identity activities within the organisation.

Measures for translating the corporate identity concept

Finally, we must turn to implementation of the identity, which has been termed a 'daily battle'. Responsibility for implementation rests with the Corporate Identity Manager who has, as her weapons of battle, a numerous and growing set of standards documents, each endorsed by the Managing Director, and a retainer arrangement with the corporate identity consultancy, who provide advice on a daily basis. The standards documents are the foundation on which the whole corporate identity structure rests, and are now to be closely allied to the whole area of customer standards within the Development Directorate.

Conservation of historical heritage

One project which was completed just before the current spending clampdown demonstrates a particularly strong link between the organisation's history, and its past and present culture, together with a response to current social pressures. This is a 'Heritage signing handbook'. 'Heritage' is a word which London Underground uses to describe inherited visible assets. This largely relates to stations of the inter-war period, including accessories such as seats, light fittings and signs, many of which were designed under the régime of Frank Pick, or under his influence. Many are outstanding examples of the architecture and design of their period and represent the Underground's 'golden age'. But the act of conserving the best of past glories is not a show of sentimentalism.

As Managing Director Denis Tunnicliffe has said: 'An organisation's heritage is something which grows from its own culture and is a highly individual phenomenon which cannot be bought or replaced'. Internally, these heritage artefacts are seen as part of 'where we come from', a tangible expression of culture and an encouragement to live up to the best of the past. Externally, respect for those objects, many of which have become part of the characteristic fabric of London, communicates a responsible and caring attitude. And conservation, by its nature, is environment friendly, another important positioning aspect.

The handbook gives objectives and strict criteria for deciding which signs should be selected for conservation, balancing historic and aesthetic merit against safety considerations, operational relevance and information value. The document will help London Underground to value these assets and also to demonstrate a positive and pro-active response to the demands of various conservation pressure groups.

Conclusions

At the end of an eventful ten-year period of conscious development of the corporate identity, questions must be asked about its success and its benefits. So far as implementation goes, it has to be said that impact was lost by not devoting resources sufficient to produce a noticeable change within a reasonable period of time. Even now, many areas of application are incomplete and the fear has always been present that changes in the organisation might upset

adherence to the chosen strategy, resulting in yet another layer of variation. However, despite big changes to top and middle management, to the organisational structure and to the corporate status itself, the aims and objectives of the corporate identity programme have been maintained. To call it a 'programme' is, in the normal sense of the word, an inaccuracy. Largely because of

Standards documents facilitate day-to-day implementation of the corporate design.

funding turn-rounds, it has been impossible to carry out tasks according to an overall strategic plan and, because of funding priorities, it has not been possible even to tackle some parts of the work in what would be, theoretically, the correct order. The current push to produce standards for all areas of corporate identity implementation is, perhaps, the most systematic contribution to implementation yet, but even that is currently held up by spending restrictions.

Internal resistance is also a problem, sometimes at line management level as already described, and sometimes in other areas of the organisation. Much effort has been devoted to information and motivation, but outbreaks of independent action still occur,

Paul Moss

Transport design consultant.

1961 Graduated in Industrial Design at the Central School of Art and Design, London.
1961-63 Junior Industrial Designer at EMI Electronics Ltd, Hayes.
1963-66 Industrial Designer with The Solartron Electronic Group, Farnborough, Hants.
1966-87 Design Manager, Hoover plc, Perivale Middlesex. Worked in US with parent company in North Canton, Ohio on several occasions on international projects.
1987-95 Design Manager, London Underground Ltd.
1995- Independent transport design consultant.

Jeff Mills

Advertising and Publicity Manager, London Underground Ltd, London.

With London Transport since the mid-sixties, mainly in commercial, research, marketing and advertising functions.

1986-92 Marketing Manager, London Underground, responsible for the introduction of market research and corporate identity into the Company, and linking customer requirements to a new signing policy and to the interior design of trains. Since 1992 Advertising and Publicity Manager, London Underground Ltd.

He is a fellow of the Chartered Institute of Transport and member of the Chartered Institute of Marketing.

supported by arguments which may make sense in an isolated, individual situation, but which work against coherence. In such a large, public and politically-influenced organisation, such problems are to be expected and are shared by others around the world. The real point about corporate identity within London Underground is that, despite problems, it is fully integrated with the culture, the management practices, the products, the environments and communication of all kinds.

It has also provided the framework used in the implementation of other projects. In concept, it represents an ideal of continuity with a respected past, projected forward in a contemporary, but timeless, way to address a present and future which is part of a rapidly-changing social and economic context. In implementation, it is a day-to-day expression of the present culture and a significant part of London Underground's striving towards quality in all aspects of its activities.

Migros was founded
in 1925 through a
personal initiative by
Gottlieb and Adele
Duttweiler. Over the
years the Company
has developed
into the biggest
private employer in
Switzerland and today
employs more than
70,000 staff. Migros
consists of 12 regional
co-operatives with
more than 1.5 million
members. The
Company embraces
the retail sector
(in 1994 there
were 568 branches),
production, and
services such as
insurance, travel,
banking and so on.
In 1994 the Group
achieved a turnover
of more than
SFr 15 billion.

M
MIGROS

Introduction

The identity of the Migros cooperative, the Swiss supermarket chain, is characterised by social obligations and the idea of serving society. Migros is an example of business success using independent, even self-willed, principles of identity. Still today, as from its inception, it is shaped by the cultural, social, business and political directives of the founding couple, Gottlieb and Adele Duttweiler.

Maja Amrein and Marcel Naegler explain the corporate culture, which is held to be a way of behaving which puts people and their environment at its centre. The values of the corporate identity result from a comprehensive philosophy and include, among other things, the culture, the own-brand concept, the environmental policy, the leadership and participation model, the federalist corporate structure and an open information policy.

'Never was the image of Migros so good.' So the generation change seems to have been successfully accomplished. A strong corporate identity stands in place of the founder and continues to communicate the ideals and principles.

Migros is different

Right from the start in 1925, Migros was moulded by the personality of one visionary man, Gottlieb Duttweiler. As the founder of Migros, he gave the Company a clear, unmistakable profile and a strong corporate personality. This was based on the idea of creating as direct a sales organisation as possible, forming a bridge between producer and consumer. Out of this idea developed the largest retail organisation in Switzerland, one which still follows the principles set by the founder, but which, by virtue of its culture, does not allow time to pass it by. The actual corporate identity of Migros finds expression through creative action based on the principles. The resultant corporate culture is not a management technique, but a way of behaving which revolves around human beings in their environment.

These are the cornerstones of the way in which Migros sees itself:

- Migros exists according to a code of ethics which gives fundamental importance to a cooperative, decentralised and democratic structure.
- Migros devotes a fixed percentage of its turnover to cultural, social and political-economic purposes.
- Migros operates a special procurement and distribution concept.
- Migros is committed to the environment.
- Migros practises a unique leadership and participation model.
- Migros cultivates a comprehensive and open information policy.

The Migros vision as a corporate identity element

In 1950, Gottlieb and Adele Duttweiler formulated fifteen propositions as guidelines to which members of the administration and cooperative council can refer when defending the Migros vision, at any time and for all time'. The basic features of the propositions can be sketched out as follows. They describe the essential characteristics of Migros and its differences from other companies.

At the outset, the first proposition states that the public interest takes precedence over that of the Migros cooperative. Also, increasing material power must be accompanied by even bigger social and cultural achievements. Closely related to this is the maxim that growth must be balanced by democracy. Such democracy has exceptionally strong roots in the Migros community. The cooperative structure has been further developed into a model for democratic decision-making. The decentralised management structure, the division into twelve regional cooperatives and the integrated cooperative alliance are among the great strengths of the Company. They

are also important prerequisites for the implementation of the vision of the founder of Migros, the main elements of which are democracy, a decentralised structure, the will to serve and the bridge function between producer and consumer.

As a rule, it is the normal goals of private enterprise which companies aim for. Turnover, profits and dividends are often the measure of all things; these economic goals are achieved through selling good products and services successfully in the market.

However Migros, according to the ideas of the founder, does not exist primarily to make money, but to serve. At the same time, the principles of economy and efficiency still apply. Altruism alone cannot be the way to reach planned targets. Migros is a means to an end, not an end in itself. So Gottlieb Duttweiler chose the cooperative structure. The articles of the Company state, parallel with Article 2 of the Swiss 'Law of Obligations' (a right in civil law), that the cooperative aims, through community self-help, to offer reasonably-priced goods and services of good to high quality, as well as cultural services, to its own members and the general public.

The Migros 'cultural percentage' as a corporate identity element

Gottlieb Duttweiler, through the 'cultural percentage fund', created an instrument which bound Migros to invest money every year, even at times of falling profits, for cultural, social and political-economic purposes. The Migros cooperative alliance spends a minimum of 1 per cent of its wholesale turnover every year; the individual cooperatives spend at least half a per cent of their retail turnovers. It is significant that these non-commercial goals are given equal status to commercial ones.

One expression of this equality is that the President of the Executive Committee (the leadership of the organisation) also heads the department of cultural and social coordination.

An important pillar of Migros' cultural activities, without doubt, are the 'Club-schools', which represent the largest adult education institute in Switzerland. They enable people to attend an extraordinarily broad range of courses under convenient conditions. The offer is conceived in such a way that it is entirely valid as a means of organising an active leisure-time programme, for the 'Clubschools' make nearly everything available from training to further education, and from games and sport to craft skills and counselling.

The participants pay about three quarters of the real cost; the remainder is taken from the 'cultural percentage fund.' Space would not permit a detailed explanation of the applications of the cultural percentage fund. The resources (1994: 107 million Swiss Francs) are spread as broadly as possible. Migros' definition of culture follows that of

the European Council, which goes far beyond what is generally understood as the meaning of the word. But then, social involvement is also important for Migros. Both in Switzerland and abroad, the disadvantaged and those in need are helped directly or indirectly. Within the framework of this support, Migros gives aid to developing countries in the Third World as well 'help for self-help' to Eastern Europe.

Migros' political activities enjoy a special status. In no way would the Company wield political power by virtue of its position as the largest retailer in Switzerland. Rather, it makes use of democratic collaboration such as initiatives and referendums, when the interests of consumers or market freedom are threatened. This is done, however, with a certain restraint to avoid accusations of misuse of power.

These political activities have their roots in the Company's history, because Migros had to fight a constant battle, during the first decades of its existence, against economic boycotts and political restrictions. Gottlieb Duttweiler therefore founded an independent

The 'cultural percentage fund' is linked to turnover and obliges Migros, every year, even in less profitable times, to use money for cultural, social, and political-economic purposes.

political party, the 'Alliance of Independents', which is still financed with help from the cultural percentage fund to this day. With this money, the 'Alliance' pursues an independent policy. It is not the 'extended arm' of Migros.

In summary, one can say that the cultural, social, business and political mission which Migros adopted in 1957 differs clearly from the philosophies of other enterprises. Numerous other companies make contributions to cultural and social activities, but nobody except Migros recognises the commitment as a percentage of turnover, thus making it obligatory to devote money for these purposes, even when business activity is at a reduced level. And this use of means is not directed towards advertising or public relations. The cultural achievements of Migros are therefore no marketing instrument, but rather patronage or targeted support.

Own-production is an important part of Migros' image.

Migros logistics and own-branding are corporate identity elements

There are many different characters in retailing. We would like to attempt to reveal the peculiarities of the way Migros distributes its goods. The fixed principles of good quality and value-for-money have already been mentioned.

However, such things can be claimed and offered by any retailer, so Gottlieb Duttweiler set further requirements about the range of goods and prices. His hypothesis demanded optimum economy of production and distribution. He disapproved of any unnecessary increases in price caused by intermediate trading. He created clear net prices and, apart from special offers, refrained from discounts. Employees pay the same prices as customers. Since, from the start, Migros was boycotted by manufacturers of branded products, Duttweiler started up his own production. His credo was that, whoever does his own production is independent from others and cannot be hindered in his activities. This vertical integration is a considerable strength and helps to differentiate Migros from other retailers. Today, own-production accounts for about a third of the range of goods on offer and adds significantly to the image of Migros.

Migros' traditional range of food and household goods is notably lacking in so-called branded products. But Migros chocolate, for example, is only available from Migros stores, at the same price everywhere. This traditional range of goods accounts for about two-thirds of the total, and behind them is the fact that Migros takes nearly a quarter of the whole Swiss agricultural production. Healthy nutrition is a further element of identity. Migros is the only retailing chain which does not sell alcohol and tobacco. In 1974, the 'Migros-Sano-Production' label for farming with regard to nature, environment and animal welfare was launched. In the non-food area, Migros produces nothing apart from detergents, household cleaning agents and cosmetics, but sells many well-known branded products with their own labels and corresponding quality standards. Own brands make up 95% of the goods on offer today. The consumer associates the Migros brand with a clear, unmistakable expression of quality and economy, i.e. a good price/performance ratio.

To complete the picture, it should be mentioned that Migros is not involved in price fixing, that dumping is forbidden, that the Migros laboratories thoroughly test all products for sale, that a well-organised department for consumer enquiries deals with the problems and questions of cooperative members and customers, and that the Company operates its own repair service.

Likewise, the relationship to suppliers is also controlled, with competition based on performance. We refer to our suppliers as partners and we often have long-lasting relationships with them. That the customary working conditions for the location or branch are met or exceeded is part of the understanding between this partnership.

The Migros environmental policy as an element of corporate identity

In 1985, through a special vision, Migros created a foundation for its environmental policy: 'We want to be exemplary in the promotion of public health and in the protection of natural resources.' 'We support effective measures for the reduction of pollution.' Effective care of the environment needs effort and perseverance. Therefore, every five years, Migros presents a comprehensive action plan based on its current

The kingfisher used in the environmental communications concept.

environmental policy. These ambitious goals can only be achieved if every member of staff is aware of the Migros environmental policy and identifies with it. The information point for environmental questions, created by the department for PR and information, works closely with those responsible for education and training. Whenever possible, environmental aspects are incorporated into existing courses constructed for various target groups. Consumers, authorities, organisations and societies will, in future, be better informed about these environmental activities. And, in this, the principle of reporting only proven evidence will be unchallenged.

The attainment of targets is also supported by an internal and external environmental communications concept developed jointly with specialists, embodied in the kingfisher. The bird stands for Migros' environmental efforts at all levels. The kingfisher is an expression of support for our environment in need of protection. The slogan 'Let's care for the environment' underlines that Migros' environmental activities can only be successful if customers also make their contribution.

*Migros retails petrol
through its own outlets.*

age for men is 65, so the Company covers
the missing three years with an additional
pension. Women in Switzerland retire at 62 in
any case. All in all, Migros offers exemplary
working conditions, which differ to a greater
or lesser extent from those of other
companies. Migros is absolutely aware of its
responsibility as the largest private employer
in Switzerland.

The Migros information policy as an element of corporate identity

Public relations is a task for the whole
company. This demands an active information
policy in the sense of clear corporate
communications, not only towards sections
of the public outside the Company, but
especially also within the Company. The
previously-mentioned 'federal' structure is
reflected in public relations activities. As
autonomous as the individual cooperatives
or affiliated companies are in their own
business, so they are in their information
policy, based on a regional network of
external and internal target groups. Thus
the nationwide corporate interests are
coordinated and presented by Migros' public
relations and information department. To
maintain and enhance the high image of
Migros implies high demands on the public
relations work. Because of the size and
importance of Migros, its activities are
of public interest and therefore exposed to
public criticism. Through an open information
policy which explains the correlation and
causes of success and failure, Migros tries
to improve the position of the Company as
a whole in the public eye. This continuous
supply of basic information promotes, as
well as credibility, trust and openness, an
understanding of objectivity, even allowing
for differing judgements and opinions. Honest
and detailed information for consumers has
been a central concern of Migros over the
years. One of the many consequences of this

Migros' participation as an element of corporate identity

Migros practises a leadership and participation model which combines functional,
material and social participation. Most visible
is the material participation, consisting of
high-interest-bearing shares which are
cashed on leaving the cooperative or retiring.
Additionally, Migros offers all members of
staff attractive rates of interest on salary and
investment accounts at the Migros Bank.
The functional participation regulates worker
participation and the right of speech within
the organisation. The staff are represented on
workers' councils and on all of the important
Migros committees.

Finally, social participation consists of close
and constructive cooperation with the trades
unions. Migros employees retire at 62, and
then profit from a very well-established
corporate pension fund. The state retirement

policy is the sheer volume of customer information on the packaging of food or non-food goods. In addition, Migros was the first company in Switzerland to introduce dating (production, sell-by and use-by) in 1976. Migros dating has become a by-word for guaranteed freshness.

A central rôle in the information policy is played by the customer dialogue in the three weekly newspapers which all cooperative members receive free of charge. Migros publishes the papers in German, French and Italian and prints over 1.5 million copies in total. Each paper has its own editor, who enjoys wide journalistic freedom. For Migros, these weekly newspapers are a very important institution. As long as they remain in their position as the largest weekly paper in the Swiss media-mix, they will continue to be one of Migros' most efficient information and PR channels, even though articles promoting the Company are strictly and clearly limited. Migros spokesmen, in addition, place paid PR text advertisements on corporate and economic, as well as social and cultural, themes. This so-called 'Zeitung in der Zeitung' ('Paper in the paper') is published in all the major Swiss titles.

Corporate identity as corporate vision

The production of the new Migros corporate film in 1992 gave the best visual instruction on corporate identity. Confronted by the challenge of presenting in ten minutes the corporate personality of Migros in a distinc-tive way, it was vital to reveal the essence of the identity. The film had to communicate the corporate identity of the Migros entity to internal and external target groups. With that, it had to elaborate on the features that distinguish Migros from other companies. Additionally, the film had to evoke an emotional response and transmit a lively corporate culture. No hard facts and figures

are given, rather Migros' philosophy and understanding of itself. Result: Migros stands for quality, logistics, environmental aware-ness, social involvement and closeness to the customer, all values which will be decisive in guiding the further future expansion of Migros abroad.

By now, everybody knows that Migros has become a strong brand. The visual identity in the form of an orange 'M' is widely recognised. And the musical 'M', the aural element in Migros' corporate identity, is just as unmistakable. This is the music of the Migros advertising, the melody played daily in Switzerland on radio, television and in cinemas for many years. Simple and catchy, short or long version, the melody can be adapted into all musical styles and, in spite of that, be instantly identified as the Migros music.

Dialogue with customers through three weekly newspapers.

Maja Amrein

*Media Consultant,
Migros-
Genossenschafts-
Bund, Zurich,
Switzerland.*

*Born 1957. Studied
law at Zurich
University, Degree
licentiate juris-
prudence. Practical
training in court and
as solicitor as well as
various other
activities, e.g. over-
seeing film production.
1985 started work
as copywriter and
PR-Manager for the
advertising agency
Edward Küng AG,
Luzern (a member
of the J Walter
Thompson Group).
1988-90 vocational
course for public
relations consultants
at the Public
Relations Society
SPRG.
Since 1991 Media
Consultant of Migros-
Genossenschafts-
Bund.*

Marcel Naegler

*Director of Public
Relations and
Information, Migros-
Genossenschafts-
Bund, Zurich,
Switzerland.*

*Born 1944. Studied
economics at Berne
University. Degree
lic. rer. pol. Scientific/
academic research
for radio and tele-
vision. 1972 Editor
at Swiss Radio,
afterwards freelance
journalist. 1978-79
Director of the
German broadcasting
service of Schweizer
Radio International
(SRI). 1980-88
Director of Press and
PR of the Touring
Club Switzerland
(TCS). 1988-90
Director of PR and
Information at George
Fischer-Konzern.
Since 1990 Director
of Public Relations
and Information
at Migros-
Genossenschafts-
Bund.*

The Migros corporate identity: an expression of continuity and change

Gottlieb Duttweiler lived the corporate culture through his great personal commitment and his goals and ideals, until his death in 1962. Much of what the founder of Migros predicted and showed is still valid today. The thoughts and behaviour of managers and staff are moulded by this well-formed system of attitudes, standards and values. The orange 'M' is today part of everyday Swiss life. Migros is obliged to this country and its people; obliged to performance, honesty and openness. The capital of the related trust confronts the new generation of Migros managers with the task of continual justification through up-to-date activities, while at the same time implementing courageous new ideas and innovations. Migros became large through this. Or, as Gottlieb Duttweiler said: 'Nothing is ever finished; never are all spaces taken. Even in the world of macaroni, plums and coffee beans there exist revolutionary ideas and the victorious breakthrough of youth.'

*Pillar Electrical was
a subsidiary of the
world's largest mining
company, RTZ
Corporation plc. The
Company consisted
of nine independent
subsidiaries. These
produced electrical
products and systems
for buildings and
were successful
strong brands in their
own right. The core
target markets were
Great Britain and
continental Europe,
with business
connections
maintained with
the USA. Turnover
in 1993 amounted
to £266 million. The
number of employees
in that year was 4,500.*

*Thanks to energetic
identity management
and the new corporate
design, the Company
achieved a
recognition value
of 75% in just one
and a half years
among its target
groups in the UK.*

Introduction

Growth, diversification and acquisitions had made the identity of a conglomerate, later to be known as Pillar Electrical, incoherent and confusing. The Group was known by the same name (MK) as its most successful operating subsidiary, which was so well known that it dominated perceptions. The name MK did not therefore represent the spectrum of services and capabilities of the Group. At a time when considerations of restructuring and renaming were in full swing, the Group was bought by RTZ following the stock market crash of 1987.

Robert Bruce describes the development of the identity structure, which provided the necessary basis for the implementation of Group strategy. A necessary element was the communication of the strategy to the individual companies within the Group to ensure that, although successful individually, they understood the benefits of Group synergy.

The new identity structure and communications strategy respected the existing company names and added the Group name as an endorsement. Through association with well-known brand names, the new Group name became established. The identity formed a sound basis for expansion and acquisitions.

A name and identity change to meet market opportunities

No company changes its name lightly; it costs too much in time and effort and involves a high degree of risk because, whatever is wrong with the existing name, it usually carries at least some goodwill and recognition value. To change a company name is to play with the very heart of corporate identification, so an analogy with a transplant is appropriate, and the corporate body must similarly be kept alive while the new vital organ takes over the functions of the old.

Here the analogy ends, for the human heart is an internal organ, invisibly carrying out its function. The corporate name – and the means for its expression and communication – is a highly visible element in a corporate identity system.

Taking into account the risks and costs involved, it is not surprising that name-changes usually only happen when the existing name is creating a barrier to corporate progress, a barrier so high that such a radical step is the only way to surmount it. In 1987, all of the available evidence and research data told MK Electric Group plc that its name had built such a barrier, and that to change it would be a positive and fruitful response to a pressing market opportunity. A name change could also form the basis of a corporate identity strategy to identify and position the Group to make the most of that opportunity.

A generic name, but misleading

MK was and is a household name in the UK, known to most people as a manufacturer of electrical plugs, sockets and switches. 'MK' originally stood for 'Multi-Kontakt' and there has been an unbroken line of development from the founding of the Company in 1919 to its present position and product range. Probably because of the visibility of the product in the domestic environment, the MK name became almost generic, and synonymous with quality in its particular area of activity. However, by the 1980s, the reality was beginning to diverge from the popular conception, not because of any departure from the quality standards which have been the basis of its success, but because MK itself was becoming a different animal, no longer just a supplier of plugs and sockets.

MK had, over several years, acquired a number of market-leading companies in related areas of activity – companies like Gent, famous in fire detection; Friedland, with 85% of the UK doorbell and chime market; Ega with its market-leading range of cable management systems; Trend, who are at the leading edge of building management control technology and Esser Sicherheitstechnik in Germany with its advanced fire alarm and security products. What was thus created was a cohesive group of companies supplying electrical products and systems for buildings, each of them a market leader in its own right.

Studying the market

So there became two MK's – MK Electric Ltd, the original manufacturer of plugs, sockets and switches, and MK Electric Group plc. The confusion which was inherent in this situation gave impetus to internal re-examination of the question 'What is MK' and, consequently, 'how should MK be seen in the market'.

Therefore we had to look at the market to establish its true nature, and this provided much food for thought, for it was, and still is, changing rapidly.

Firstly, there were the general effects of consolidation and concentration, with a smaller number of bigger competitors, the growth of Do-It-Yourself superstores, the increasing presence of professional property management groups, and the concentration of market share on a smaller number of larger construction companies.

Secondly, there had been changes in the law which increased the product liability of specifiers, causing them to seek external advice and reassurance, an obvious pointer to the need for a leader in the field. Thirdly, the increasing adoption by the construction industry of fast track design-and-build and shell-and-core techniques had led to more exacting product and systems specifications. Fourthly, the emergence of design consultants as major specifiers had a big impact; and, finally, product technology was moving ahead fast. Big changes were also happening in the areas of building control, security, energy management and fire detection.

As a result of these changes, building services were taking an increasing share of overall construction costs (from 18% in 1980 to 30% in 1987). The opportunity and potential for growth was plain and the MK Group of companies was ideally placed to take maximum advantage.

A victim of its own success

Or was it? It certainly had the products, the brand names, the capacity and the expertise. But what about the means for communicating this message of MK as the leading supplier of electrical products and systems for

Historically, and still today, MK is Britain's best-known manufacturer of plugs, sockets and switches.

buildings? With monotonous regularity, target audiences associated the MK name with plugs, sockets and switches: 'everything they ever do will be hidden under their plugs and sockets image' and 'It's hard to see MK as any more than plugs and sockets. I suppose MK is a victim of its own success!'

The conclusion, confirmed by research, was that a new name and a new identity was necessary, certainly to distinguish MK Group from MK Electric Ltd, but principally to enable it to grasp the opportunities offered by the changing market, to position and identify itself as 'the leading supplier of electrical products and systems for buildings'. It had, of course, been recognised very early that there should be no disturbance of the individual subsidiary company names. As it was put by one retail buyer interviewed during market research: 'They shouldn't change the Company brand names. They're worth money to me.' The 'Single Business Units' (SBUs), as we refer to them, were, of course, aware of this and were somewhat suspicious of any hint that might mean their own identities could be usurped by a group identity, especially one which was not known in the marketplace.

Setting the stage for the identity structure

The cooperative strength of the SBU's was very much needed to form the basis of the identity launch strategy, with the new name 'piggybacking' on the established names until it had enough strength to take on its full function as a communicator of Group strengths, lending overall competence associations and supporting new ventures and acquisitions.

The theory was sound and readily accepted. But what should the new name be? Naming, personal or corporate, is a tricky business,

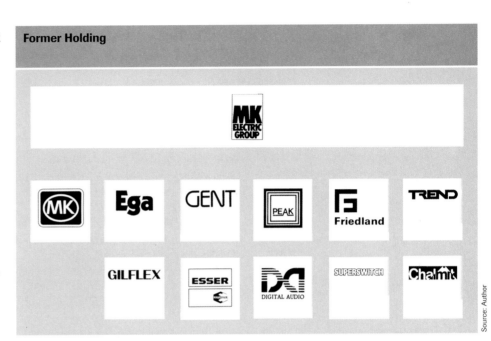

Former Holding

Source: Author

fraught with practical and emotional problems. Little did we know it, but we were about to be relieved of all those problems. In November 1987, on so-called 'Black Monday', the London stock market crashed. Share values collapsed and we became the first dawn raid takeover prospect of the new post-Black Monday era. Legrand of France and The RTZ Corporation had entered into a battle to buy the MK Electric Group. The victorious party was RTZ and in January 1987, MK became one of the main groupings within RTZ Pillar, the industrial division of the RTZ Corporation. The two other main groupings were Pillar Aluminium and Pillar Engineering. It was natural and inevitable that we should become known as 'Pillar Electrical' and this was to be the case.

Our aspirations for our Group were left undisturbed by RTZ Pillar, who readily agreed to our marketing strategy and supported us in our efforts. With the naming problem so fortuitously solved, we were therefore left with three tasks: to express the name visually, to find a corporate identity system to express our strategy and structure and to introduce the changes both internally and externally. It was at this point that corporate identity considerations came into prominence, and we appointed a consultancy to assist us in this sensitive task. Although they were able to demonstrate their credentials and impressive track record, there is a tendency for all clients to feel that their own problem is special, that there are certain pitfalls peculiar to their own circumstances that will throw a spanner in the works. For the 'driver' of the project on the client side, there is always the worry that the board will reject what has been jointly conceived and painstakingly assembled. It was in this sort of atmosphere, in a company rocked by a major culture shock, with an MK Electric Group board and an RTZ Pillar board to convince, that we started to work with the consultants.

Cultural complexity and management involvement

Because of the cultural complexity of the situation – which would have been quite enough even if only a name-change had been involved rather than a complete change of ownership also – it was vital that we first assessed the internal atmosphere, if only to be aware of the scale of the communications task which lay before us. In fact, the internal aspects really led the work.

The consultants therefore carried out wide-ranging, in-depth management interviews, which not only yielded much valuable information, but also focused the various minds on the issues involved and the potential benefits to be gained from reaching our desired positioning as 'the leading supplier of electrical products and systems for buildings'. At the same time, awareness of the strategic importance of the corporate identity process was established and was generally well accepted, following some

initial scepticism. We were mostly dealing with managing directors of substantial or growing businesses, which belonged to a group which had a distinctly 'hands off' approach to their day-to-day running. Some companies, such as Friedland, had very well-developed and cohesive corporate cultures which had grown up over many years. Others, such as Trend, were young and dynamic, at the leading edge of new technologies and growing fast.

One company, MK Electric, naturally saw itself as the senior partner, a position which performance actually justified. But all, including MK Group, were encouraged to realise that RTZ's approach to managing their subsidiaries was not dissimilar from that to which they had become accustomed.

In fact, the whole corporate identity process would have been necessary even if we had not been bought by RTZ. The new name would have been different, of course, but the launching of the name, along with a new positioning, identity and marketing strategy, would have been the same. There was a sense, in some of the larger SBUs, of 'nothing really changing', a feeling that the Pillar endorsement would be relatively unimportant and unnoticed, although the smaller companies looked for a back-up of financial stability for their day-to-day operations. At this point, the marketing strategy which drove the original, pre-Pillar, thinking towards a new name for the Group, was somewhat overwhelmed by the post-takeover priorities, but it was shortly to reassert itself.

Defining process, objectives and criteria

When the consultants had finished the interview process, we sat down with them to work out the exact processes by which we would:

- formulate the communications strategy,
- create an identity structure for Pillar Electrical,
- find a visual expression for Pillar Electrical and
- launch the identity internally and externally.

The objectives we jointly drew up for the identity were that it should:

- represent Pillar Electrical as an 'umbrella' marketing support organisation in relation to the SBUs,
- help the Group to establish a leading position in the marketplace, and
- position Pillar Electrical as the leading company supplying electrical products and systems for buildings.

A companion set of criteria was produced at the same time. These were as follows:

- The identity must create a presence for Pillar Electrical which is appropriate, understandable, open-ended to future acquisitions and visible in relation to the SBUs.
- The identity must play a major rôle in differentiating Pillar Electrical from both its UK and European competitors.
- The identity should be appropriate to the Group's target audiences in its main marketplaces, reflecting those aspects of Pillar Electrical which they most value.
- The structure of the Group should be clearly expressed for both internal and external audiences.
- The identity should not hold any negative associations in Pillar Electrical's market places.
- The design will be used on a wide variety of items from vehicles to business cards – it must, therefore, work equally well in both very large and very small sizes.
- The identity will also be an important vehicle for communicating Pillar

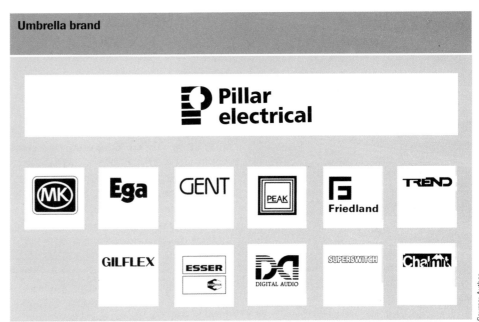

Umbrella brand

Source: Author

Electrical's key qualities:
- innovative and entrepreneurial in the way it seeks new opportunities for application of its products
- applications-oriented in terms of using technology to service customer needs
- problem-solving
- authoritative – taking a rôle as commentator on the trends and developments in the industry
- quality-oriented – more than merely a platitude in the case of Pillar Electrical. The SBUs have a tradition of producing high quality products
- associated with buildings, and
- not overtly 'high tech'
- For the smaller companies in the Group it is important that Pillar Electrical be communicated as:
  - reliable
  - solid
  - secure – a safety net

In thinking about the communications strategy, and the identity structure to support it, we had to take a view on the value of the

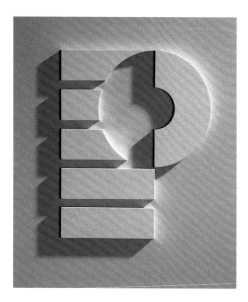

*The initial letter of
the logotype.*

identities of the individual SBUs. We already knew from our earlier market research that the names were indispensable, but now it was decided that no immediate disturbance to the existing visual identity elements of the SBUs would be made.

Mandatory and optional endorsements

There was no way in which change to the SBU identities would have been either beneficial or practical at this time. There was little to be gained, and much to be lost, although the Group resolved that, after the establishment of Pillar Electrical, SBU identities would be assessed on an individual basis and changes or improvements would be made where necessary and appropriate. So the way forward was via an endorsed approach, where the SBU identities would remain intact and undisturbed. Expression of Pillar Electrical would be as a mandatory endorsement on SBU stationery, publications and signs and as an optional endorsement on advertising, packaging and vehicles. Pillar Electrical would thus gain its presence and profile mainly by 'hitching a ride' on its brands, allied to a very modest amount of direct promotion, although Group corporate items such as the annual report would address financial markets and investors. Of course, the success of this process depended on the SBUs using the endorsement in a correct and consistent way, the prerequisite to which was an appropriate, strong and distinctive visual treatment of 'Pillar Electrical'. It has to be admitted that the name 'Pillar Electrical' is not the best start for an endorsement which will usually appear at very small sizes. The name is long, partly generic, and 'Pillar' has absolutely no association with the business activity of the Group. You may wonder at this point why Pillar Electrical could not simply adopt the style of the other 'Pillar' groupings within RTZ. The answer to that is that those other

'Pillars' simply did not have a coordinated style. Pillar Electrical therefore had no alternative but to go it alone although, later, the others emulated the lead by adopting a similar consistent approach.

Developing a mark

It was the consultants' strong recommendation that the initial 'P' of Pillar be adopted as the 'corporate thumbprint'. This was based on the reasoning that the whole name was too long to be stylised as a logotype which would then need to be reduced to a very small size. On the other hand, a completely abstract, new symbol would need to be learned by target audiences, whereas 'P' would at least give a hint as to the word which followed. Design of the mark followed the objectives and criteria in the brief. It was presented to Group management in a rational, detailed and objective fashion which allowed them to take strategic decisions in an area (aesthetics) where businessmen often feel insecure and uncomfortable. The presentation went very smoothly. Of course, some discussion points were raised and dealt with, but no significant changes were either requested or made, and the subject was referred upwards to the RTZ Pillar board. We were very happy with the outcome. and with the 'P' mark which had been created. It was strong, simple and distinctive, lacking any fashionable element which might lead to premature obsolescence, something which was endemic among identities conceived in the late 80s. But it was not to be all plain sailing.

An uncomfortable experience

As part of the consultancy's normal procedures, the proposed mark had been sent to their trademark agents for a health check. The result was not clear-cut, so they submitted it to two further agents for second and third opinions. These two gave their opinion that our 'P' did not conflict with anyone else's mark, so everything was put in process for preparation of a design manual and a major internal launch event.

In the meantime, our legal department, concerned by the one view which was equivocal, had decided to get an opinion from our own lawyers. They decided that there could be a potential clash with one particular mark, owned but not used by a competing company. To us, this potential clash seemed a very distant possibility, but the seeds of doubt had been sown and we tried to resolve the situation by approaching the holders of the problem registration direct. No reassurance was forthcoming, so the reluctant decision was taken that our beautiful 'P' had to be changed.

A date had already been fixed for the internal and external launch, so time was extremely limited. Because the design had been so well 'sold' and was considered to be appropriate for the task, as well as being liked, there was considerable disappointment. Very fortunately, and in a commendably short space of time, the consultants were able to modify the original design in such a way that the lawyers felt able to pronounce it safe. There was all-round relief that we did not have to start again from scratch, but this was not a comfortable experience!

Identity launch strategy

In formulating the launch strategy for the identity, we came to the conclusion that the external launch would be a fairly modest affair. Trade advertising, a corporate brochure and some PR activities sufficed to bring the name to the attention of most targets, the main job of consolidating the profile being left to the endorsement process described

earlier. Internal launch of the identity was a different matter. In the atmosphere of shock and uncertainty which prevailed following the 'dawn raid' on MK Electric Group, we had to communicate our message of opportunity and strategic response in no uncertain fashion if our aims were to be fulfilled. We had to win hearts and minds, convincing independent-thinking SBU managers that their companies were integral parts of a group which was going to provide leadership in the field under the banner of 'Pillar electrical', a completely unknown name.

The annual managers' meeting was chosen as the event for the launch. The audience was thus assured, and the consultants proposed that, as part of this launch strategy, we should produce a short audio-visual programme which would both explain and motivate, and that this should form the centre-piece of the event. The concept was that the audio-visual could be introduced by the Chief Executive at the meeting, then transferred onto video, including the CE's

'Pillar electrical' used as an endorsement to the well-known brand of an SBU, in this case MK Electric Ltd.

'Pillar electrical' as it appears on corporate communications items.

Robert Bruce

*Formerly Group
Marketing Manager,
RTZ Pillar Ltd,
London, UK.*

*Born 1944 in Yorkshire.
Leicester University.
After period
in management
consultancy, joined
Electrical Division of
The Delta Metal Group
as Divisional Marketing
Manager. Entered
area of mergers and
acquisitions with
Consolidated Gold
Fields-ARC as Director
New Business
Development. To MK
Electric as Special
Projects Executive
and Group Marketing
Manager. After
acquisition of MK by
RTZ moved to Group
Marketing Manager
of RTZ Pillar.
On sale of RTZ Pillar
to Caradon, moved
to General Manager,
Marketing BBC
Resources Directorate
at the British Broad-
casting Corporation.*

introduction, for showing to a wider internal audience. (It has since been used to communicate the Group's overall marketing philosophy to acquisitions and to new recruits.)

Although the production costs were high in relation to the total corporate identity programme costs, the results justified the expenditure. The audio-visual was at the same time succinct, professional, impressive and persuasive. It did not seek to 'sell' the strategy by hype, nor to blind with science nor talk down to the audience, but to explain it with reference to all the background information and evidence, building up the case for the strategy, the name-change and the corporate identity measures with clarity and watertight logic.

Acceptance and implementation

Thus presented, all was accepted with enthusiasm, not based on being seduced by over-glossy persuasion, but on good understanding of the facts and intentions. The Pillar Electrical culture had arrived as it meant to go on.

To ensure correct implementation of the visual identity, both on Pillar Electrical corporate material and as an endorsement on SBU material, we produced a design manual, divided into four sections: basic elements, corporate applications, SBU mandatory applications and SBU optional applications. Eventually, the Pillar Electrical 'P' was extended in its use to include the other Pillar groupings within RTZ.

Measuring the results

Concerning the results: externally, we tested the level of awareness of Pillar Electrical, 18 months after the launch, among relevant targets. We found that around 75% of those questioned were aware of the Group and at least some of its attributes. Considering the relatively low-key nature of its introduction, we felt that this was a highly satisfactory result.

Internally, we have implemented various changes and developments in line with the identity strategy. To say that it has been easier than it would have been without the corporate identity process must be true, but is not quantifiable. What we can say is that our aims and motives are clearly understood and accepted, which facilitates action. Corporate identity is concerned with the future, with providing solid foundations for the implementation of ambitious strategies, with nurturing credibility in key market areas. It is a long-term thing. We were satisfied that we had performed the prerequisite task of informing people, first internally and then externally, of our nature and of our aims. Through the programme, we contributed to changing the culture and the outlook of the organisation. We were satisfied that we had a basic identity which would serve as a good foundation for our plans, a pad from which to launch exciting new developments.

Time would add value to our new identity and the investment would ripen. Our identity became the embodiment of our leadership position.

Siemens is a leading worldwide manu-facturer and distributor of industrial products in the electrical engineering and electronics sectors, including research and development in these areas. Business activities include energy generation, trans-mission and distribution; production technology; propulsion, switchgear, information technology; automation technology; private communications systems; public com-munications networks; security technology; transport technology; automotive technology; medical technology; semiconductors; passive components and pipes.

Headquarters of Siemens AG are in Berlin and Munich. Siemens employed around 377,000 staff worldwide in 1994, with a Group turnover of DM 84.6 billion.

SIEMENS

Introduction

An international nature and global business activity have been part of Siemens' mission since the Company's foundation. So cultural openness and internationality are the essential characteristics of its identity.

Siemens' concept is that all its expressed visual characteristics should credibly visualise the style of the business. Those characteristics should be a visible framework, revealing the unity of the products and expressing the Company's attitudes and expectations.

Julius Lengert describes Siemens' conceptual credo, the essential basis which conveys the technical powers of the engineers and the corporate culture. He explains the quality and consistency which is necessary to ensure that all products express 'belonging', and he makes clear how consistency is achieved – consistency in the sense of a recognisably universal attitude which unmistakably brings to mind the name of Siemens.

Corporate design at Siemens is understood as a complex, interlinked system which includes graphic design, communications and architecture; as an expression of identity which makes attitudes visible; and as a visualised code of behaviour and the self-imposed expectations of the Company.

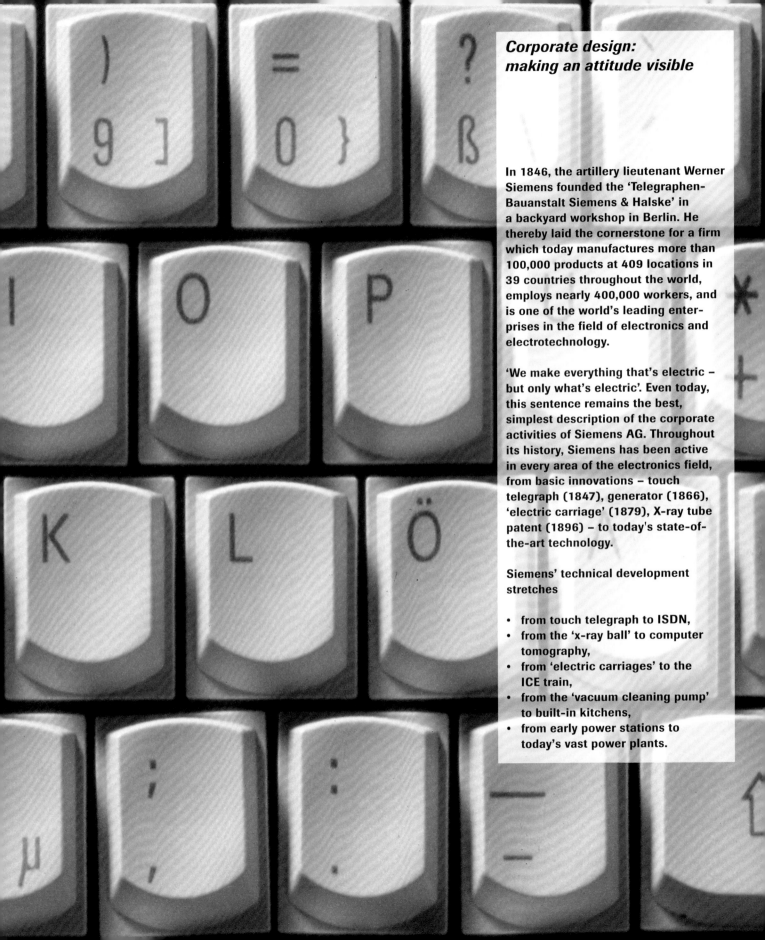

Corporate design: making an attitude visible

In 1846, the artillery lieutenant Werner Siemens founded the 'Telegraphen-Bauanstalt Siemens & Halske' in a backyard workshop in Berlin. He thereby laid the cornerstone for a firm which today manufactures more than 100,000 products at 409 locations in 39 countries throughout the world, employs nearly 400,000 workers, and is one of the world's leading enterprises in the field of electronics and electrotechnology.

'We make everything that's electric – but only what's electric'. Even today, this sentence remains the best, simplest description of the corporate activities of Siemens AG. Throughout its history, Siemens has been active in every area of the electronics field, from basic innovations – touch telegraph (1847), generator (1866), 'electric carriage' (1879), X-ray tube patent (1896) – to today's state-of-the-art technology.

Siemens' technical development stretches

- from touch telegraph to ISDN,
- from the 'x-ray ball' to computer tomography,
- from 'electric carriages' to the ICE train,
- from the 'vacuum cleaning pump' to built-in kitchens,
- from early power stations to today's vast power plants.

And Siemens has been internationally oriented from the very beginning. Eight years after the Firm was founded, the first foreign branch opened in Russia, where the Tsar commissioned Siemens to install a telegraph network. Shortly thereafter, English-based business activities led by Wilhelm Siemens, the brother of the Firm's founder, led to the founding of Siemens Brothers Ltd in London, which was mainly responsible for producing telegraph cables. In France, the enterprise Siemens Frères introduced the first 'electric tramway', an international sensation, at the World Exposition in Paris in 1867.

Developing a European telegraph network, constructing the telegraph line from London to Calcutta, and laying underwater cables – especially the sensational Transatlantic Cable, which linked Europe with the 'New World' – were all projects that continued Siemens' close collaboration with partners from many different countries.

Siemens engineers'
uniforms in Russia.

Ever since its founding, therefore, Siemens has seen internationality and global business activity as a matter of course. From the very beginning, this international character posed the problem of how to conform to individual, national expectations and requirements while at the same time preserving a distinct corporate identity. It has generally been axiomatic at Siemens that the best policy is to adapt to each country and behave 'according to local customs'. The Company still follows this principle today. The Firm's guidelines state that 'We see ourselves as an integral element of the national economy, with a responsibility both to society and the environment'. In order to be seen and respected as a power to contend with and a potential business partner, however, it was absolutely necessary to develop a recognisable international identity. That this will toward self-representation was born of necessity was demonstrated by a curious situation in old Russia. After the telegraph

network had been installed in the Tsar's Empire, it became clear that the Russian authorities were not adequately tending to the maintenance of the equipment, which led to frequent interruptions on the line; Siemens was therefore assigned with reorganisation. This was an extremely lucrative task, as it was a long-term commission which could be counted on to bring in regular sums of money; but it was also problematic in that the German engineers, as foreigners, had trouble gaining the necessary respect from their Russian employees. To solve this problem, the Tsar authorised the Siemens engineers and electricians to be issued their own uniform; this made them recognisable as representatives of the Firm, and gave them a semi-official status, and thus the respect that had been lacking, among the population.

This uniform had to be designed with considerable tact and sensitivity, as it couldn't seem to compete with other uniforms. The designs were carefully thought out and purposefully, sensitively attuned both to practical requirements and the political and psychological climate in which they were to be worn. Cultural openness and internationality don't have to oppose the development of a national identity. One impressive example of this is the 'Siemens-stadt' (Siemens City) in Berlin.

Berlin was, and remains, Siemens' company headquarters. Regardless of its extensive international involvement, Siemens wants to be seen as a German firm. One of Werner von Siemens' major achievements was aid to the development of German patent regulations and industrial standards. Only by protecting the product from imitations and the inventor from the theft of his intellectual achievement, Siemens believed, could German industry become more highly regarded both at home and abroad, and the tag 'Made in Germany', which was originally pejorative, become a sign of quality.

After the industrial revolution, technical and industrial development led to work being centralised in factories, which developed into plants of ever-increasing size. These plants gave rise to a whole new organisational, sociological and cultural problem situation. It had never before been necessary to bring so many people together in one place: this meant providing for their transportation, feeding them during the day, setting up their workspaces and organising their work schedules. Employers, furthermore, had never before had to furnish employees with a sense of belonging, of identity; before industrialisation, when artisan shops were the norm, identity came with a profession. It is only in the age of industrialisation and mass production that the worker's increasing alienation from his work has become a problem.

Constructing the 'Siemens City' was an attempt to find a solution to this problem, and it is fair to say that the attempt was successful. For the public as well as for Siemens employees, the complex was a symbol for economic success and social involvement, as well as for a special kind of company culture: a symbol, in short, of company identity. This identity is partly shaped by design elements, above all by the architecture. The site contains buildings by every renowned architect of the period, including Gropius and Scharoun; the greatest influence, however, is that of Herdtlein's industrial architecture. Herdtlein understood how to translate the discipline and factual purism – the essence of technology – into a formal vocabulary which, over the years, has lost none of its validity or appropriateness.

From the very beginning, then, Siemens had a clear identity, was recognised inter-nationally, and projected a positive image, especially in insider circles. In consequence, the Company's public image was characterised by a certain restraint, a note of understate-

ment. Its design elements – its corporate design – were equally restrained and unobtrusive. The corporate logo was white on a blue background. Advertising – both images and typefaces – was corseted within a fairly tight set of formal regulations. Company architecture so adapted to the prevailing local styles of individual sites that the buildings became purely functional, without a trace of fashionable or spectacular design. The Firm was like a sturdy ocean-going ship, crossing the sea time and again along tested routes, reliably, unspectacularly, and without incident.

As time went on, however, a global market gradually developed, bringing with it an ever-growing number of competitors fighting for the same shares of the market and using every method, including aggressive marketing, to win it. It became clear that Siemens' traditional organisational structures and ways of thinking were no longer adequate to the demands of the new situation. In 1990, therefore, the Company was reorganised and divided into fifteen autonomous business areas.

Siemensstadt (Siemens City) 1930, painting by Scheuritzel.

Apartment block in Siemensstadt, architect Hans Scharoun.

*Development of the
Company's logotype –
1926, 1969 and today.*

Siemens' product range stretches

- from keyboards to factory technology
- from car telephones to the Eurosprinter locomotive
- from dentists' drills to motors
- from PCs to orthodontic X-ray equipment
- from factory automation technology to street lamps

Given the wide range of products and activities, the designers of Siemens' corporate identity are faced with this question: how can a firm with fifteen autonomous, independent, internationally-operative profit centres prevent centrifugal force from dissipating the Company's overall identity; and how, instead of this, and in spite of the Company's complexity, can one preserve a kind of unity within this multiplicity, a single corporate identity?

Identity can be defined as 'the correspondence of standards to reality'. Siemens' standards which it applies to itself are first-rate technology, quality, seriousness, internationality, modernity.

The Company's guidelines assert that

- Our goal is to provide our customers with the most useful products and services possible.
- We want to maintain constructive, long-term relationships based on mutual trust with our partners the world over.
- Our Company's success is based on the creativity and motivation of our employees.
- We see ourselves as an integral element of the national economy, with a responsibility both to society and to the environment.

How can these standards be expressed, conveyed visibly and tangibly as a company-wide stance?

First, by installing central control and supervision for all of the Company's design activities. All 'design activities', therefore – architecture, advertising, and design – are organised in a central department. Its task is to develop corporate design concepts and strategies for ways to apply and maintain these concepts throughout the Firm. The tool most important for this is a Corporate Design (CD) Manual which defines the Company's philosophy of design and contains rules for the practical application of this philosophy. The manual's task is to guarantee a visual identity for the Company which is internationally valid and without contradiction. Its goal is not to set in stone every detail, every conceivable eventuality; rather, its rules give as much leeway as possible. The principle is: rules where rules are needed; and room for free play in special situations, to find solutions to new developments. The manual, therefore, is not an instruction book, but rather describes a design philosophy unique to Siemens: making an attitude visible.

Second, by developing and applying a consistent design concept which expresses this philosophy credibly in all of its formal and other aesthetic characteristics, every element of the Company's appearance is a manifestation of its philosophy.

Siemens product design

Of all of the elements of our Company image, such as advertising, Company buildings, letterhead, packaging, trade-fair stands and vehicles, our products are the most important. They are a major part of the Company's identity and Company culture. It is products that define a company to the public; through direct, concrete contact with products, the customer experiences, perceives, and judges the Company. Therefore, a product's appearance has special significance in the communication between the Company and the customer: not only in terms of the customer's decision to buy or the product's chances of market success, but also in terms of the Company's identity. When we say 'design is performance made visible', we refer, of course, to the visible, tangible performance of an individual product; but product design, if it is consistently carried out and maintained, also expresses something else: the attitude of a firm. And this, in turn, is closely associated with the entity we term 'corporate identity'.

Such an identity is not visible so much in individual situations as in a consistent, fundamental, predictable stance, a philosophy that extends to all of the Company's thinking and activity.

Seen thus, product design is an attitude made visible, the visualised principles of a firm's activity and the standards it sets for itself. How one uses and applies product design as a factor in a company's culture varies from company to company. A company which is active in only a single area can try to define itself mainly through its product design, and demonstrate its corporate identity mainly in this manner.

In the case of Siemens, the situation is quite different. Siemens, first of all, manufactures more than one hundred thousand products. Many of these, admittedly, are not 'designed' as such. Still, at least a thousand products do need to be designed. Secondly, some 90% of these products are capital goods, products for which design has a different value, a different function, and a different priority than it does in the case of consumer goods. Thirdly, these products are developed, produced and marketed around the world.

Fifteen 'firms within a firm' develop various products independently of one another; yet the products have to be made to harmonise visually both with each other and with the

overall appearance of the Company. These products have only one thing in common: they carry the Siemens trademark.

At Siemens, therefore, design has two main tasks: it should function as a kind of visual bracket, making it clear that the various products are related; and it should express the Company's philosophy and standards. And these tasks do not serve only to gain better market position for the products themselves. Even more, they serve to define the Company's philosophy, its style, its culture.

Siemens' design philosophy is summed up in the credo of Chief Designer Herbert H. Schultes:

'We describe this philosophy, our basic approach to design, as "technical-aesthetic", because it employs a reduced formal vocabulary as the best way to express the technical accomplishments of our engineers.

Classical capital goods become consumer goods, and design expresses this.

We use basic geometric forms for housings, bringing sculptural forms into play only in areas where people come directly into contact with the equipment, with their hands, their ears, or their eyes.

We don't want to draw attention to our products or try to win people over with avant-garde, futuristic designs. On the contrary, we allow a certain amount of tradition to show through, however innovative the product. Our customers see our Company's strengths as being in tradition and innovation. Quality and unified corporate appearance are the most important requirements for our product design. Unified doesn't mean uniform: we're not aiming at standards, stencils, or patterned repetitions of the same shapes. Rather, we aim at a "unified appearance" in the sense of a recognisable design approach that's reflected in every product, a continuity which is immediately identifiable and signals to the viewer or the user that this is a Siemens product. Only thus can we achieve the synergetic effect we aim for; only thus can

design truly become that which it can and should be: an effective factor in market competition.'

A unified overall design concept is one thing; special market conditions, competitive situations, product-specific requirements and surroundings are another. At Siemens, therefore, typical long-term products receive a long-term, 'classic' design, while consumer products with their short-lived designs, which are becoming increasingly prevalent in the Siemens product range, are oriented toward current, contemporary design trends. In addition, certain product requirements are born of the individual product's environment: hygienic requirements in the field of medical technology; the need for extra durability in the automation and energy fields; or the necessity for home appliances to fit into living spaces and environments. The first command-ment remains unchanged: our products have to reflect the attitude, reputation, and standards of the Firm Siemens, whose name stands for the quality of all of its products;

Design awareness is expressed in the 'technical aesthetic' of, above, the satellite station at Raisting and, right, the dental workstation 'Sirona C1'.

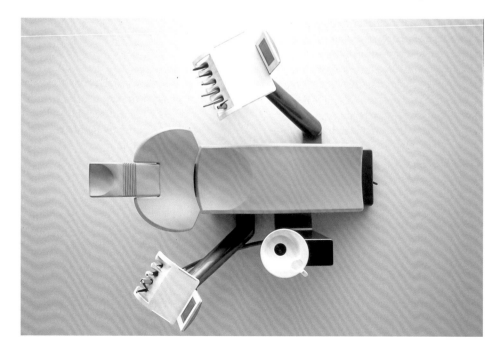

and they should, through a unified design vocabulary, allow the customer to recognise a unity within their multiplicity and variety. The same goes for other components of the Company image, such as packaging and trade-fair stands. Here, too, the goal is to create a recognisable design stance within a tremendous variety and number of objects. Siemens manufactures more than one hundred thousand products, which are all delivered to the customer in some kind of packaging; and Siemens is represented at trade fairs throughout the world with stands of all shapes and sizes. We hope to create a unified image from this tremendous multiplicity.

Siemens architecture

Aesthetic tastes change with the times; but a long-term product such as a building has to maintain its continuity and credibility over the years, and cannot, visually, shut itself off. Using the general, timeless formal vocabulary of the 'classical modern', we have created handsome, impressive company buildings. This vocabulary is expanded to incorporate such elements as current values and the 'genius loci' of each individual site. What makes Siemens buildings recognisable as such is not the routine repetition of patent solutions; rather, it is the recognisability of a certain design approach and the adherence to certain individual architectural solutions: railings, lights, signs, stairs. In addition, we employ a set repertoire of colours, materials, flooring, and display systems. Logical strictness and precision of thought – the basis of all technical achievement – demand an individual design expression. We therefore use a technically-oriented colour palette: white, silver, light grey, anthracite, with certain considered colour and design accents. By using materials with technical grace, precise forms, and visibly organised technology, we further attest to the fact that 'we are a technology firm'.

Siemens advertising

Every advertisement contributes to the image of the Firm as a whole. Every advertisement therefore has to be designed with this in mind. The basic design elements outlined in the CD Manual help to define the arena within which the designer's creativity can unfold. At the same time, they ensure that all of the messages will share a common orientation and contribute to the trust-worthiness of the Siemens image. They give enough room for free play for designers to create advertisements which are both individual and full of ideas. As well as visual unity, of course, economic considerations play a major rôle in the way that the CD rules are followed and applied. For a global enterprise such as Siemens, it is especially important to be able to stage local, regional, national, or international appearances quickly and economically. Corporate design, therefore, is not only a way to convey our Company image; it is also a strategic instrument which helps us to uphold the value of our name and be able to communicate quickly in the market.

The future

A corporate design is a complex, networked system. In such a system, every element affects every other, directly or indirectly. Just as a chain is only as strong as its weakest link, so is a corporate design only as strong as the weakest design statement within the complete design system. There's no such thing, therefore, as a design element which is incidental or unimportant. It is simply not true that some design elements are less important than others, and can therefore be overlooked or neglected. Every design statement has an effect. And if it doesn't have a positive effect on the corporate identity, then it has a negative one. Either it supports a company's image, or it damages it.

SIEMENS

Leo oder Lea ?
Hauptsache gesund.

SIEMENS

Wenn schon
Stinker auf der Straße,
dann vierbeinige.

*Advertisements
from the corporate
identity campaign.*

Dr Julius Lengert

*Freelance adviser to
Siemens AG, Munich,
Germany.*

*Born in 1936. After
studying philosophy
and cultural anthro-
pology, he has been
an independent
design consultant and
freelance adviser of
many years' standing
for Siemens AG.*

*Dr Lengert's principal
areas of expertise
are design culture,
business culture,
industrial culture,
the quest for identity
in the day and age of
the faceless society
and technological
civilisation.*

A convincing, effective corporate identity
assumes that every design element and
statement is of equal quality and importance.
In a large enterprise such as Siemens AG,
this is no easy thing to bring about; it
requires a high level of organisation and
communication. A design manual laid out
as an encyclopaedic reference work can
only serve as a basis, a point of departure.
Time and again, it happens that an on-site
designer follows the sense of the old Russian
proverb 'Heaven is high, and the Tsar is far
away' – that is to say, 'No one is likely to
notice exactly what it is I'm doing here' – and,
for reasons of time or cost, settles for the
next-best, the quickest, the most economic
solution. As stated above, this always takes
its toll on the overall quality of our corporate

design. We are therefore planning to take a
next step and digitise on computer network
the information which is set out in a linear
manner in the CD Manual. The information
will thus be even more easily accessible; it
will be simpler to select everything applicable
to a given situation, and therefore easier to
apply it in practical terms within a given
design. This will increase efficiency, lower
costs, and guarantee design unity. Note
that this applies only to the realisation of
the principles of our basic design credo,
the application of our design philosophy.
The creative element – fortunately or
unfortunately – can't be digitised. In this
area, now as always, competent designers
are called for, designers with imagination,
intuition, and a view to the whole.

*Veitsch-Radex AG
is an Austrian
manufacturer of
refractory products
for primary industry.
The Company's main
customers are steel
makers, along with
cement, glass, lime
and non-ferrous
metal manufacturers
and processors.*

*The Company is the
result of a merger in
1993 between two
Austrian competitors
in refractory products,
Veitscher Magnesit-
werke AG and Radex
Austria AG. Thanks
to the successful
image and goodwill
transfer from the
merged companies to
Veitsch-Radex AG,
the Company is now
a world market leader
in certain segments
of the refractory
industry,with products
being exported to
more than 100
countries. At the end
of 1993, Veitsch-
Radex employed
3,496 persons, 68%
of those in Austria,
and achieved a
turnover of 5.6 billion
Schillings.*

Introduction

Development of a corporate identity at the time of a merger is always a demanding task. When the two companies have been competitors for over a century, and when the merger also involves reductions in capacity, relocation and plant closures, as well as staff reductions of around 30%, the potential for conflict is clear.

With two product lines overlapping to a large extent, and in a competitive market situation which was characterised by structural crises, recession, overcapacity problems, price wars and dumping, the external circumstances were also the worst imaginable.

Dr Friedrich Nemec, the Chairman of the merged business, here tells how corporate identity was used as an instrument of crisis management in coping with the merger process; how the corporate identity development was achieved through a culture analysis, a new direction in cooperation, a common mission and a positioning strategy; and how, at the centre of the identity, a multi-branding strategy helped to preserve market share and, ultimately, ensure survival.

Corporate identity: contributing to the success of a merger

Corporate mergers are easy things on paper. Balance sheets, resources, purchasing power, logistics and organisational interfaces are all readily combined in theory. But corporate culture as a critical factor for success is almost always neglected. Companies are social structures with characteristic cultures. If this is not taken into account, there can be an unpleasant awakening, because then, no matter how well calculated, the synergetic equation will not function.

A merger situation is additionally aggravated if the two companies involved, which for nearly a century were competitors, must suddenly work together. Former rivals then have to change their view of the world from one day to the next, work together and present a united front. For most members of staff, this is hard to understand and even harder to implement. Resistance and cultural crisis are almost inevitable. Where then lie the synergies which should have been achieved through free and constructive cooperation of all employees of the constituent parts? How can such a situation be overcome? How can one be sure that, with such a start, the merger will be successful?

*Logotypes of the pre-
merger companies,
Veitscher Magnesit-
werke AG and
Radex Austria AG.*

The two best known refractory products
manufacturers in Austria, from which
Veitsch-Radex emerged, had to cope with
such a merger at the end of 1992. The
background, strategies and means for the
successful implementation of this unique
merger, which opened a new chapter in the
history of Austria's magnesite industry, are
described here.

The starting point and the context

The merger of 'Veitscher Magnesitwerke AG'
with 'Radex Austria AG' to form 'Veitsch-
Radex AG' was a response to challenges
which arose from dramatic economic and
political upheavals. The main customers for
refractory products are the prime industries
of steel, non-ferrous metals, concrete,
limestone and glass. Growth potential was
therefore generally only seen in developing
countries. In the industrialised countries,
markets were stagnant or shrinking due to
new technological developments or through
relocation of production facilities in developing
countries. In addition, the refractory industry
was characterised by global overcapacity.
As a consequence, severe price battles broke
out between manufacturers.

The structural problem was aggravated
by economic difficulties resulting from the
recession. Turbulence on the European
economic scene, a severe steel crisis,
increasing unemployment and problems in
Eastern Europe all added to the difficulties.
The crisis in the steel industry was persistent
and, this industry being the principal customer
for the products of both companies, capacity
problems increased and cut-throat price
competition became the order of the day. To
add to the problems, there was dumping of
competing products from China and Eastern
Europe, and costs were rising inexorably.
It had become impossible for both companies
to earn proper returns on the basis of existing

corporate structures. To adapt to these
developments, indeed to ensure long-term
survival, it was decided to merge the
refractory activities of both companies into
one combined enterprise under one management as 'Veitsch-Radex AG für feuerfeste
Erzeugnisse'. Through this, it was hoped that
potential synergies would be realised.

The merger presented all involved with great
challenges and some painful steps had to be
taken to secure the survival of the fledgling
company. Indeed, the merger involved a far-
reaching restructuring programme which
included a reduction in capacity, staff lay-offs
and closing of some sites. Although these
measures were alleviated by social planning,
they remained hard for the individuals
involved. Additionally, head office functions,
which until then were handled by each
partner individually, were newly focused on
one office in Vienna. This meant further
personnel problems, from redundancy to
work-related relocation.

The fact that the product ranges of the
former competitors overlapped made it
even more difficult. This overlap was so far-
reaching that experts warned against the
merger and predicted some frightening
scenarios. The board now faced the most
important strategic question for survival:
how the new combined product programme
should be structured. Everyone was
unanimous that both ranges should remain,
so that no market share was lost to the
competition. The question was how this
could be achieved.

The restructuring measures and these many
unresolved questions led to unfavourable
reactions and to protests by staff and the
local population around the sites. How
should this nascent company react to the
justifiable concerns of staff and public?
How should the seemingly unmanageable
task of a successful merger be carried out

under these conditions? What could restore the troubled cultural balance of the two and what could create a common system of values?

Corporate identity as solution and project process

The board saw the necessity of creating a common mission as part of a common strategy for the new Veitsch-Radex AG. Bearing this in mind, the designated board of the soon-to-be-merged company called in an external consultant with special expertise in the field of corporate identity development. In the briefing discussions with the consultants it quickly became clear that integration could only be achieved through construction of a corporate culture which combined the strengths of both companies. The new corporate identity should serve to overcome emotional barriers and form a strategic framework for the merger. It should confirm the continuity of the basic values of each of the companies with their backgrounds of strong tradition, but it should also express the change resulting from the integration of the two. Targets, values and expectations should then be made clear internally and externally so that performance potential, activities, offers and areas of business were communicated.

The new Company also needed to create market presence, both for itself as a whole and for its product ranges. How the new Company should be seen by clients, market partners and public, needed to be defined. What was its particular competence and performance potential? How could it be differentiated from competitors? What position should it attain in the minds of customers and other target groups in the market? These were all questions which would be answered through a comprehensive corporate identity strategy.

How, then, was the corporate identity of Veitsch-Radex AG developed? In cooperation with our external consultants, a phased project plan was drawn up. Because of the fixed merger date, the project was carried out under severe time pressure right from the beginning. The approach was structured as follows:

• carrying out of a status quo strengths and weaknesses analysis
• recommendations on measures for corporate identity development
• working out of a positioning strategy (corporate vision)
• development of a differentiation strategy for product ranges
• conceptualisation of a new corporate design
• implementation of introductory measures

In developing a new corporate identity, the boards of both constituent companies had decided to accept the challenges of the merger actively, thus creating a new shared company with a new quality.

How the status quo strengths and weaknesses analysis was carried out

Existing documentation, which gave information on the history, organisation, strategies, products, services and competitive environment of both companies, was scanned. On the basis of briefing discussions with the board and the knowledge gained from the desk research, discussions were held with management and staff in the form of individual interviews to lay the basis for development of a new common identity. One aim of the interviews was to determine self-perceptions and perceptions of the other: that is to say, what did a Veitscher employee think of his own company, then of Radex, and vice-versa? In addition, further information on both corporate cultures as

The commitment and motivation of each and every worker is an essential aspect of corporate success.

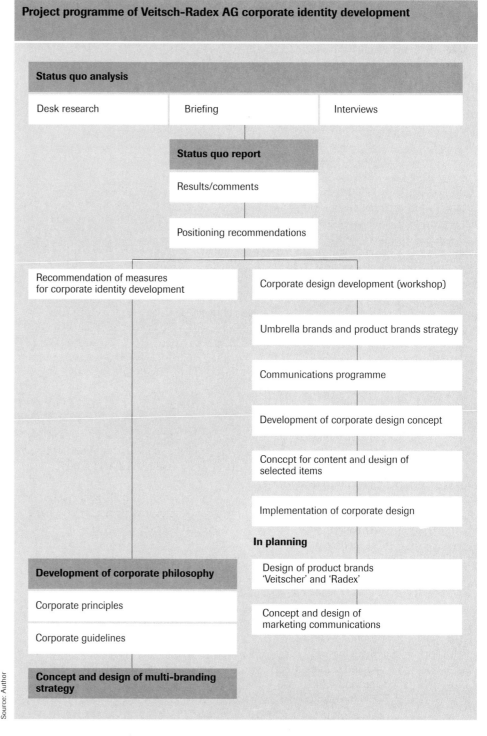

Project programme of Veitsch-Radex AG corporate identity development

Status quo analysis

| Desk research | Briefing | Interviews |

Status quo report

Results/comments

Positioning recommendations

Recommendation of measures for corporate identity development

Corporate design development (workshop)

Umbrella brands and product brands strategy

Communications programme

Development of corporate design concept

Conccpt for content and design of selected items

Implementation of corporate design

In planning

Design of product brands 'Veitscher' and 'Radex'

Concept and design of marketing communications

Development of corporate philosophy

Corporate principles

Corporate guidelines

Concept and design of multi-branding strategy

Source: Author

well as perceptions of staff concerning further development of the new Company were to be surveyed. However, the rôle of the interviews as a motivational measure was not underestimated. Through them, a possibility was opened up for active dialogue on the new corporate concept and the prevailing atmosphere, particularly the willingness of individual members of staff to support the development of a corporate identity. In this way, the interviews were the starting point for the active involvement of staff in the development of the corporate identity. The evaluation of existing documentation and the results of the interviews both proved the assumption that the issue of corporate culture was a particularly critical factor within this merger. It became very clear that this component would have a strong influence on whether or not the merger would be an economic success.

Those involved agreed that two widely differing cultures had to be integrated. One of the managers interviewed said pointedly: 'The problems lie in the two different cultures and in local patriotism.' Great scepticism was expressed as to whether the merger would work. In addition, those who had to move to Vienna feared for their jobs because of the necessary 'downsizing' of staff numbers and the fear of being uprooted from familiar surroundings. Radex was more directly affected by the restructuring than was Veitscher, as the latter boasted higher productivity and more modern production facilities. This gave many Radex employees the feeling that they were the losers. Because of the specific situation of the merger and the related crisis, many members of staff felt a particular need for harmony and for the development of an esprit-de-corps. They did not know where they stood and they waited for signs and signals which would give them direction for the future. Loss of an opponent in the market also seemed to be a problem. Up to the time of

the merger, there was always the other as a standard by which to measure oneself. This Austrian competition was often a catalyst for technical development and a starting point for peak performance on both sides. Staff agreed that, within the process of unification, it was necessary to define new competitors to ensure the leading technological position of the Company.

In the analysis, strengths and common points which could be built on became clear. The Veitscher Magnesitwerke AG was, amongst other things, characterised by a high degree of production automation, a close-knit organisation, excellent research and an outstanding source of raw materials. The Radex Austria AG, on the other hand, had strong marketing expertise, great flexibility and improvisational talent in its staff and also excellent research. The product quality and market penetration of both companies was comparable, but emphases were different. Many members of staff had a common background in that they had attended the Montan University in Leoben (the European university for the coal and steel industries) and this gave a good basis for the development of an integrated corporate culture. The creativity and innovative force achieved by combining research should also be emphasised.

The Austrian roots of both companies were another important thing that Veitscher and Radex had in common. Through the merger, Veitsch-Radex at a stroke became one of the world's most important manufacturers of refractory products, so the industrial implications of the merger for Austria were unparalleled. The development of a common corporate culture was not regarded, by those involved, as important only for internal relations. Externally, customers were irritated and this feeling was stoked up by competitors. Doubts about the new Company's credibility and ability to succeed could only be satisfied through the consistent actions of all members of staff and through convincing external presentation. The leading circle was unanimous in its agreement that one of their first tasks was to win over employees for their new Company.

Open-minded managers and employees receptive to change, willing to overcome existing barriers, were therefore essential factors in the advance towards a common cultural development. Despite misgivings, those affected were aware of the fact that, to survive in the market for refractory products, the merger of the companies, the restructuring and the downsizing of staff numbers, had to be carried through. The merger and the project for corporate identity development created great hopes for the future. Following the analysis, the development of corporate goals and values was an urgent necessity. Clear statements concerning the future of the Company were awaited. A positioning – a corporate vision – also had to be worked out.

Developing a positioning

The target positioning, the corporate vision for Veitsch-Radex, was developed out of the information gained during the status quo strengths and weaknesses analysis. The positioning, as a formulated self-perception of the Company, describes how the Company wants to be seen by its target groups and which position it wants to achieve in the market. The positioning devised takes into account the strengths of both companies and combines them so that they harmonise and enhance each other synergetically. For all employees, the positioning is both a challenge and a commitment. The main statement was as follows:

The Veitsch-Radex AG is a globally-active Austrian company in the refractory industry. As a future-oriented, strongly-performing

and solid company, it presents its profile through professional, customer-oriented, innovative and sophisticated products and problem-solving systems. Towards staff, customers and shareholders, the Company sees itself as a socially responsible, ecologically aware, communicative and responsible partner.

This statement was supplemented by detailed clarification of the individual aspects. For example, the following is an extract from the clarification of the aspects 'professional, demanding and competent':

Professional, competent action and thinking by all employees, from research engineer and skilled production worker to applications technician and salesperson, is a prerequisite for extensive process, product and system know-how. We are aware that the professionalism and competence of all members of staff is decisive in determining the quality of our performance. We view our employees as our most important corporate resource, which should be encouraged and supported.

Together with the positioning, the aims and requirements for the new Company were given. To reach these goals and to live up to them in everyday corporate life, the involvement and cooperation of every-one was necessary. A whole series of measures was recommended by the consultants, developed on the basis of the insights from the analysis. The most important concerned the development of a differentiation strategy for product ranges, the creation of a new corporate design and the development of corporate guidelines.

Differentiation, key to the multi-branding strategy

Against the background of maintaining and even broadening the combined market potential, Veitsch-Radex had to aim its product strategy even more than before to meet customer needs and the demands of the market. Before the merger, Veitscher marketed its products under the brand name 'Anker', while Radex used its own name as the brand. The product ranges of the partners, which previously were in competition to each other, overlapped in some areas. What was to be done? Both ranges were successfully established in their respective markets. Eliminating one of the two brand names would have led to a significant loss of turnover. On the other hand, the new Company could not possibly sell two similar products under two different brand names to the same customer. Loss of credibility would have been inevitable.

A detailed analysis of the product ranges showed, however, that both Veitscher and Radex possessed quality and the highest technological competence. Because of that, it was decided to develop them further as independent ranges, each with their own profile.

Both ranges differed somewhat, partly through technical characteristics (raw materials, physical qualities) and partly through inherent system and process know-how. In addition, there were geographically-biased customer preferences. In some parts of the world, Radex had a larger market share, in others Veitscher was strongly preferred. These market shares and levels of recognition, disproportionate to user segments, were attributable to former corporate politics as well as to the differing state of market development in individual countries.

The transformation of product ranges into brands within a multi-branding strategy was the logical outcome of this knowledge. It was decided to maintain the existing range structures, and therefore the high level of customer confidence they enjoyed, and to

The 'Anker' and 'Radex' brands.

develop them further into brand profiles. Although the goodwill inherent in the names did not appear as a positive item on the balance sheet, it represented a value which the Company did not want to deny – nor should it have done! The brand values would be actively developed and used for the Company's benefit through a differentiation strategy. This strategy included reinforcing existing distinctions between the brands, as well as active differentiation between them in areas in which identical products coexisted. The multi-branding strategy, under the common corporate umbrella, became a feature of the corporate policy. It guarantees strategic coordination of brand management, built around the positioning.

Creation of a new corporate design

A further important measure within the development of the corporate identity was the new corporate design. It had to be one of the first visible signs of unification, a flag under which we could set out to face the new circumstances. It had to convey the new structure and positioning. The combining of the two companies, the new 'quality', had to be made visible. The mark for Veitsch-Radex includes the new corporate name and interprets the subject matter of the positioning. It symbolises the mountain as the traditional source of raw material (magnesite, with its singular qualities), and the bricks of a high temperature oven, representing the applications know-how. However, the corporate design does not just consist of the mark. There is a complete corporate design system, which forms a visual framework for the consistent appearance of all items of communications which originate from the Company.

involvement of all members of staff at the time of introducing a new corporate identity. Communication of change took a key rôle in the implementation of the positioning and the corporate design. What use are the clearest positioning and the most beautiful design if no-one knows about them? A vital element in this process was the internal promotional event for the introduction of the new corporate identity, which took place on the day of the merger in front of the top management. The event was initiated by a

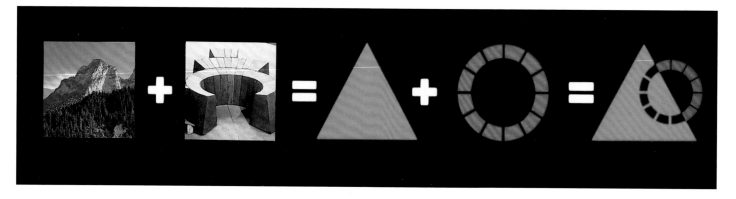

The new logotype reflects the new Company name and the positioning.

Everything, from delivery notes and letterheads to product brochures, is subject to these obligatory design principles.
The corporate design is thus of practical benefit in everyday work. It rationalises the information flow internally and optimises the communications impact externally. It expresses the unity with which all members of staff of Veitsch-Radex face economic, ecological and social challenges.

The introductory event

The merger of the former competitors has brought various changes. Each and every member of staff was affected by the changes, which create insecurity if they are not communicated clearly. Change also awakens expectations, and this can be used to foster a positive climate for the acceptance and

discussion between a moderator and the board of Veitsch-Radex. The moderator led the event by asking the board questions, to which they replied with brief explanations. Through this form of presentation, it was possible to convey to staff in a vivid way the essential aspects of corporate identity, starting with the background to the merger and proceeding through the target positioning and the multi-branding strategy to the corporate design.

For successful implementation of the new corporate identity, it was considered necessary to involve staff in active consideration of the positioning and the corporate design. This was encouraged by sending a personal information package to each member of staff. The presentation event and the accompanying measures generated a momentum which carried over into everyday work.

Development of corporate principles

The development of the corporate identity did not come to an end with the introductory event. It is an ongoing process. A corporate identity must be continually further developed, indeed lived, so the positioning had to be interpreted in a way which made it relevant to everyday work. What does 'For our staff, colleagues and society in general, we are the socially responsible, ecologically aware, communicative and open-minded partner' mean, for example? How does this confession of social responsibility manifest itself in a crisis such as we had to face during the merger? The practical meaning and consequences of these statements for day-to-day work and business had to be established. The corporate vision statements had already been explained in the corporate brochure and in the board's statements during the introductory event, but these interpretations were not taken to the point where they could serve as concrete measures, commitments and targets for daily activities.

To meet this need, workshops were held with employees. The first task allotted was the interpretation and detailed development of the corporate vision. The second task was the further working out of the multi-branding strategy which was such an important theme for the Company. The workshops were characterised by intensive and focused work by all participants. With moderation by our consultants, discussion and positive argument took place with the greatest involvement and interest. The workshops not only brought constructive results, but also helped to enhance personal relations between employees of both former companies through an atmosphere of camaraderie. The ongoing implantation of corporate principles and of the multi-branding strategy is achieved through further training measures, which involve all departments and employee locations.

Conclusions and future outlook

What have been the successes related to the development of the corporate identity in the first year of life of the newly-merged Company? Just as the success of a company cannot simply be preprogrammed by adding up turnover figures, so a unified corporate identity cannot be achieved by pressing a button. It is a dynamic process, which has to be carried out through the will of the board and of all employees. The responsibility lies with every individual to be an example through his personal commitment and active promotion of the success of the Company.

Cultural changes need time. The symbolic change of culture happened virtually overnight, but true internationalisation is going to take longer. Taking into account the very difficult context, great progress was made during the first year in the task of filling the process of a new cultural development with life. Financially, too, Veitsch-Radex reached a turning point at the end of 1993. The restructuring measures and the measures for developing a corporate identity having been established, in the second half of 1993 the downward trend was reversed. In comparison to the first half of the year, turnover improved even in static trading conditions. In addition, massive cost savings were implemented and, as a result, the operating deficit was reduced by half. In the middle of 1994, the Company reached break-even, and made a profit of 2% on turnover by the end of the year. It was able to pay a dividend again and move back towards its old position as a blue-chip company. In spite of all doubts, the multi-branding strategy has emerged as an

Dr Friedrich Nemec

*Chairman
Veitsch-Radex AG,
Vienna, Austria*

*Born 1932 in Preß-
burg, Czechoslovakia.
After a diploma
engineering course
in technical physics,
doctorate in tech-
nological sciences,
1956 commenced
work for Veitscher
Magnesitwerke-
Actiengesellschaft.
Numerous activities
within the organisa-
tion, but mainly in
the area of research.
1969 Member of the
board with responsi-
bility for production.
1982 additional
responsibility for
research and develop-
ment. 1986 Chairman
of the board.
1989 retirement and
consultant on future
issues. 1991 re-
appointed. Since
the merger in 1993,
Chairman of Veitsch-
Radex AG.*

important success factor for the merger. In the difficult market situation of a recession, we not only safeguarded the existing market share of the Company, from a defensive position, but we even gained additional market share. The multi-branding strategy will now form the basis for Veitsch-Radex's further development. The Company will concentrate its selling efforts on increasing its market presence in the developing countries with growth potential, such as those in the Far East and South America. Besides the refractory business, engineering activities will be built up. Within this general framework, an entry will be made into the field of environmental engineering, where an immense market is emerging, to which Veitsch-Radex can bring its know-how. The consistent implementation of the proven, customer-oriented quality concept, built around the new corporate identity, will further strengthen the competitiveness of Veitsch-Radex. The Company has achieved the merger with the help of the corporate identity strategy, and so can face the future with self-confidence.

Since its foundation in 1950 by Willi Fehlbaum, Vitra has developed into one of the most renowned suppliers of furniture for public and private environments. The Company is still a family business and is headed by Rolf Fehlbaum. Vitra employs around 570 at its production sites in Weil am Rhein and Neuenburg in Germany, Blotzheim in France and Allentown in the USA. Vitra has further subsidiaries in Austria, Belgium, Switzerland, Great Britain, The Netherlands, Spain and the USA. Headquarters and head office are in Weil am Rhein and in Basel-Birsfelden, Switzerland. Since 1983 turnover has increased from DM 66 million to DM 247 million in 1993.

Introduction

The special feature of Vitra's identity is its foundation in design pluralism. That means, above all, in the personalities of the renowned designers who create the products, in the personalities who represent the creative ideal by appearing on Vitra chairs in the Company's advertisements, and in the personalities of contemporary architects who, with their individual sense of style, create the Company's buildings. And, not least, it is in the personality of the person who runs the Company – in our case Rolf Fehlbaum – which forms the identity.

Rolf Fehlbaum describes the philosophy and implementation of Vitra's identity, which is receptive to influences and innovation, and which holds to the concept of variety. In fact, Vitra's identity philosophy is based on diversity, complexity and contradiction. The principle is to create space in which various personalities can exercise their creativity. In this way, an open-minded identity is created, with quality and authenticity as its themes.

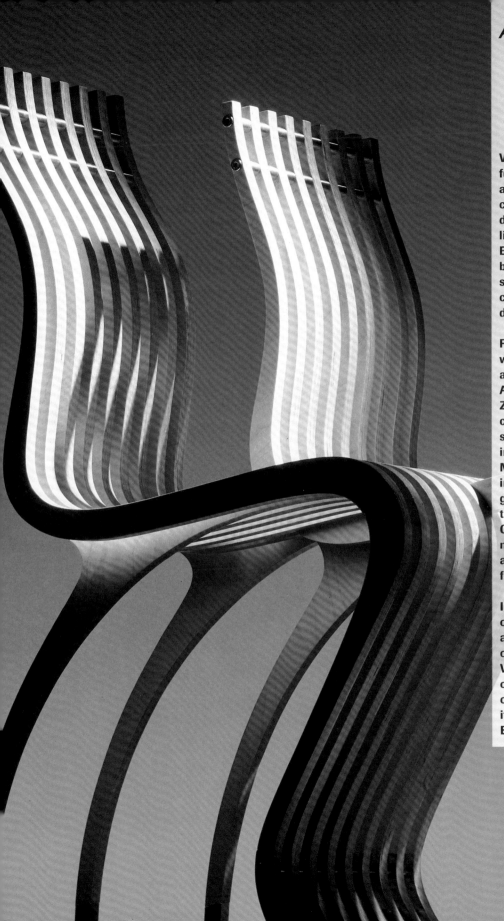

A pluralist identity

Vitra manufactures and distributes furniture for offices, public spaces, and for the home. Products are created in cooperation with important designers. The programme is pluralistic: classics by Charles and Ray Eames, office chairs and furniture by Mario Bellini and Antonio Citterio, stacking chairs by Philippe Starck, chairs and objects by other prominent designers.

For their own buildings, Vitra works with a broad palette of contemporary architects with varying styles: Tadao Ando, Frank Gehry, Nicholas Grimshaw, Zaha Hadid, Alvaro Siza. Vitra's customers, too, are pluralistic: airlines such as Lufthansa; important banks, industrial companies including Mercedes-Benz, Apple, and Coca-Cola; institutions such as the German government in Bonn; offices such as the European Common Market Commission in Brussels; small and mid-sized firms; free-lancers, as well as innumerable private persons who furnish their homes with Vitra products.

In order to gain a deeper understanding of its own activities, Vitra has become active in a broader context. Among other things, Vitra founded the Vitra Design Museum with its large collection of modern furniture and its changing exhibitions organised by its own staff and loaned to important European and American museums.

Attitude and philosophy

Spaces and their furnishings influence the
well-being and behaviour of inhabitants
and users. Vitra has made it its business to
develop furniture and furnishing concepts
that stimulate, inspire and motivate on the
one hand and, on the other, that take into
account the physical aspects of well-being
(ergonomics, safety, comfort and so on).
Design, choice of materials and production
methods are founded on ecological
principles such as longevity and recycling.

ecological, and other factors. All great
designers do this. On top of this, they lend
their products or buildings a magic, an
energy, that rubs off onto the observer or
user. This energy is never used up but is
transmitted again and again for years and
sometimes decades. Such products are
classics. Strong design stimulates and
motivates and is also a sign through which
the user's own value system can be manifested, his identity communicated. This
added value guarantees longevity; products
created in this spirit last longer since neither
their stability nor their charm pales. Great
designers are not merely clever craftsmen.
Their strength lies in the possession of a
vision of their work within the context of their
era and society and an antenna for the future.

Vitra history and product development

Vitra history begins at the end of the 1950s.
Willi Fehlbaum, the Firm's founder, had seen
Eames' furniture while on his first visit to the
USA and had tried to secure manufacturing
rights to it.

This furniture, light and comfortable, was
completely new. With technology never before
utilised in furniture design, it was beautiful in
a new way. For the first time wood was bent
three-dimensionally, thus allowing for an
anatomically improved seat edge. Plastic
was introduced to series-produced furniture
to achieve a new price-performance ratio.
In an effort to gain lightness, materials were
welded and aluminium was cast. Furniture
was created that is still, today, 40 or 50 years
later, a product of our times. It became clear
that furniture can be much more than a
practical and comfortable utilitarian object;
a chair can express a world and is highly
expressive of the identity of its user. Charles
and Ray Eames are considered to be the
most important designers of this century.
Their interests were far-reaching: folk art;

*Lounge chair and
chaise (Eames).*

For many years Vitra has worked with an
open programme including important
designers from several different cultures.
Vitra's goal is the attainment of ecological
results with special products. In the last
10 years, Vitra's entirely self-financed sales
have risen from 66 million to 247 million DM.
Good design shows a good price-performance
record and is, first and foremost, the fulfil-
ment of obligations, that is a confrontation
with functional, economic, ergonomic,

their film and multivision-show collection whereby they developed a new kind of short film, multivision as a new kind of communication, and toy design to inspire children to live out their own creativity. Foreign cultures were also a stimulus. For Nehru, the Eameses wrote a report that led to the creation of the Design Institute in Ahmedabad. Through Charles and Ray Eames the simple act of building or designing furniture was projected onto a larger plane of life and work to become much more interesting and challenging. Light transparent design ruled the first phase of Vitra activities. In the 1960s, the confrontation was with plastic, then infiltrating furniture manufacturing for the first time, and its new possibilities for form and colour. A lasting contribution to this era is the Panton Chair.

In the 1970s, another ideal took hold and has remained dominant to the present day: ergonomics. The fact that human beings are not made for sitting for a period of many hours was recognised. It was then that the ergonomic chair was born. Vitra developed the Vitramat, a chair that was aesthetically innovative in its time and one that made ergonomics easy to experience. The confrontation with the ideal ergonomic chair continues to preoccupy Vitra today. New approaches are tried again and again in an attempt to optimise the play between support and movement.

A new issue arose in the early 1980s for which Vitra constantly seeks new solutions, that is the search for inspiring contemporary office environments. Due to new demands placed on employees, the new office of interconnected personal computers must be completely different. It must become a lively place in which workers are stimulated and gain enthusiasm for common goals and projects. Departing from here, cooperation with Mario Bellini began. Bellini had gained much experience in his work with Olivetti and office machines. Although he had designed

several pieces for residential spaces, he had never before attempted an office chair. In order to do justice to the future blurring of boundaries between home and work spheres, Vitra wanted to bring to an office environment increasingly dictated by machines, elements that were reminiscent of more private, intimate home life. Even the names of these products were intended to express a different office image. They were called Persona, Figura, and Imago. Aside from extensive research into office themes, Vitra also became involved in other design issues. In the 1980s, assuredness as to what modern, up-to-date form actually was fell apart. In all areas, these were the 'design explosion' years. Vitra experimented with new materials and new techniques. The Vitra Edition was one type of research, an instrument intended to test new possibilities and new relationships to designers. Projects arose with Ron Arad, Richard Artschwager, Coop Himmelblau, Paolo Deganello, Frank Gehry, Jasper Morisson, Shiro Kuramata, Gaetano Pesce, and Borek Sipek, among

Top: Panton chair.

Below: Aluminium and Soft Pad Group (Eames).

Top: Louis 20 (Starck).

*Below: Figura and
Imago chairs (Bellini).*

others. Vitra's pluralist approach resulted from these experiments. Another new theme that sprang up in the 1980s was that of ecology. In the intense confrontation that followed, it became apparent that Ray and Charles Eames had also been exemplary in this regard. Their ideal of the use of a minimum of material, their concept of longevity and the patina of age, the possibility of replacing those parts most accident-prone during a product's life, and the use of recyclable materials were all answers to the ecological challenge. Later, Vitra introduced the ideas that had appeared so obvious to the Eameses into its own product development and manufacturing:

• longevity
• recyclable materials
• low diversity of materials for simplification of material separation
• use of recycled materials
• easy exchangeability of defective parts
• environmental consciousness in manufacturing methods
• less packing material

Thus a product by a designer who had been condemned as an eccentric was created: Louis 20 by Philippe Starck. The chair consists of only two parts: a blown polypropylene body creating volume with a minimum of materials and an aluminium bridge fitting so seamlessly into the plastic body that it can be fastened to it with only five screws. The chair is extremely robust for long lasting use. Later disposal is easy since the product consists of only two easily separable materials. Both materials are recyclable; the aluminium has already been recycled once. This is an example of change in design to meet new ecological needs and of the fact that ecologically-sound products need not come across as green manifestos. Thus ecology is no 'sacrifice' if integrated into the design process from the product's inception.

In the office sphere, Vitra continued with a designer who followed directly in the Eames's path: Antonio Citterio. Citterio's design statement is discreet and yet very much his own style. He is successful in combining his own experience in varying disciplines in a manner that is familiar yet new. Thanks to Citterio's architectural experience, the designer has been able to create objects that are never isolated but that always relate to other objects and to their space. Thus, products have arisen that lend the office environment lightness and animation. One of Citterio's latest chair, Axion, has a very discreet aura and has been designed according to strict ecological rules. Here an ergonomic plan has succeeded. A new succession of movements following the Scandinavian School's creed with a seat that can be lowered in the front combines with the German hypothesis of the importance of movement while sitting. With Citterio, Vitra also developed the manager programme Spatio, elegantly simple furniture that avoids old stereotypical power symbols. With Mario Bellini, Vitra had already made the leap from chairs to other office furnishings in its

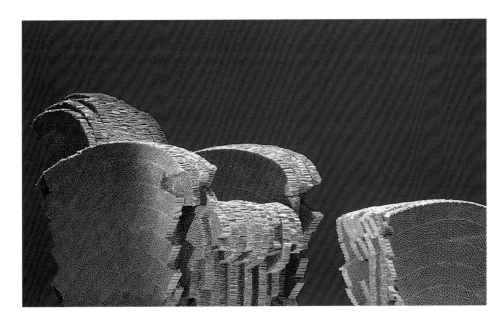

Little Beaver (Gehry).

Metropol series. *Metropol* brings a new mood to the office. The workspace is no longer seen as a static unit but rather as a collage of variable elements that can react to technical innovations with third level and electronic possibilities while nonetheless creating atmosphere. Today, Vitra creates total environments and, often in cooperation with architects, conceives whole projects such as that for the German government.

Communications

It has only been in the past ten years that Vitra has consciously tried to build up the power of its brand name. Aside from products and classical advertising, the architecture and activities of the Vitra Design Museum have been responsible for the diffusion of the Vitra name. Pierre Mendell, of Mendell & Oberer, Munich, has created the graphic image while Hans Hansen, Hamburg, is the photographer for all the products. Vitra does not limit its work with Mendell and Hansen to clearly defined commissions. At regular meetings, Vitra's developments and

communications needs are discussed with them and new solutions are found. In the field of classical advertising, Vitra has followed a simple path for years. This path is in tune with Vitra's dialogue with creative personalities. A special person is photographed while seated on a Vitra chair.

This image is published with no commentary other than that of the Vitra address. Decisive to these images is the style and personality of their photographer, Christian Coigny, who never demotes his models to the position of mere advertising carriers. At present, more than 100 images have been created, featuring Miles Davis, Patricia Highsmith, John Cage, Yehudi Menuhin, Audrey Hepburn, Robert Rauschenberg, Billy Wilder, Jack Lemmon, Charles Bukowski, David Hockney, Jeanne Moreau, Roman Polanski, Robert Wilson, Margarete Mitscherlich, Wim Wenders, Pina Bausch, Peter Ustinov, Roy Lichtenstein, and Martin Scorsese, to name only a few. The photographs were shown at an exhibition at the Musée d'Élysée in Lausanne in 1993. The personalities featured in them represent Vitra's creative ideal.

Advertisement – dialogue with creative people (Miles Davis).

Vitra architecture

Vitra has been consciously creating its own architectural image since 1982. After a fire levelled the Vitra site, the Firm decided to build a new factory by the English high-tech architect Nicholas Grimshaw. After his first building was finished, Grimshaw was commissioned to develop a master plan for the whole Vitra site. His ideas focused on the idea of 'corporate identity architecture' that could be utilised at every site built by Vitra. This idea was called into question in 1984 when Claes Oldenburg and Coosje van Bruggen installed their sculpture at the north end of the factory site. Balancing Tools, a kind of gateway formed by a giant hammer, screwdriver, and pliers, was the keynote for a new architectural concept. Instead of corporate identity architecture, inherently a non-site specific architecture, the concept of constructing a vital, non-interchangeable place arose. Non-interchangeability and vitality were planned to arise from the meeting of differing (but never coincidental)

architectures. For each future building task a different architect was commissioned. The choice of architect was made after careful analysis of the brief and of the new architecture's relationship to neighbouring buildings. Thus Frank Gehry has created the inviting Vitra Design Museum with an accompanying factory. Zaha Hadid has built the dynamic fire station, Tadao Ando the meditative conference centre, and Alvaro Siza a delicately articulated factory consciously subordinated to the rest of the built site. During the course of this work, consciousness of the Vitra site was upgraded to transform its identity from a location on the outskirts of Weil am Rhein to a new urban gateway to the city. This position will determine Vitra's future architectural planning. Vitra's architectural concept counters the dreariness of industrial parks and the demonstration and confirmation of power represented by closed corporate architecture. Clarity and uniformity are replaced by complexity and the multiplicity of unexpected relationships.

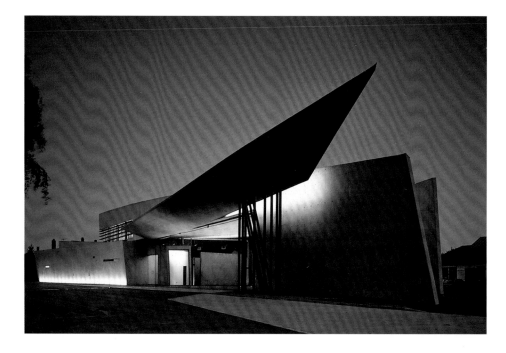

Vitra Fire Station by Zaha Hadid.

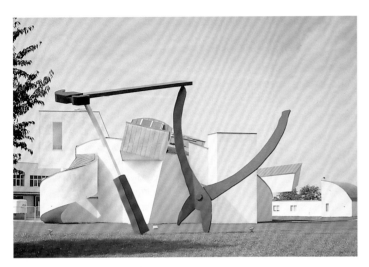

Vitra Design Museum

In cultural affairs Vitra acts as a 'self-sponsor.' The Vitra Design Museum was opened in 1989. The first idea was that of a modern furniture collection accessible to the public. This idea led to the building and, inspired by the museum's director, Alexander von Vegesack, to a totally different concept, that of the founding of an independent institution to confront historic and contemporary design issues through the media of exhibitions, workshops and publications with Vitra as main sponsor.

Today the collection comprises approximately 1,600 pieces of modern furniture and is one of the largest in the world. Exhibitions are created from pieces from Vitra's own collection and other material. Vitra Design Museum exhibitions have travelled to such famous museums and institutions as the Centre Pompidou in Paris and the Cooper-Hewitt Museum in New York, as well as to cities with a great backlog in demand for the subject of design such as Prague and Warsaw. The exhibitions Czech Cubism (1991), an historic retrospective of the era between 1919 and 1925, and Citizen Office (1993), a confronta-tion with the office realities of tomorrow by

designers Ettore Sottsass, Andrea Branzi, and Michele De Lucchi, drew wide acclaim. The Vitra Design Museum also publishes catalogues, produces miniatures of furniture classics, organises student workshops, and lends parts of its collection to other museums. The year 1993 saw 40,000 visitors to the museum and Vitra's architecture. These visits and numerous press reports have greatly contributed to a positive Vitra image. The museum's presence on the Vitra site and the daily confrontation with the best objects wrought by the history of design have had a clear effect inside Vitra. This constant confrontation has become a decisive motivating factor for all employees. Visitors, too, are aware of this climate of unusual competence.

Conclusion

Vitra's identity is not only based on the clarity, discipline and rationalisation of the Firm's various activities. On the contrary, the Vitra programme – whether one thinks of product design stretching from Eames to Starck or of architects from Tadao Ando to Zaha Hadid – is characterised by multiplicity, complexity and contradiction. This is the

Vitra Design Museum by Frank Gehry.

Conference pavilion by Tadao Ando.

Dr Rolf Fehlbaum

*Managing Director
of Vitra GmbH, Weil
am Rhein, Germany.*

*Born 1941 in Basel.
Studied social sciences.
Doctorate in the
utopian socialism of
St Simon, co-founder
of art publishing
house, editor at film
production company,
consultant for further
education in architec-
ture in Munich.
Since 1977 member
of the management
team at Vitra.
Since 1983 has been
building an extensive
collection of furniture
of the modern age.
Initiator of the Vitra
Design Museum.*

*1991 honoured with
the prize of the
Industrie Forum
Design Hanover (iF)
for outstanding
achievements in the
area of design
promotion and the
public conduct of
design activities.*

difference between Vitra's efforts and most
other identity efforts. Standardisation and
streamlining are reduced to the minimum.
That keeps the Firm lively and changing and
helps it to renew itself. Vitra's identity rule is
to create space for the creativity of the most
highly varied personalities.

Vitra's identity is open – but not open to all
sides. Behind Vitra's various activities stand
the principles of quality and authenticity that
guard it from arbitrariness and confusion.

Definitions of corporate identity, corporate culture and other terms vary widely, not only from country to country, but also from expert to expert. This short glossary gives the definitions we have adopted and refers particularly to the first three chapters.

Corporate behaviour dimension
This dimension is understood as the total of all corporate actions which contribute to the identity, be it as a planned result through the corporate culture, or even accidental or arbitrary.

Corporate communications
Corporate communications are all internal and external information means and measures which aim to influence perceptions or behaviour.

Corporate culture dimension
The corporate culture embraces all cultural conditions, contexts and aims of a company. It is the main value system, developed in a continuous process, which shapes the behaviour of staff and is expressed through it.

Corporate design
Corporate design is a design system specific to a given company. This includes the visual style of all manifestations such as products, promotion and environments, and all the characteristic elements such as typographic style, colour and form.

Corporate guidelines
The corporate guidelines contain actualisation and interpretation of the corporate principles for individual areas of business activity and functions. They therefore explain the relevance of the corporate principles to the actions and behaviour of all employees, departments, functions or whatever.

Corporate identity
Corporate identity is the aim and process by which the strategically-planned self-portrayal of a company is developed externally and internally.

Corporate image
Corporate image is the perceived picture which external target groups have of the company.

Corporate principles The corporate principles define the mission, targets and values of a company. They form the basis of, and standards for, all corporate actions.

Holistic corporate identity strategy In a holistic corporate identity strategy, the identity-relevant factors of corporate culture, corporate behaviour, market conditions, market strategies, products and services as well as communications and design are planned and developed on the basis of a target positioning to create a unique and consistent corporate identity for all relevant target groups.

Market conditions and strategies dimension This dimension includes all conditions, objectives and strategies which relate to the market or result from it.

Multicultural The multicultural approach facilitates the inclusion of all cultures which exist within the company or its contexts, along with their specific peculiarities, in the development of the strategy.

Positioning Positioning is the process in which the company is assigned a clearly defined position, derived from its self-perception, to differentiate it from the competition. The positioning encapsulates the aimed-for identity, and therefore how the company perceives itself, how it wants to be perceived, how it needs to behave and how it wants to be understood.

Products and services dimension This dimension incorporates all aspects connected with products and services, such as product design, ergonomic qualities, product benefits, value for money and customer services.

Picture acknowledgments

ABB   All ABB, Mannheim

Ford   All Ford Motor Company – photographic library

Henriettenstiftung   p. 73, Henriettenstiftung, Hanover
                  p. 80/81, Henrion, Ludlow & Schmidt, London

IBM   All IBM UK, Portsmouth

INSEAD   p. 102, J. E. Pasquier / Rapho
                  All others INSEAD, Fontainebleau

Keller   All Henrion, Ludlow & Schmidt, London

KLM   All KLM, Amstelveen

Krups   p. 127/130/131/134/135, Krups, Solingen
                  p. 133/136/137, Henrion, Ludlow & Schmidt, London

London Underground   p. 142/143, London Transport Museum
                  All others Henrion, Ludlow & Schmidt, London

Migros   All Pressedienst MGB, Zurich

Pillar Electrical   p. 163, ZEFA, London
                  All others Henrion, Ludlow & Schmidt, London

Siemens   p. 173/177/178, Studio Koller, Munich
                  p. 174/175 upper, Siemens Museum, Munich
                  p. 175 lower, Architekturfoto D. Leistner, Mainz
                  p. 176, Siemens Fotostudio
                  p. 179, Foto Fössel, Munich

Veitsch-Radex p. 183/184/185/189, Veitsch-Radex AG, Vienna
                  p. 190/191, Henrion, Ludlow & Schmidt, London

Vitra   Product photography, Hans Hansen
                  Advertising photographs, Christian Coigny
                  Architectural photography, Richard Bryant, Andreas Sütterlin